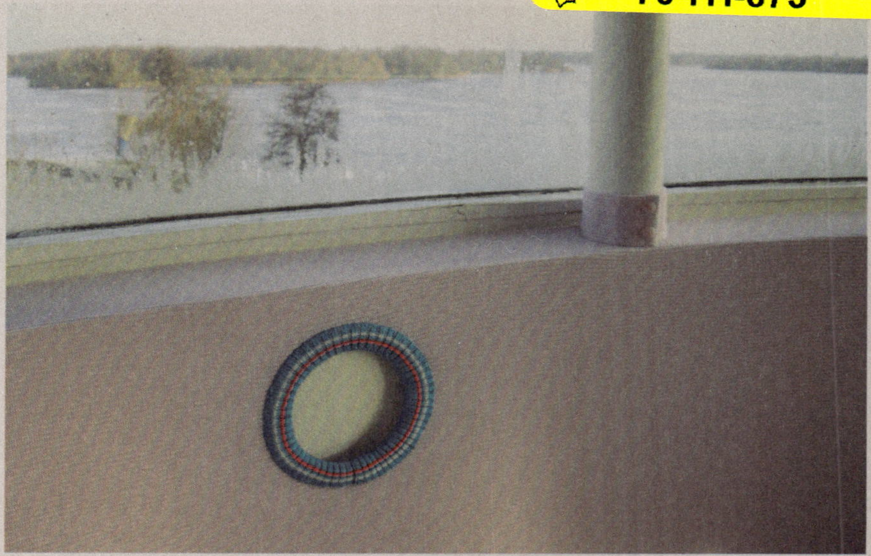

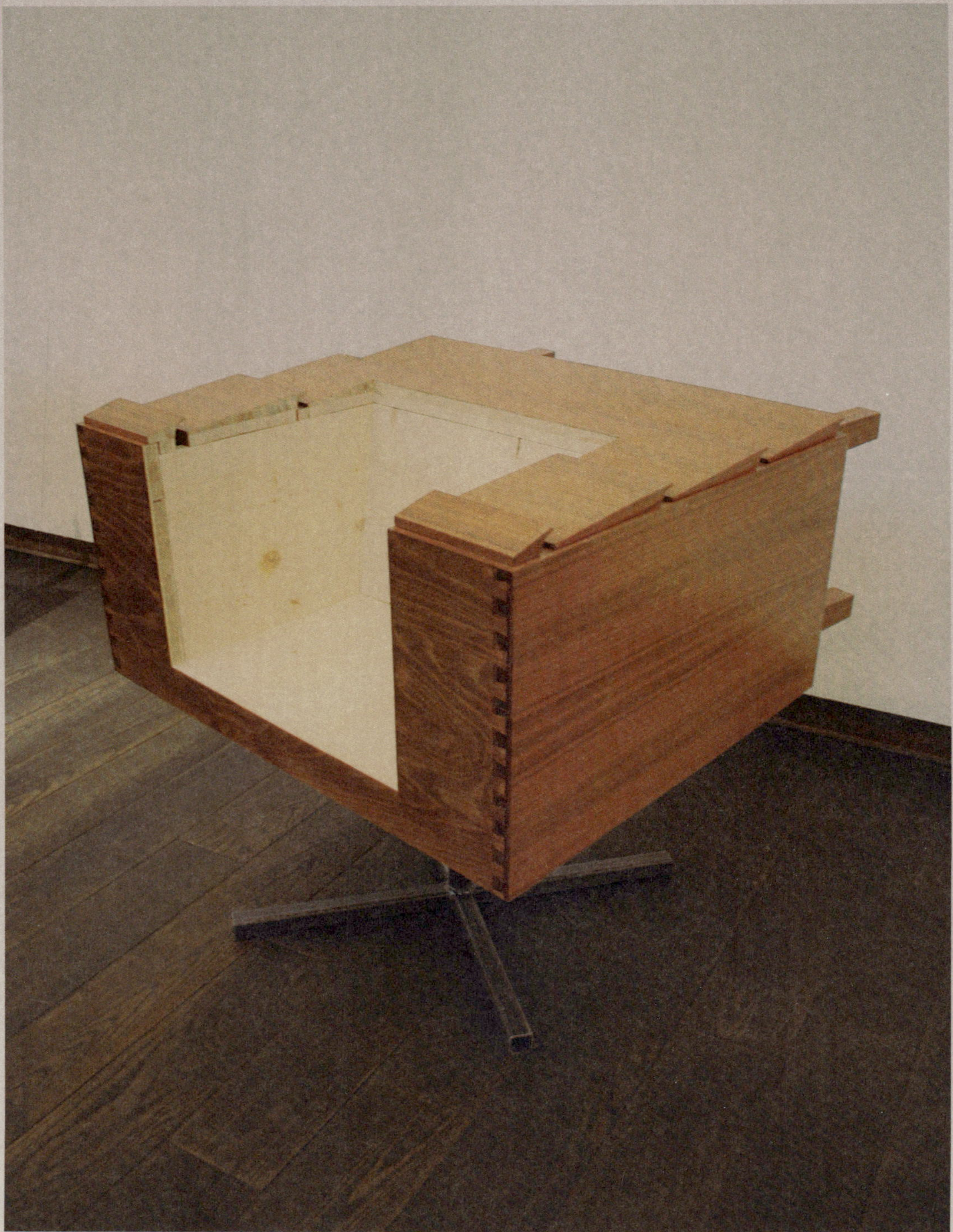

Erwin Wurm *Wear Me Out*

Edited by Middelheim Museum, Antwerp/Gemeentemuseum, The Hague
With an interview with the artist by Sara Weyns, Benno Tempel, and Laura Stamps, and an introduction by Menno Meewis, Philip Heylen, and Benno Tempel

HATJE
CANTZ

Contents/Inhoud

Foreword

Austrian artist Erwin Wurm seeks to engage museums and institutions in his artistic processes. We visited him a year ago in Vienna to invite him for an open-air exhibition at the Middelheim Museum. It soon became clear that his existing artworks would be more than ample to compile a fascinating and inspiring exhibition, and that's exactly what we did. The results have been on exhibit at the Middelheim Museum since the start of summer 2011. Together, these monumental pieces form a representative body of the artist's work. As mentioned, the works had already been created, and many of them previously featured in various catalogues.

He did, however, specifically produce a new comprehensive artwork or *Gesamtkunstwerk* for the Braem Pavilion, the exhibition pavilion of the Middelheim Museum. The artwork incorporates the architecture of the building; the artist also exhibits reconstructed furniture, and presents performative sculptures. We thought it would be interesting to focus on the new work in this catalogue, rather than presenting the more familiar, monumental open-air works. This provides us with an opportunity to put on view previously unpublished—and in some cases entirely unexhibited—projects, works, and drawings.

During the conceptual phase, it became clear just how deep Wurm delves into the heart of the art of sculpture: the human form coupled with gesture, attire, and "chairs" form the cornerstones of his work. This was also expressed in his groundbreaking *One Minute Sculptures*. Under the guise of his often-humoristic works, he conducts serious studies into the origins and limits of sculpture. This made him the ideal choice for an exhibition at the Middelheim Museum, the open-air museum for sculpture.

From June 25, 2011, GEM, The Hague's museum for contemporary art (part of Gemeentemuseum Den Haag), hosted the first major exhibition of Erwin Wurm's work in the Netherlands. All of the sculptures, photographs, drawings, installations, and *One Minute Sculptures* emulate ties with the concept of sculpture—are in fact forms of sculpture—and clearly reflect aspects of society today. Wurm examines topics such as consumerism, striving for status, dealing with shaky norms and values, and the relationship between people's physical and mental states, in a light-hearted and fascinatingly amusing manner. Wurm captures the spirit of contemporary sculpture like no other, and is therefore instantly at home in the settings of GEM.

The artist's earlier and more recent creations are discussed in an interview hosted by Benno Tempel and Laura Stamps (the director and curator of Gemeentemuseum Den Haag respectively) and Sara Weyns (curator of Middelheim Museum).

The recently acquired Psychos (Small Psychos), 2010 were on exhibit at GEM. These works are included in the catalogue. We would like to thank Erwin Wurm, Claudia Salzer, and Leni Michl (Studio Wurm); Sara Weyns and Pieter Boons (Middelheim Museum); Laura Stamps and Mandy Prins (Gemeentemuseum Den Haag); Markus Hartmann (Hatje Cantz); and last, but not least, Dimitri Jeurissen and Sander Vermeulen of BaseDesign.

Finally, it should be noted that this marked the first solo exhibition of this scale of Erwin Wurm's work at a museum in either the Netherlands or Belgium. Not a moment too soon!

Menno Meewis
Director of the Middelheim Museum

Benno Tempel
Director of the Gemeentemuseum Den Haag

Philip Heylen
Alderman of Culture and Tourism Antwerp

Inleiding

De Oostenrijkse kunstenaar Erwin Wurm is een van die kunstenaars die een museum of instelling deelachtig maakt aan zijn artistieke processen. Toen we hem in Wenen bezochten met de vraag naar een openluchttentoonstelling in het Middelheimmuseum, bleek er al vlug voldoende bestaand werk te zijn voor een boeiende expositie. Het resultaat was in de zomer van 2011 te zien in het Middelheimmuseum: een mooi overzicht van Wurms monumentale werken die samen een beeld gaven van zijn oeuvre en al in verschillende catalogi waren opgenomen. Voor het tentoonstellingspaviljoen in het Middelheimmuseum, het zogenaamde Braempaviljoen, maakte Wurm ook een nieuw werk, een *gesamtkunstwerk* dat de architectuur van het gebouw bij het kunstwerk betrok. De kunstenaar toonde er omgebouwde meubels en organiseerde er performances.

We vonden het een boeiende denkpiste om de catalogus toe te spitsen op het nieuwe werk, eerder dan de bekende monumentale openluchtwerken nog eens af te beelden. Op die manier kregen we ook de kans om projecten, werken en tekeningen die nooit eerder gepubliceerd werden – en in sommige gevallen zelfs nooit eerder getoond – aan het publiek voor te stellen. Tijdens het ontstaansproces werd duidelijk hoezeer Wurm tot de kern van de beeldhouwkunst gaat: zowel het menselijk lichaam als de beweging, de kledij en de 'zitmeubels' vormen de bouwstenen van zijn werk. Dit kwam al tot uiting in zijn *One Minute Sculptures*. Onder het mom van vaak humoristische werken voert hij een ernstig onderzoek naar de oorsprong en de grenzen van de beeldhouwkunst. Dit maakte van hem de geknipte kunstenaar voor een tentoonstelling in het Middelheimmuseum, het Antwerpse openluchtmuseum voor beeldhouwkunst.

In het GEM, het museum voor actuele kunst dat een onderdeel is van het Gemeentemuseum Den Haag, opende een kleine maand later, op 25 juni, de eerste overzichtstentoonstelling van Erwin Wurm in Nederland. De getoonde sculpturen, foto's, tekeningen, installaties en One Minute Sculptures verhielden zich allemaal tot het begrip 'sculptuur' – het zijn in feite allemaal vormen van sculptuur – en hadden een duidelijke relatie met de huidige maatschappij. Consumeren, het streven naar status, de omgang met onzekere waarden en normen en de verhouding van geest en lichaam zijn onderwerpen die Wurm als vanzelfsprekend lichtvoetig onder de aandacht brengt. Hij vangt de tijdgeest als geen andere hedendaagse beeldhouwer en was daarom ook helemaal op zijn plek in het GEM.

In het interview dat Benno Tempel en Laura Stamps, respectievelijk directeur en curator bij het Gemeentemuseum Den Haag, en Sara Weyns, curator van het Middelheimmuseum met de kunstenaar voor dit boek hadden, komen zowel de oudere werken als de meest recente projecten aan bod.

Het GEM nam ook het werk dat voor de collectie aangekocht werd, op in de catalogus: Psychos (Small Psychos) (2010).

Wij danken Erwin Wurm, Claudia Salzer en Leni Michl (Studio Wurm), Sara Weyns en Pieter Boons (Middelheimmuseum), Laura Stamps en Mandy Prins (Gemeentemuseum Den Haag), Markus Hartmann (Hatje Cantz) en last but not least Dimitri Jeurissen en Sander Vermeulen van BaseDesign.

Tot slot nog de vaststelling dat het, zowel in Nederland als in België, de eerste maal was dat Erwin Wurm een grote, museale eenmanstentoonstelling kreeg. Niets te vroeg!

Menno Meewis
Directeur Middelheimmuseum

Benno Tempel
Directeur Gemeentemuseum Den Haag

Philip Heylen
Schepen voor cultuur en toerisme Antwerpen

Middelheim ceiling, 2011
Middelheim Museum,
Antwerp
Photo: Ottomura

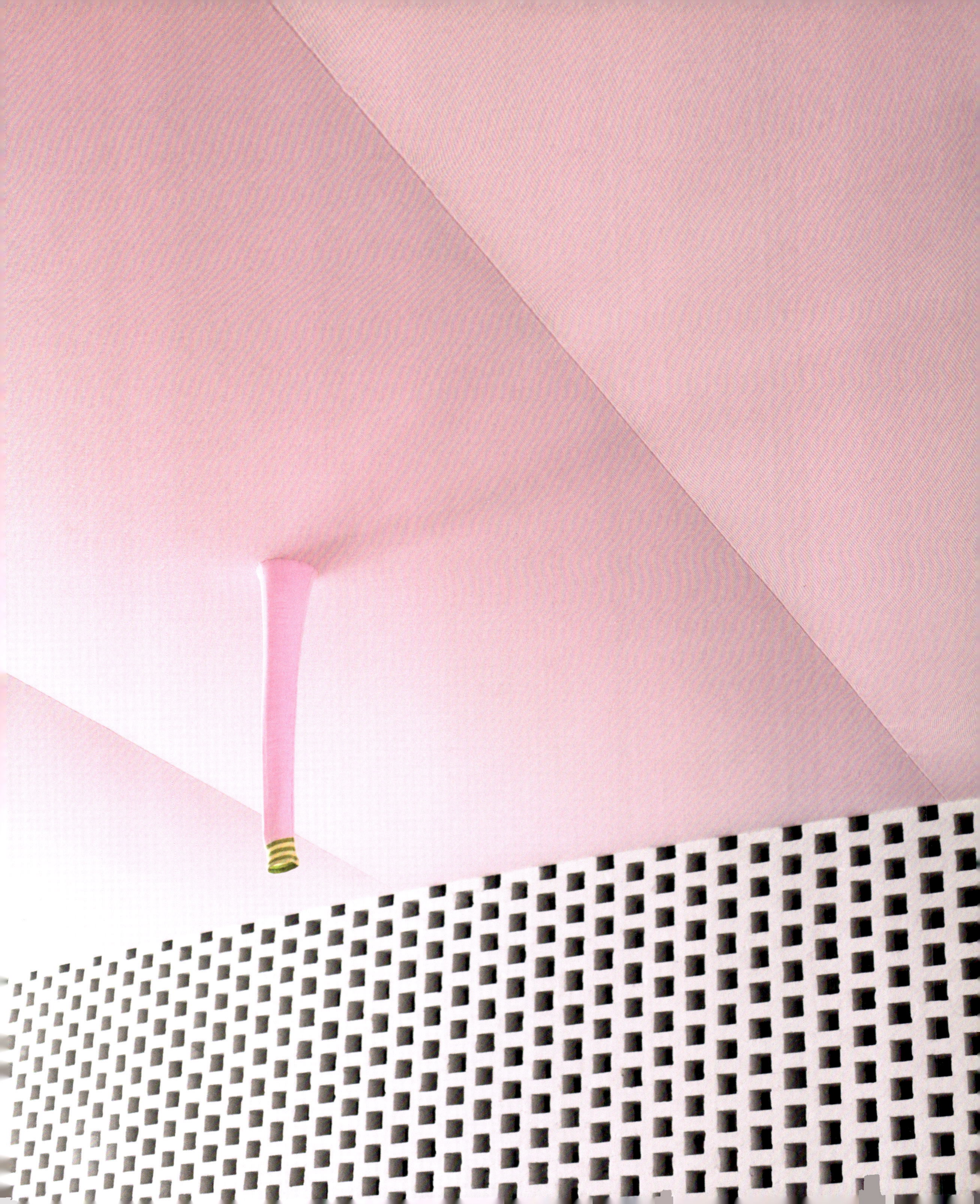

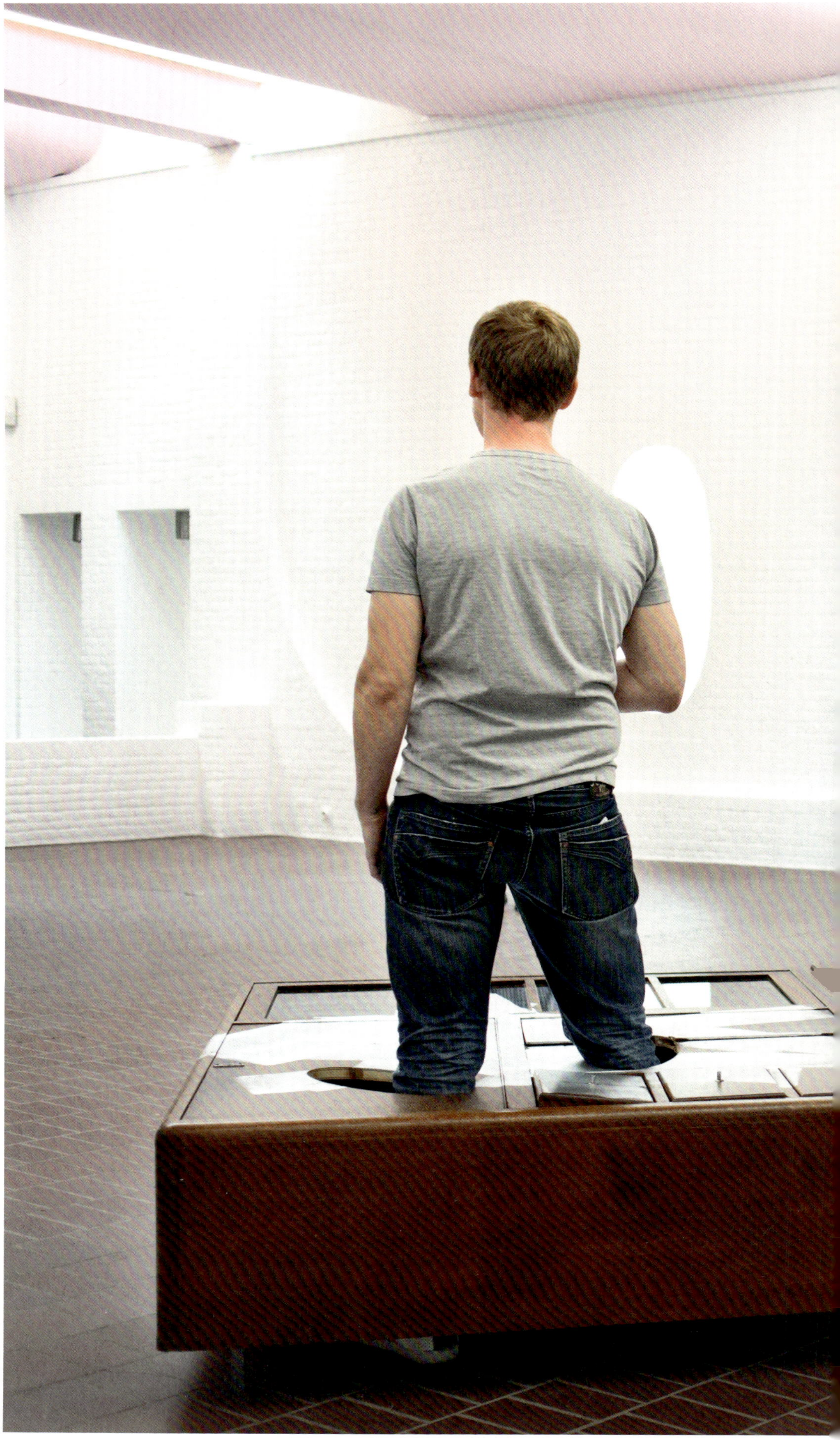

Performative Sculptures: Drinking Sculptures, the public is invited to open the drawers, take the glasses and bottles out and drink. The piece is realized when the performer is drunk.
2011
Middelheim Museum, Antwerp
Photo: Ottomura

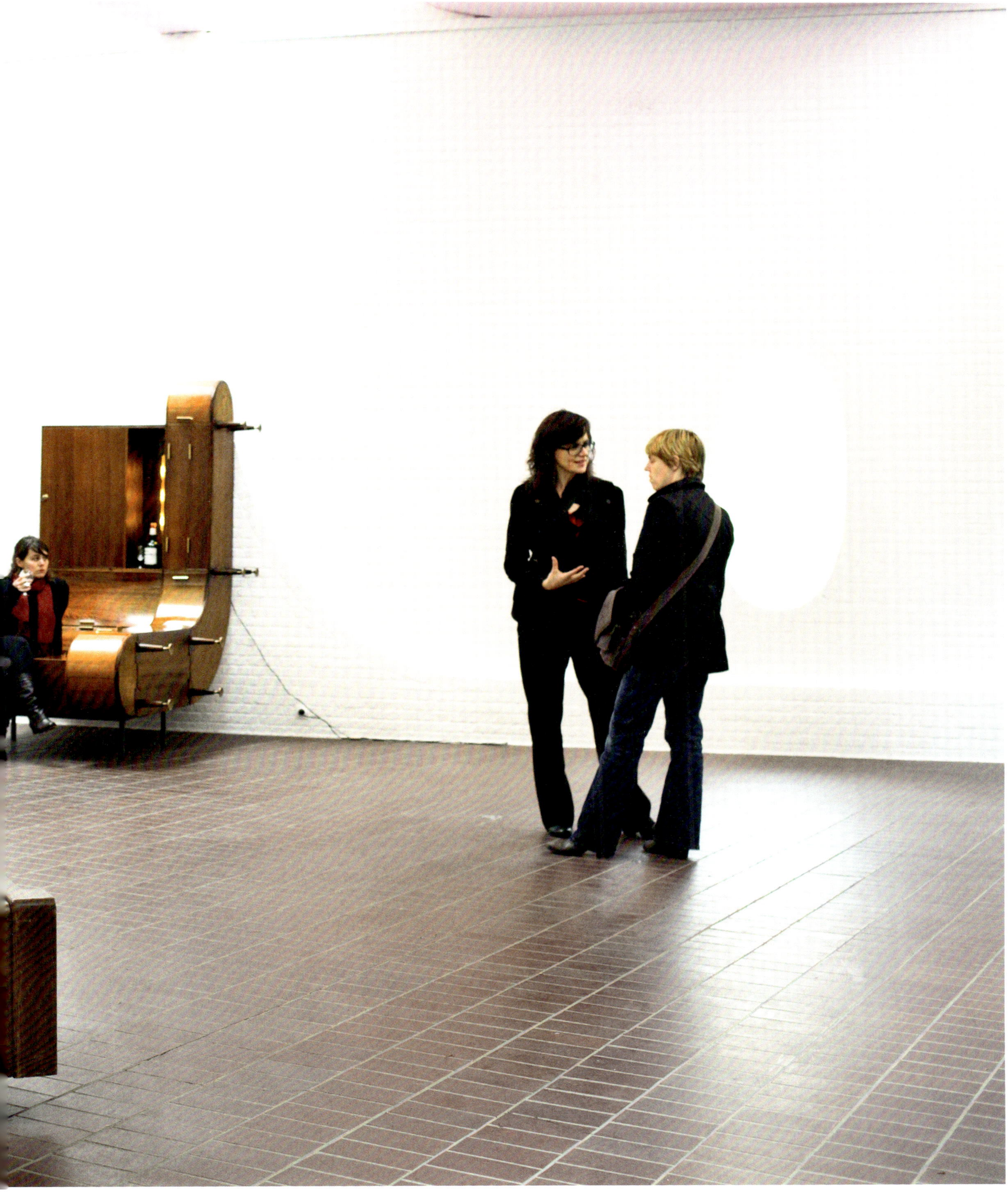

Performative Sculptures: Drinking Sculptures, the public is invited to open the drawers, take the glasses and bottles out and drink. The piece is realized when the performer is drunk.
2011
Middelheim Museum, Antwerp

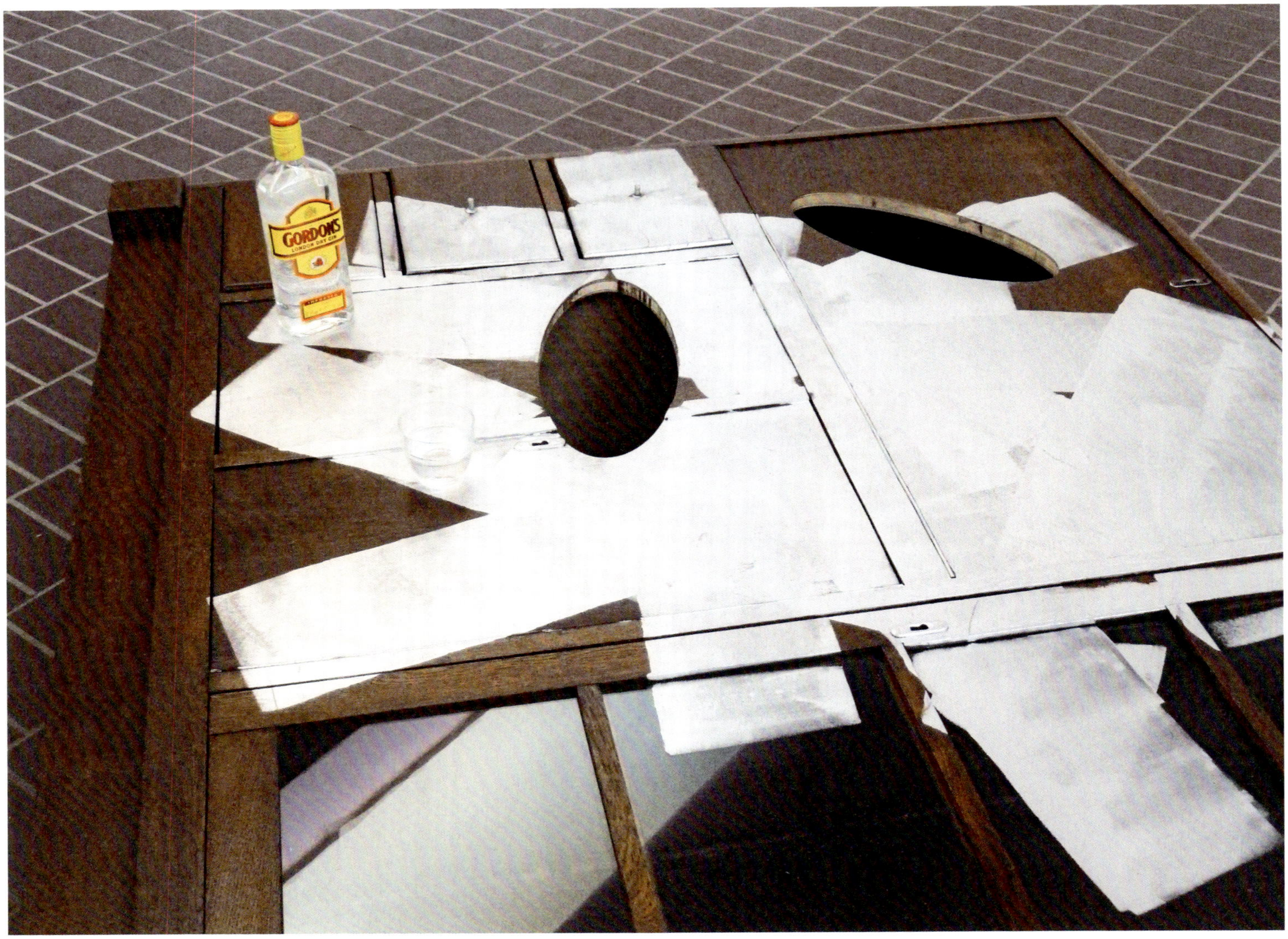

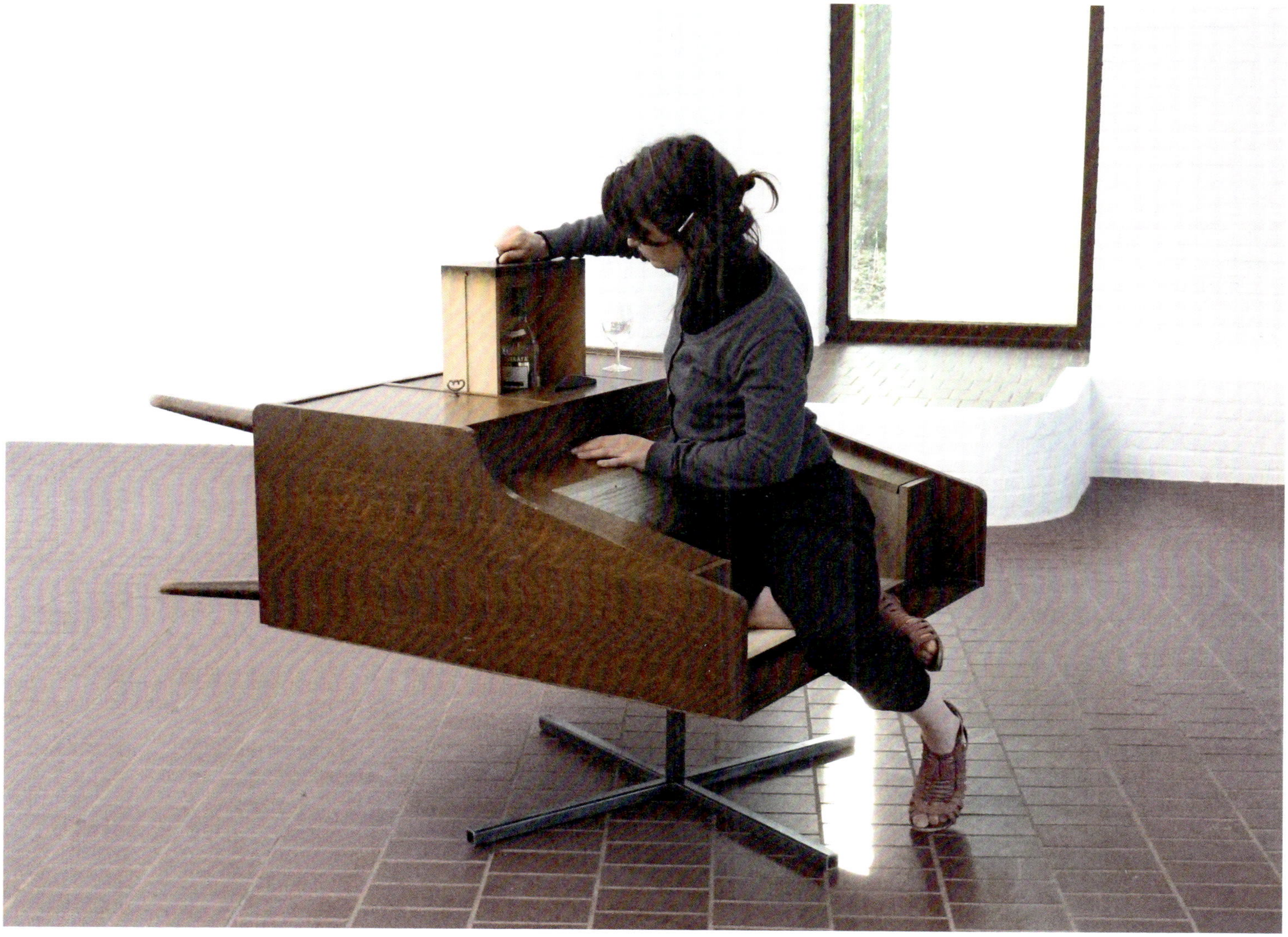

Performative Sculptures: Drinking Sculptures, the public is invited to open the drawers, take the glasses and bottles out and drink. The piece is realized when the performer is drunk.
2011
Middelheim Museum, Antwerp
Photos: Ottomura

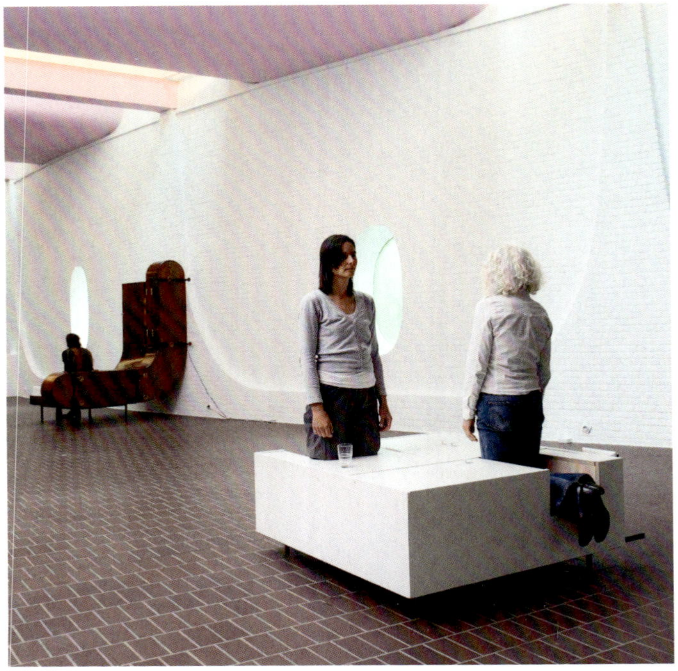

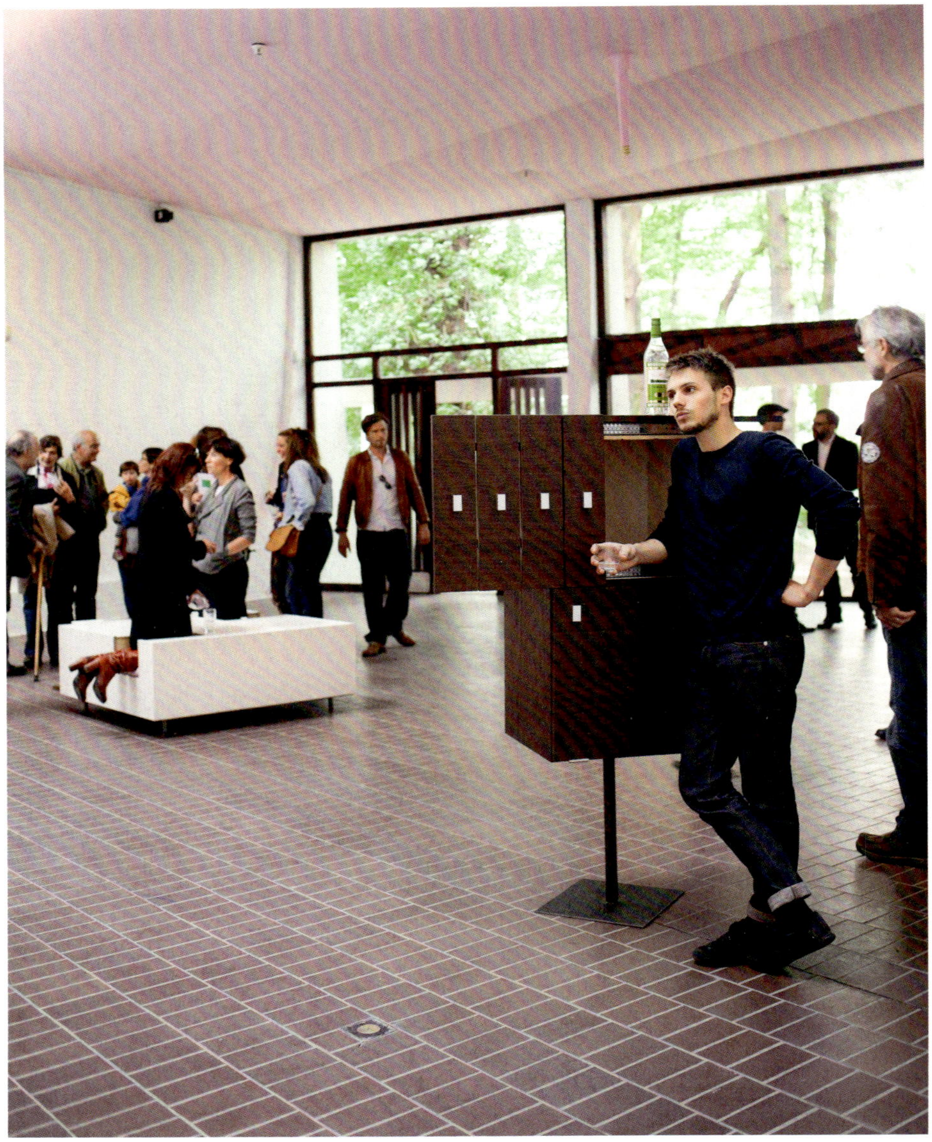

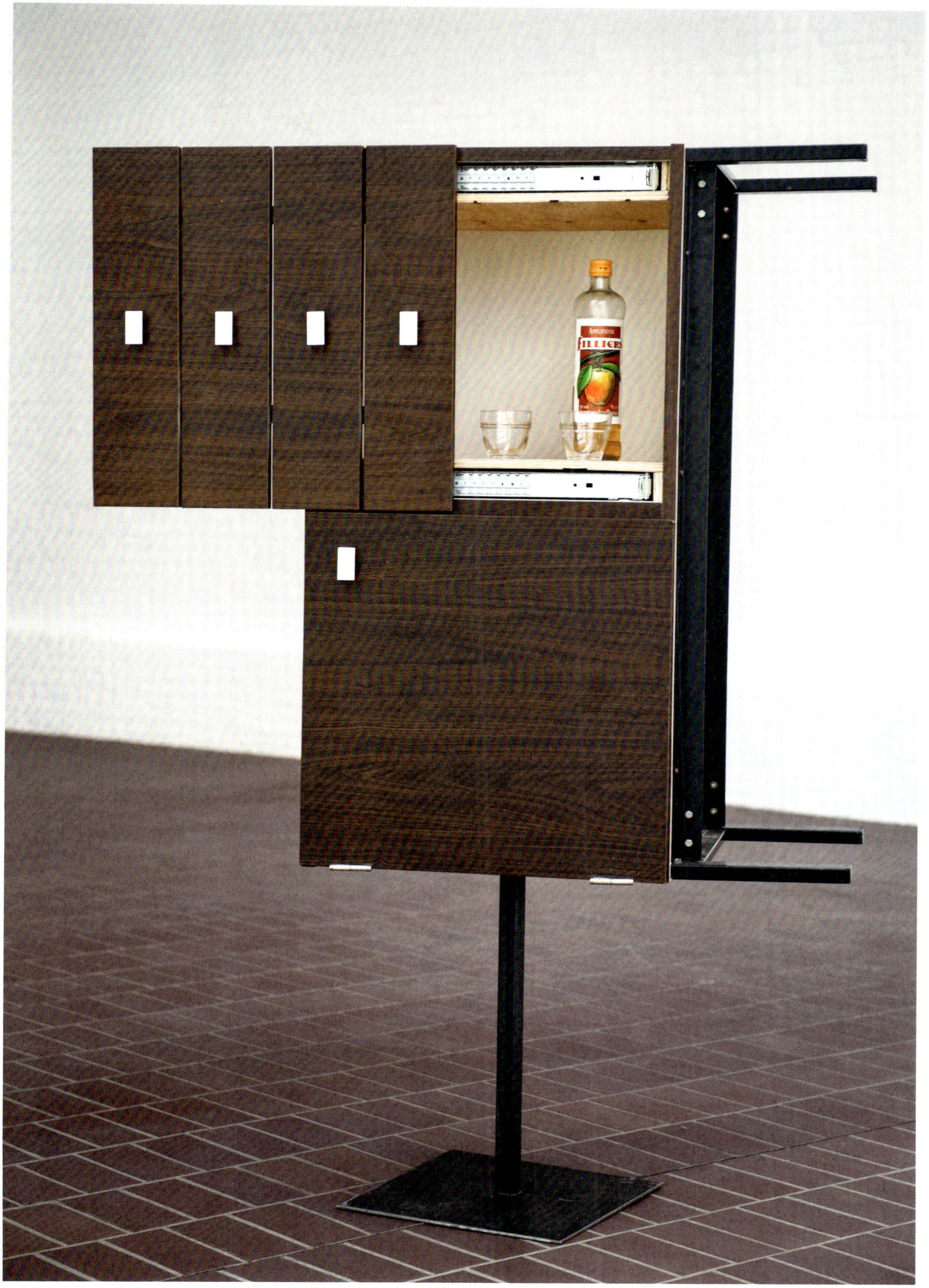
FILLIERS

Performative Sculptures: Drinking Sculptures, the public is invited to open the drawers, take the glasses and bottles out and drink. The piece is realized when the performer is drunk.
2011
Middelheim Museum, Antwerp
Photos: Studio Wurm & Ottomura

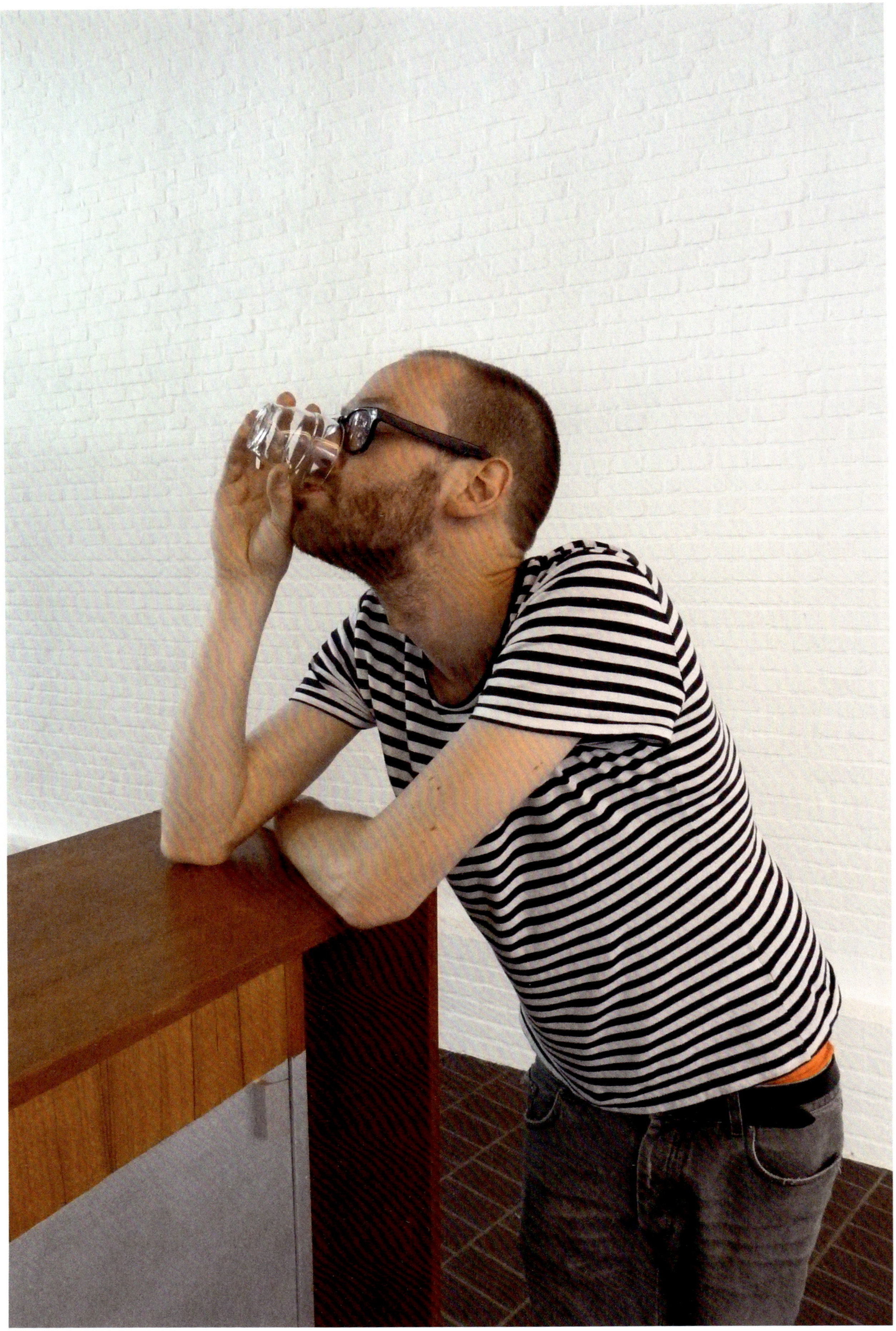

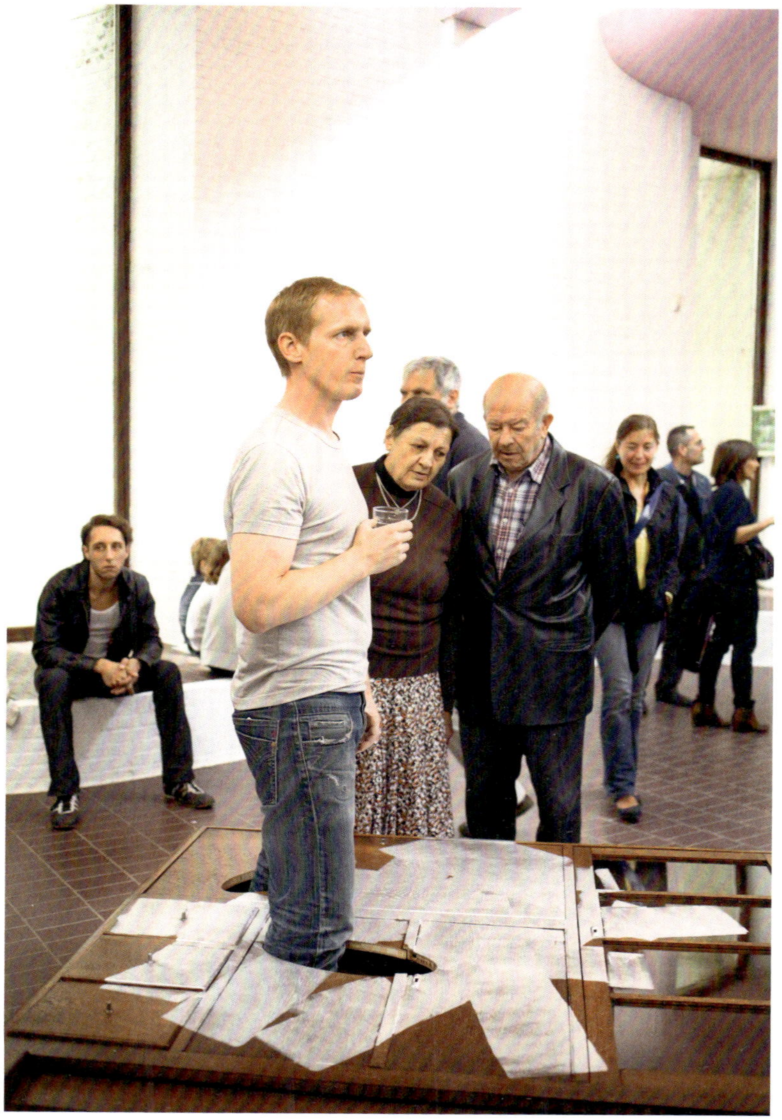

Performative Sculptures: Drinking Sculptures, the public is invited to open the drawers, take the glasses and bottles out and drink. The piece is realized when the performer is drunk.
2011
Middelheim Museum, Antwerp
Photos: Ottomura

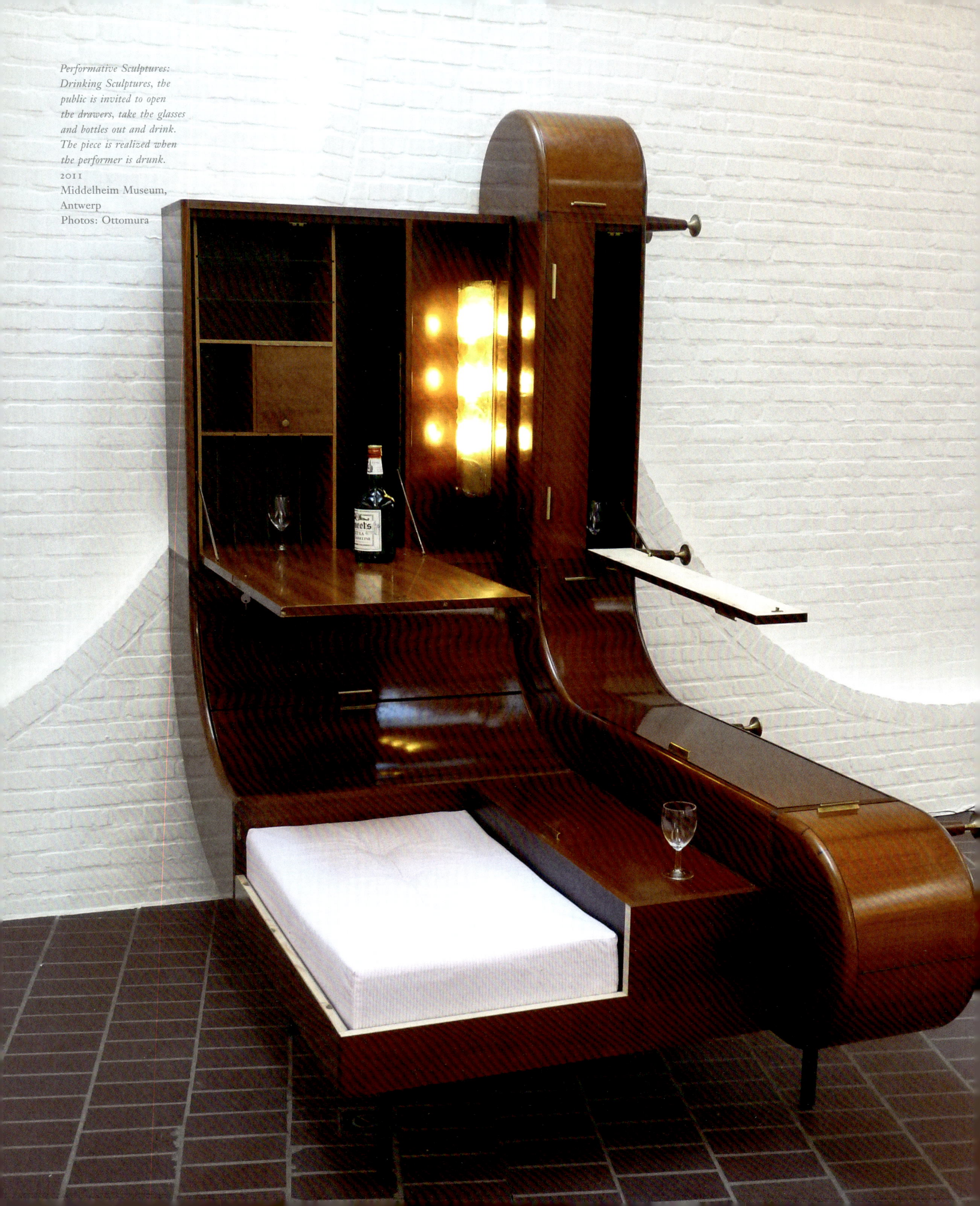

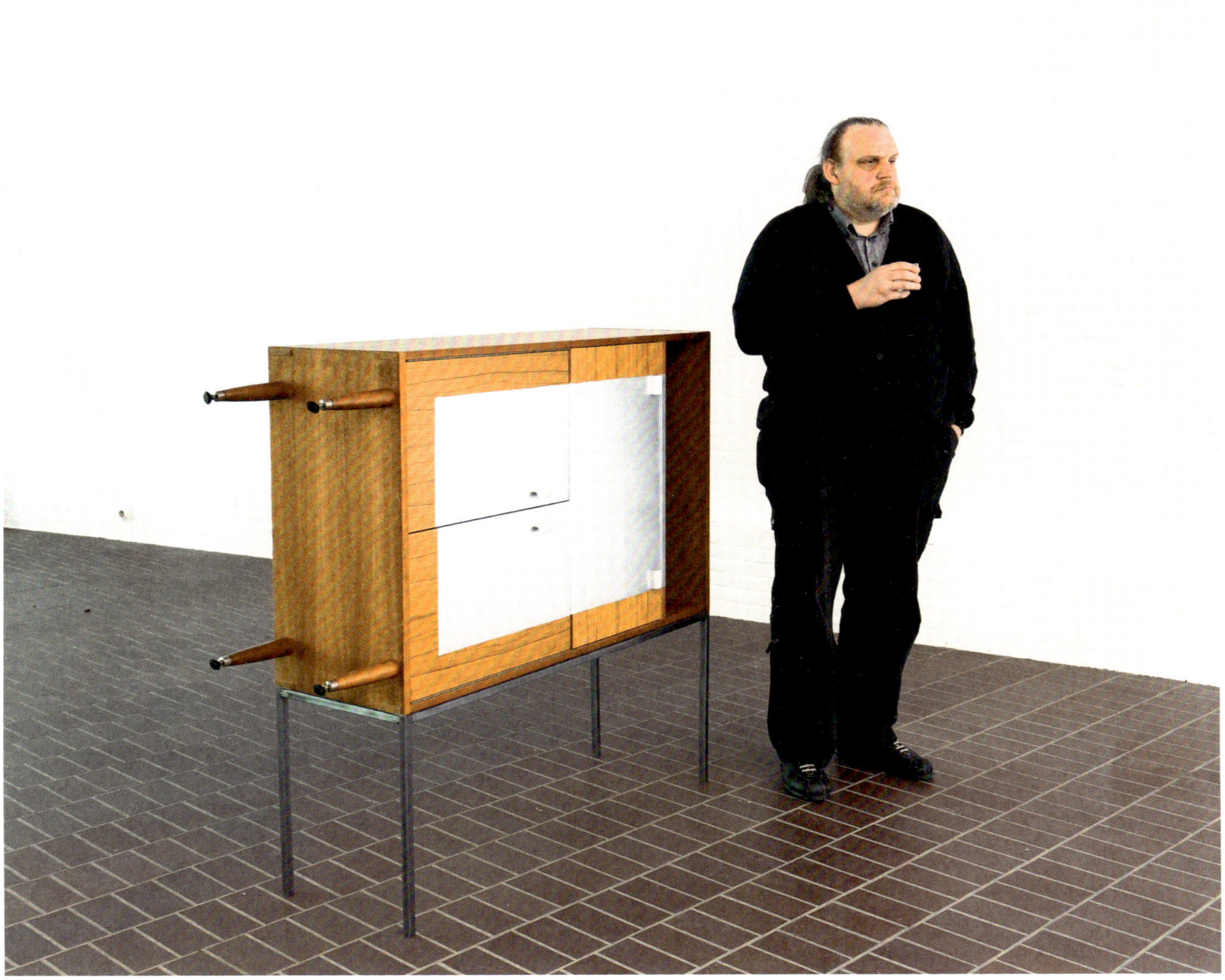

Doppelbank für Trinker, 2011
Wood, metal, glass, bottles
79 × 181 × 82 cm
Installation view, 2011
MAK, Vienna

Groom, 2010
Photo: Christian Wind

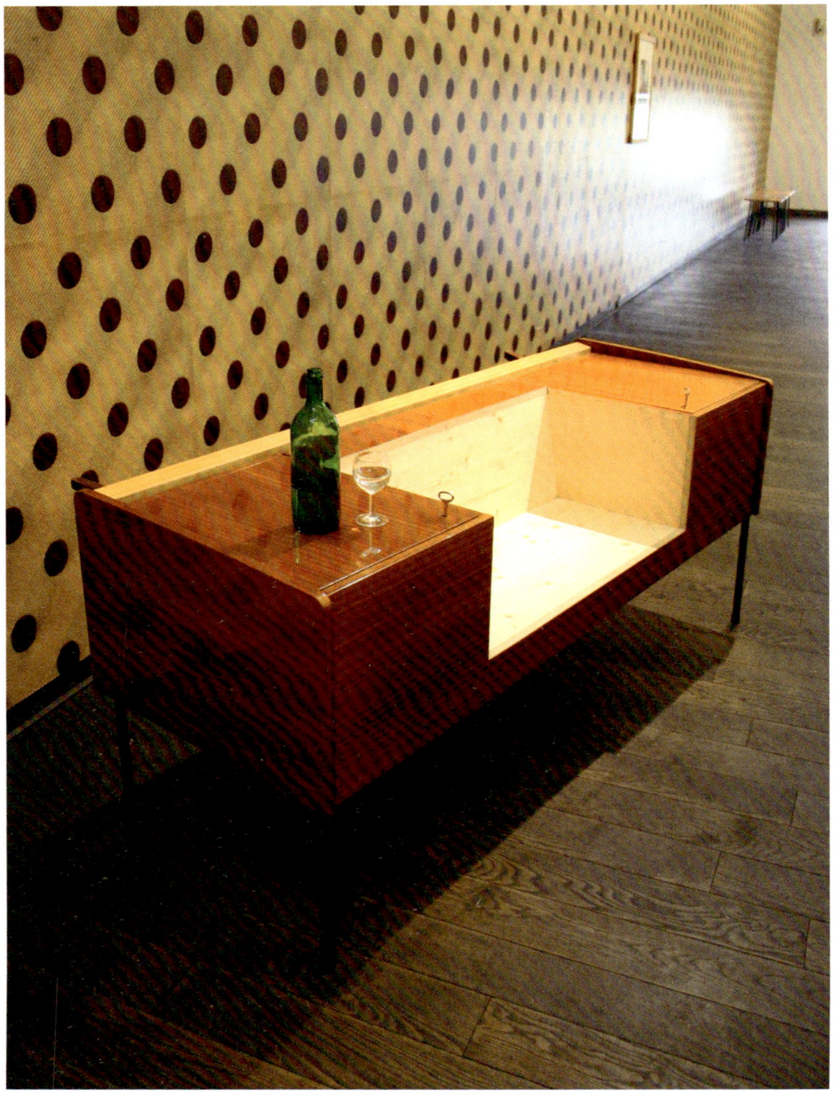

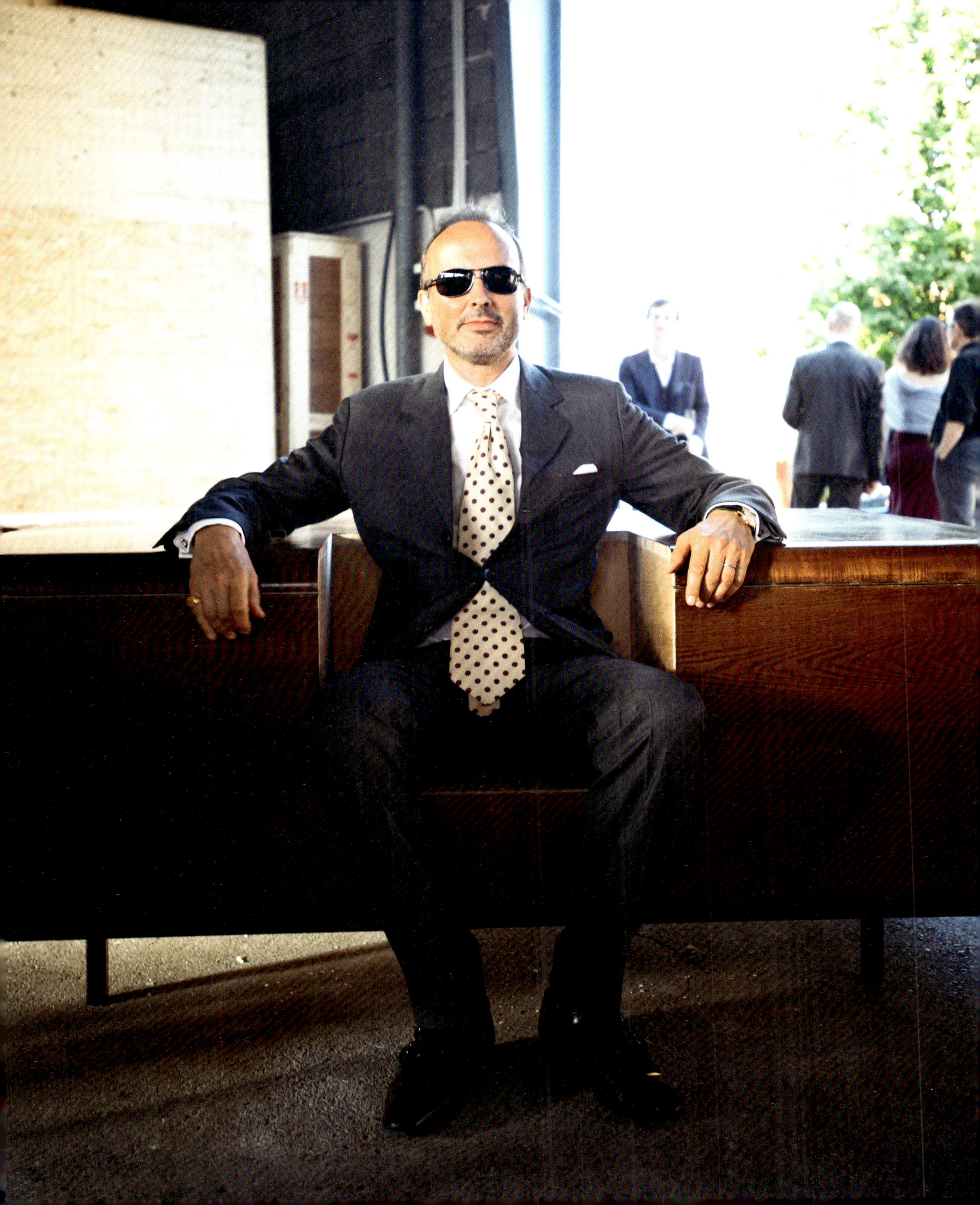

Untitled, 2011
Wood, tubs, lacquer
81 × 175 × 44 cm

Performative Sculptures: Drinking Sculptures, the public is invited to open the drawers, take the glasses and bottles out and drink. The piece is realized when the performer is drunk.
2011
Middelheim Museum, Antwerp
Photo: Ottomura

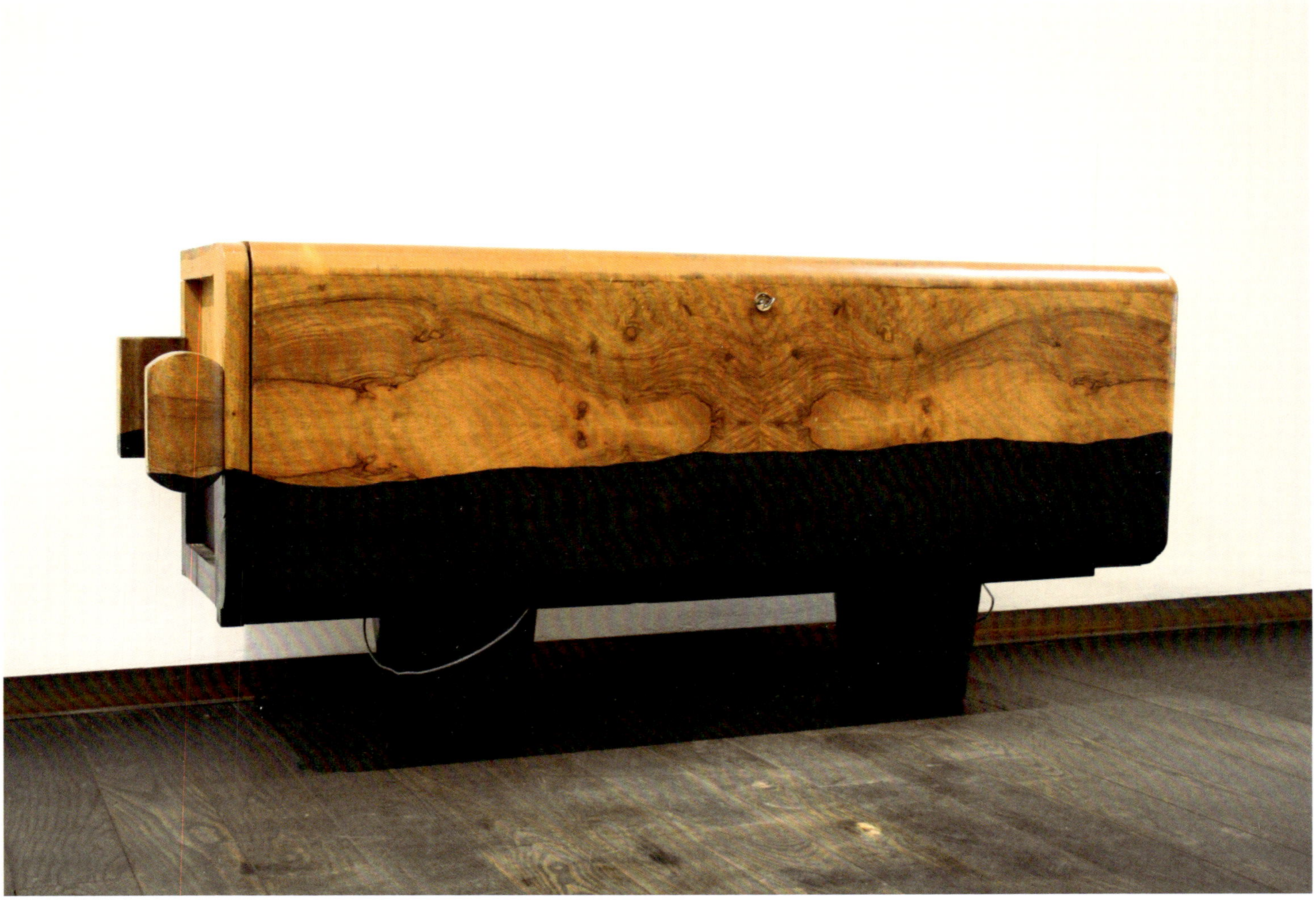

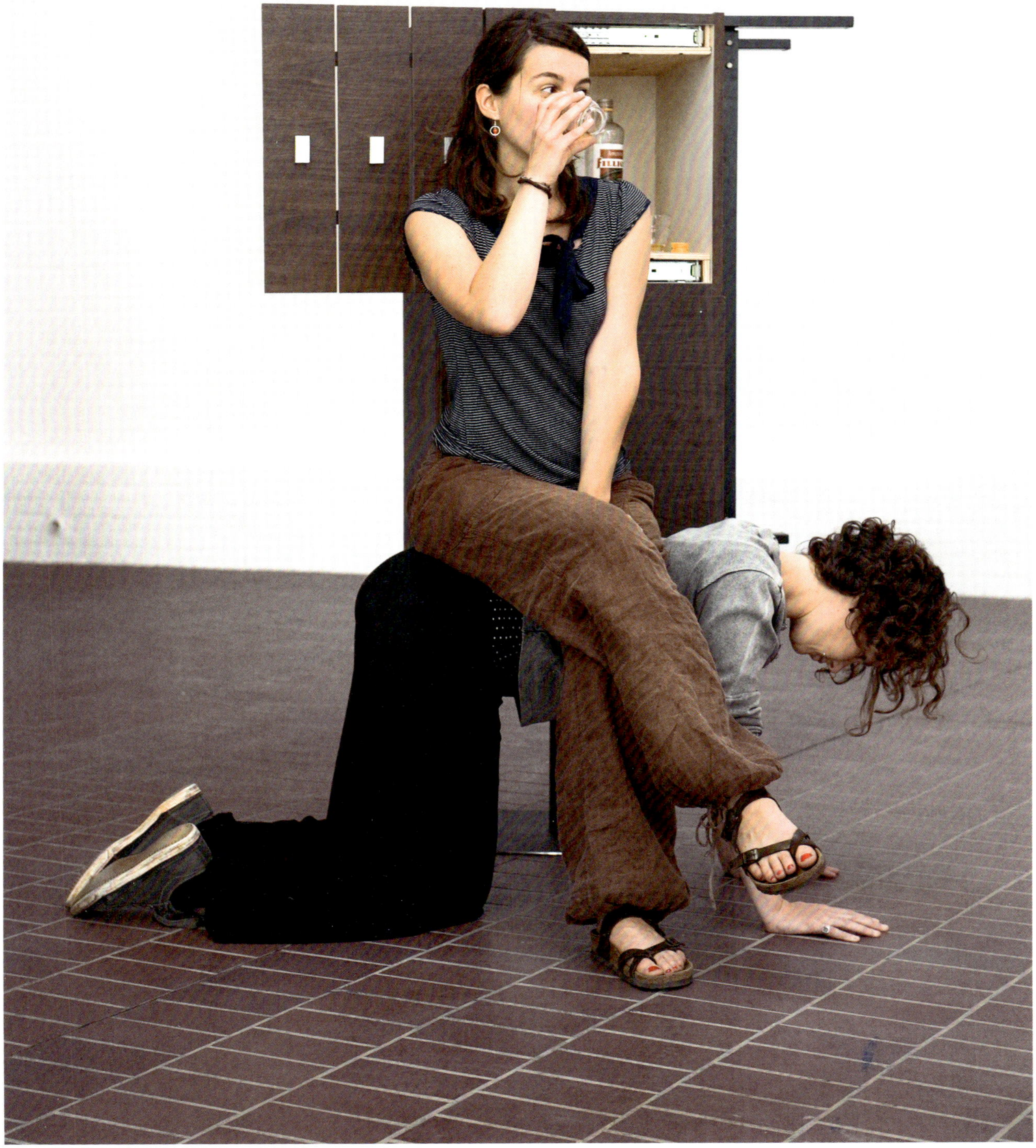

Punschkrapferl, 2011
Wood, metal, lacquer,
glass, bottles
84 × 149 × 108 cm
Installation view, 2011
MAK, Vienna

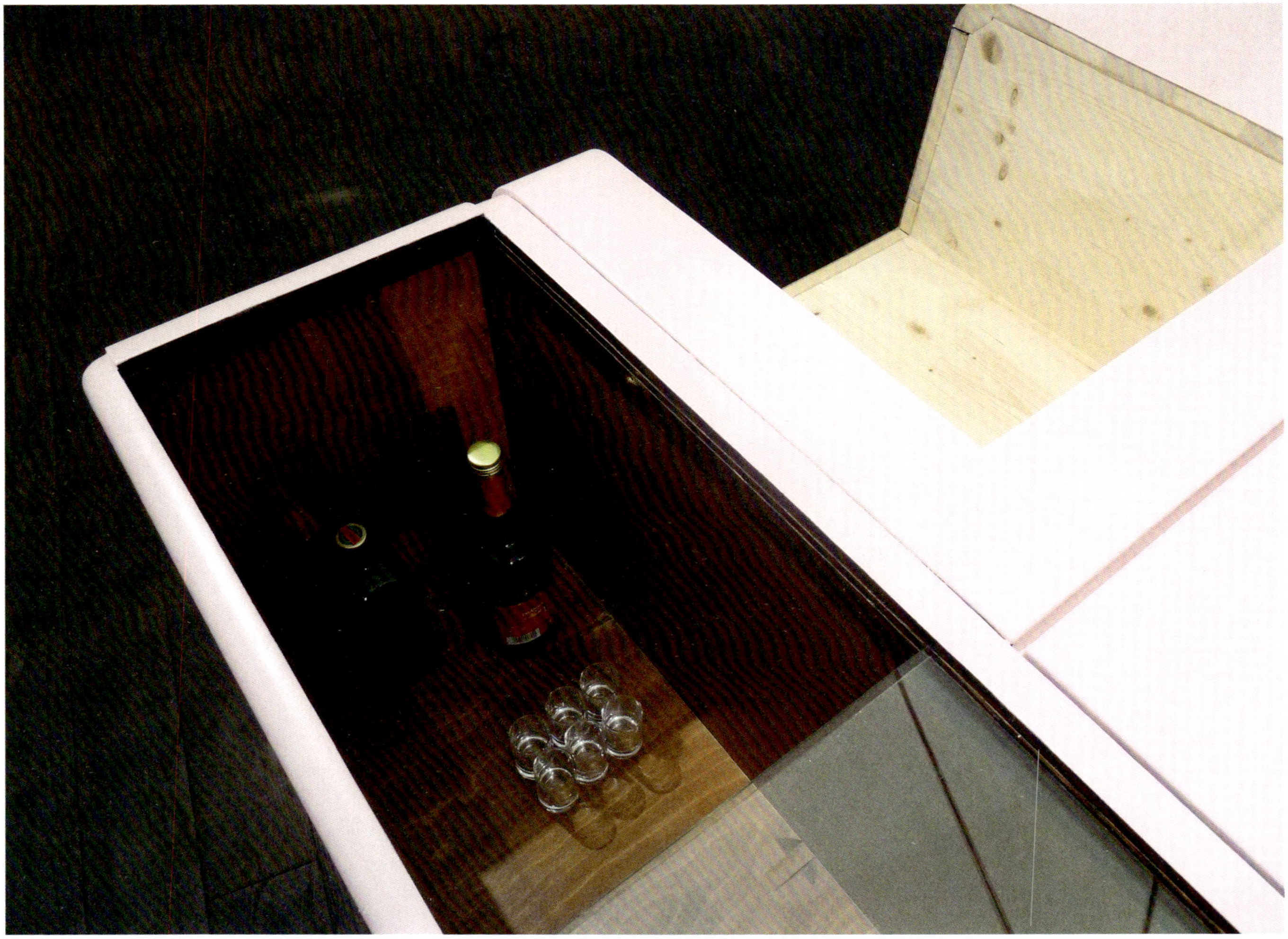

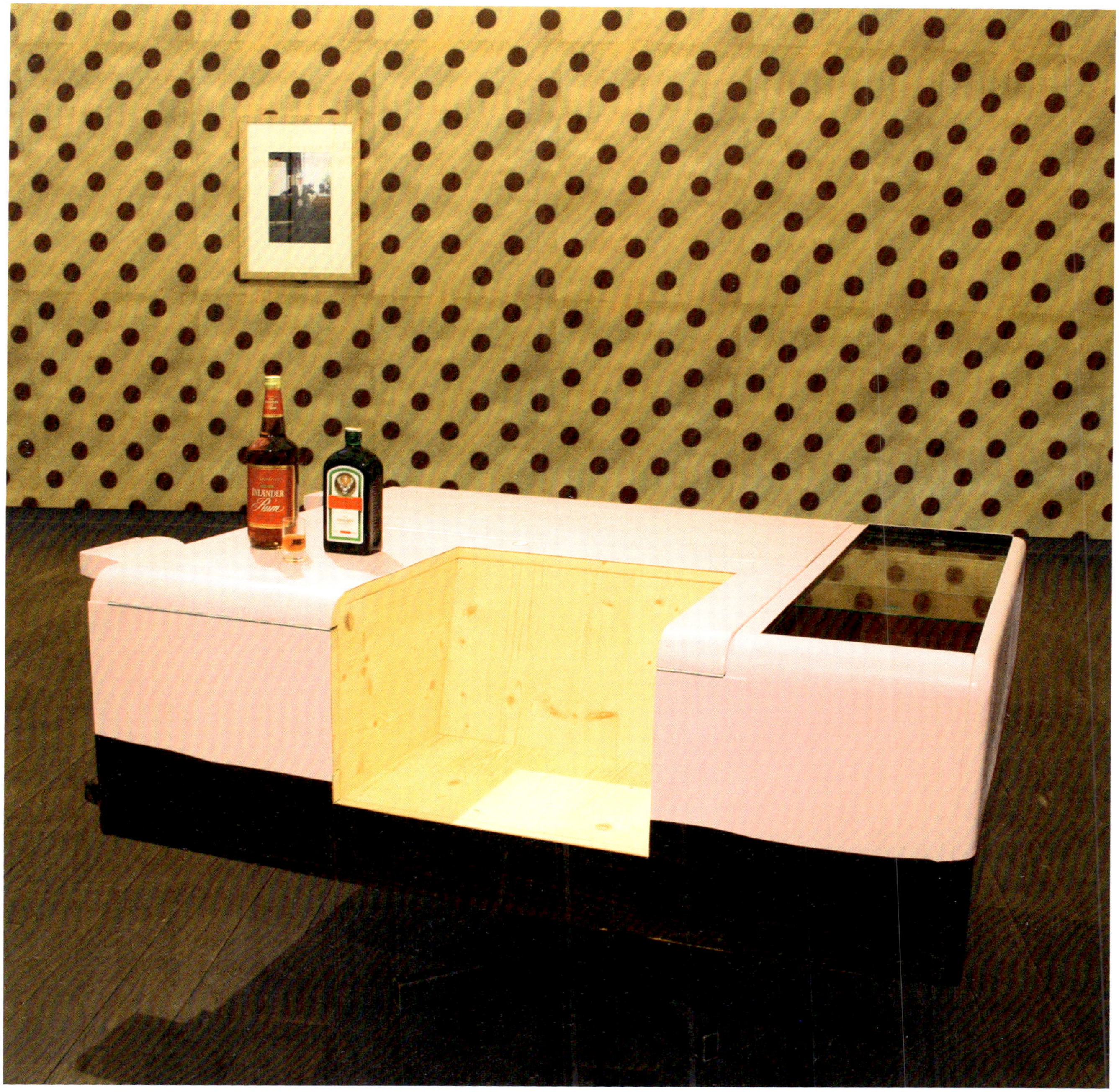
INLÄNDER
Rum

Beistelltisch, 2011
Wood, metal, glass
57.5 × 83 × 77 cm

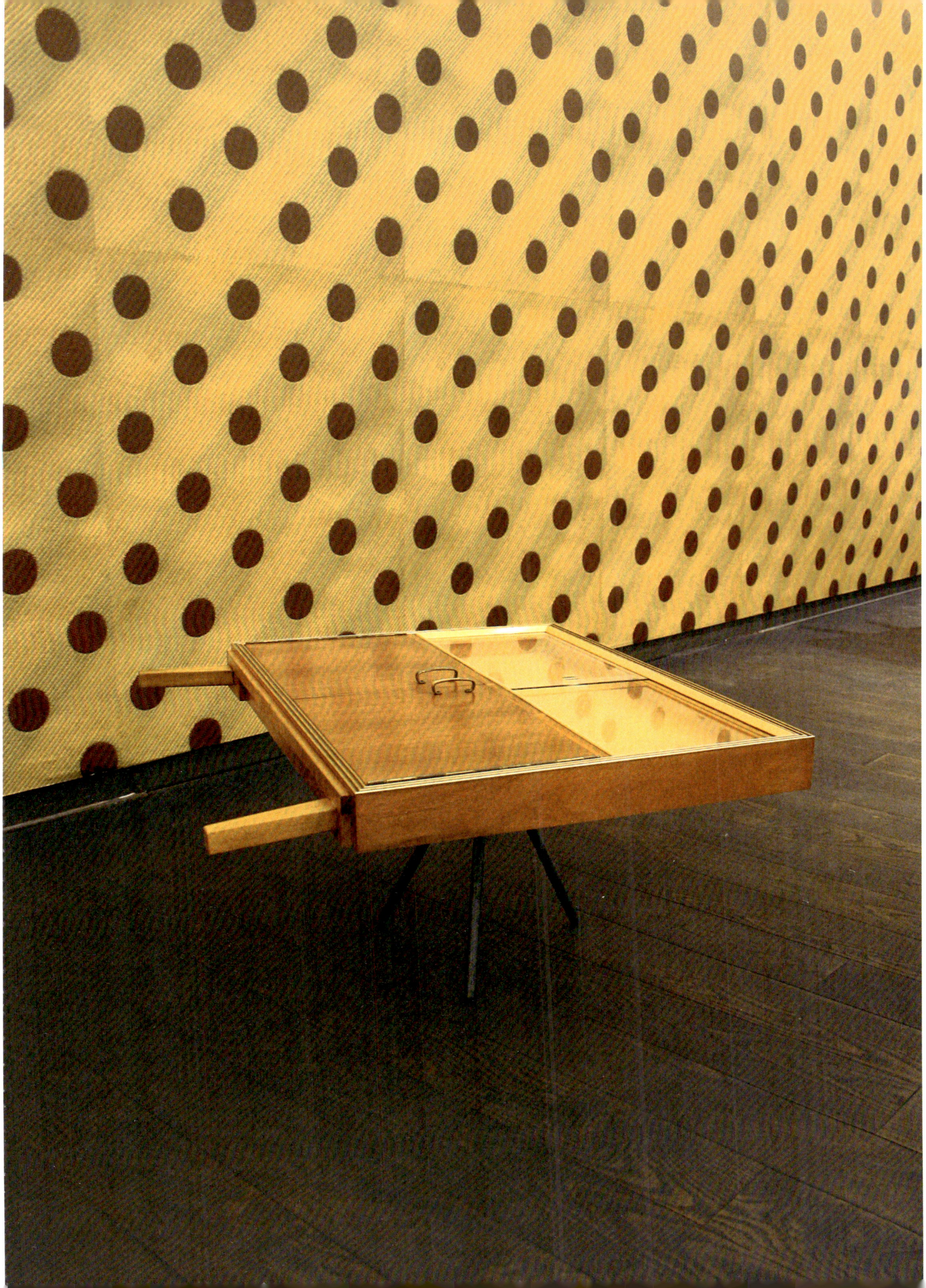

Untitled, 2011
Paint on c-print
40.5 × 30.3 cm

Untitled, 2011
Paint on c-print
30.3 × 40.5 cm

Kredenza, 2011
Wood, metal, glass
214 × 193.5 × 43 cm

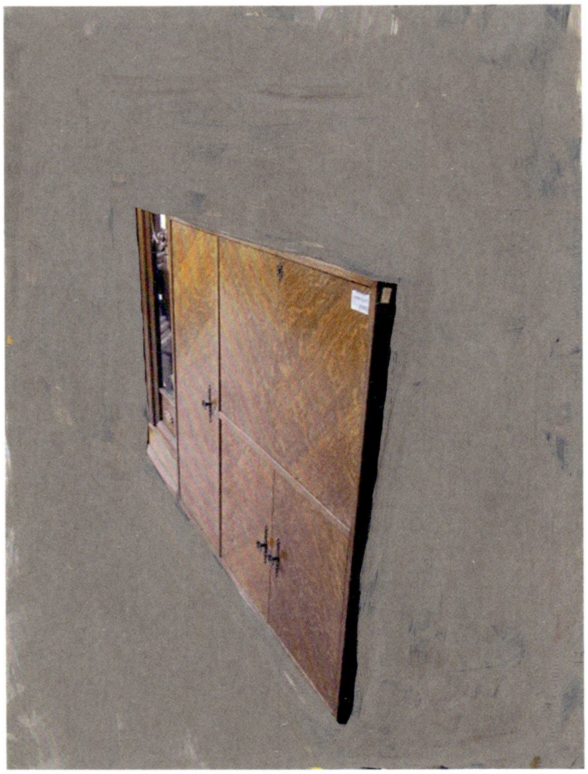

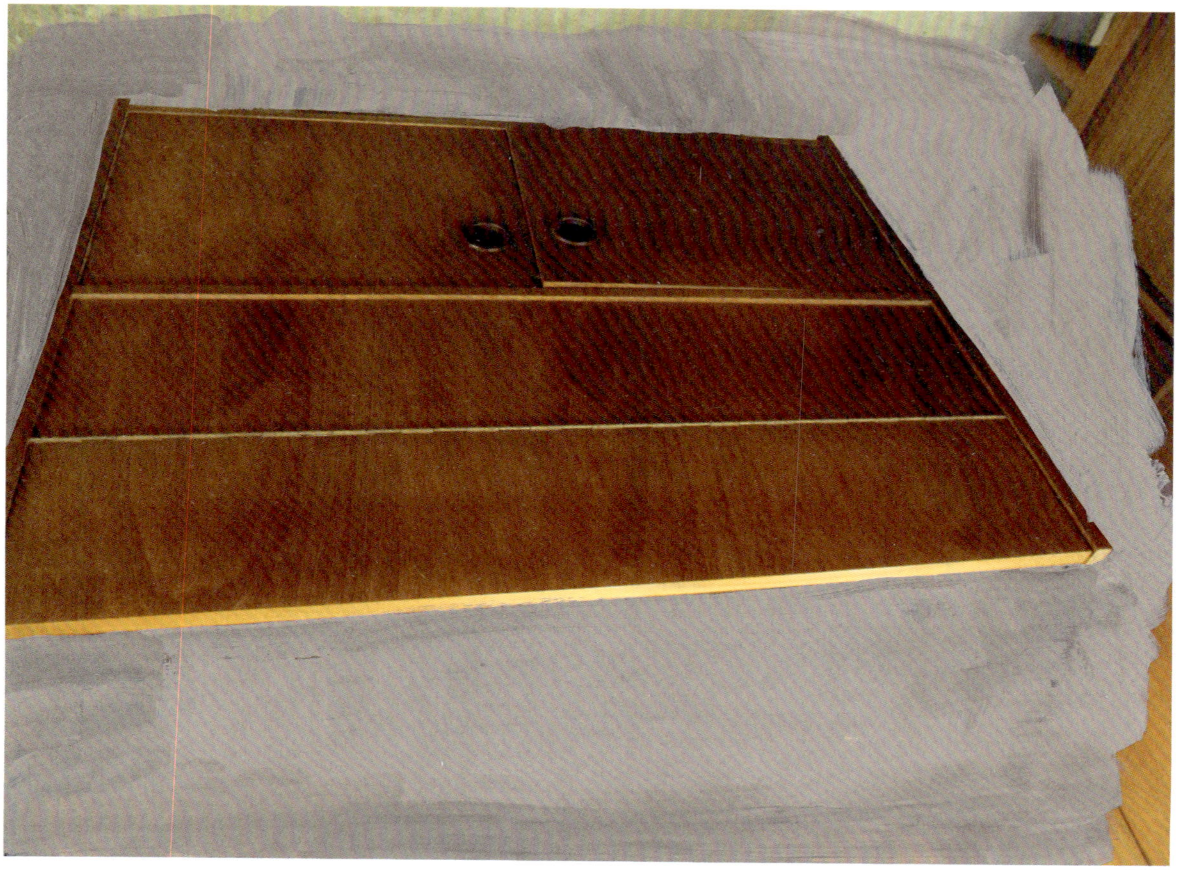

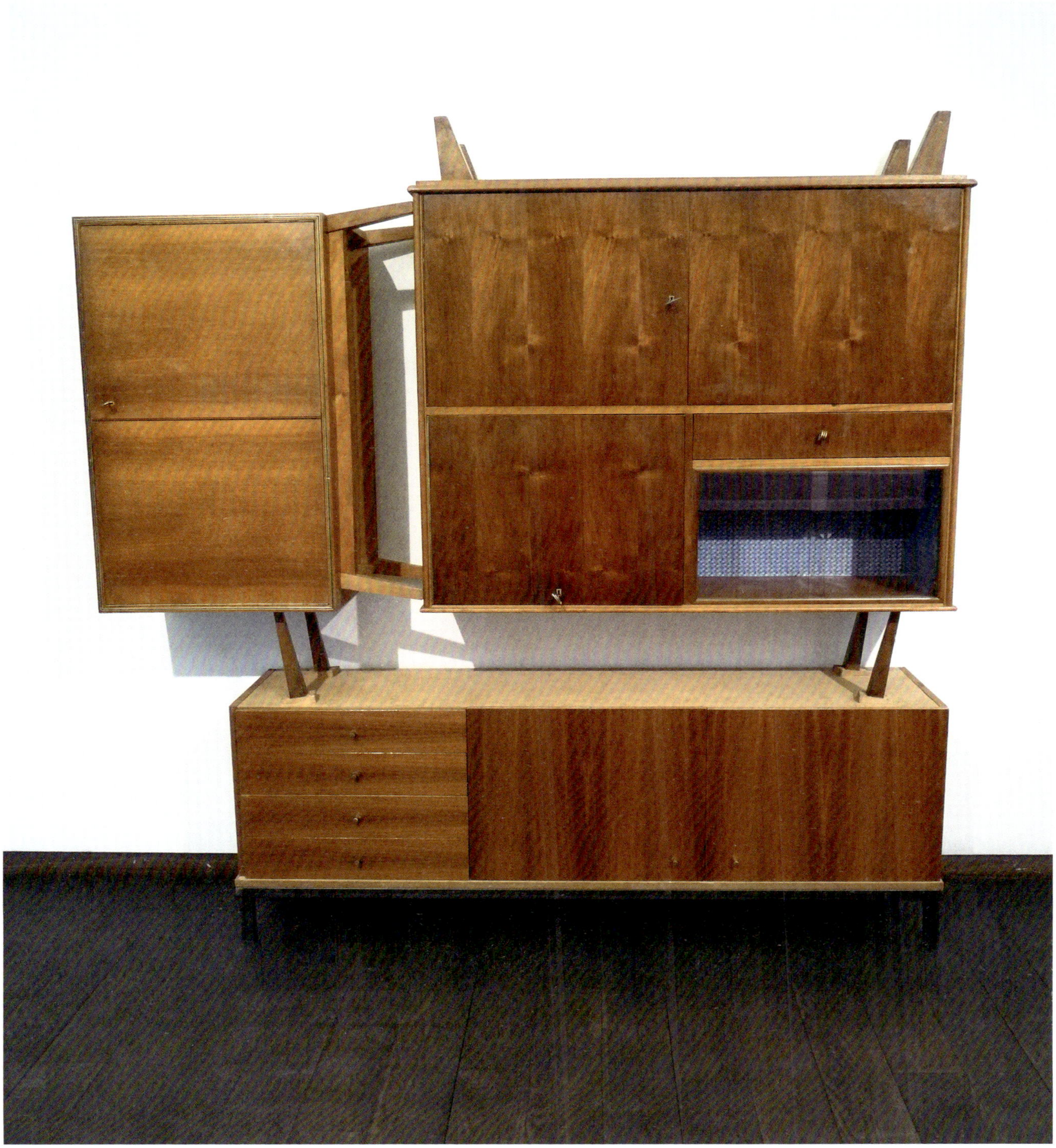

Untitled, 2011
Paint on c-print
30.3 × 40.5 cm

Ich schlucke deinen Müll, 1995
Felt-marker on magazine
29.9 × 16-22.2 cm

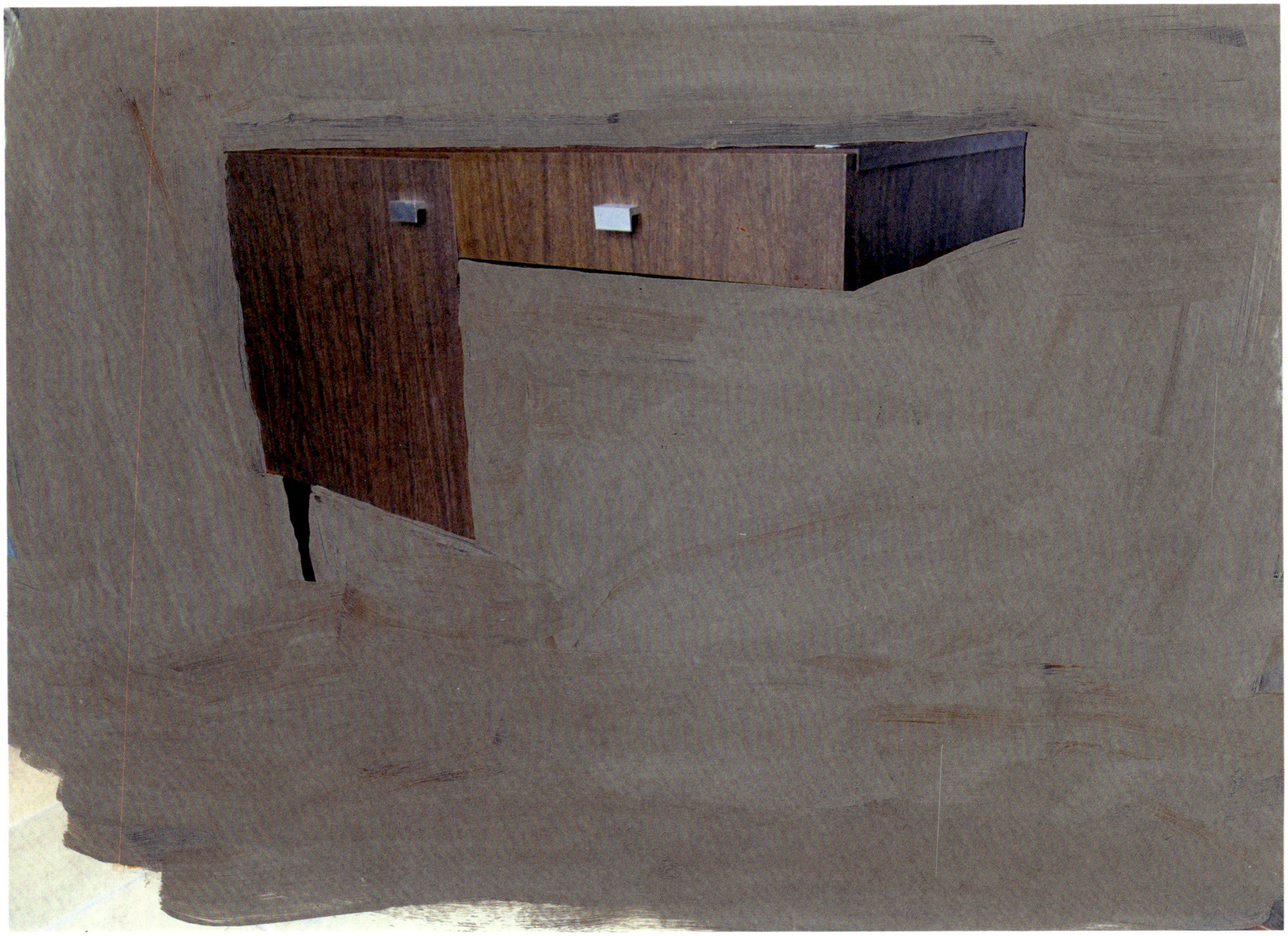

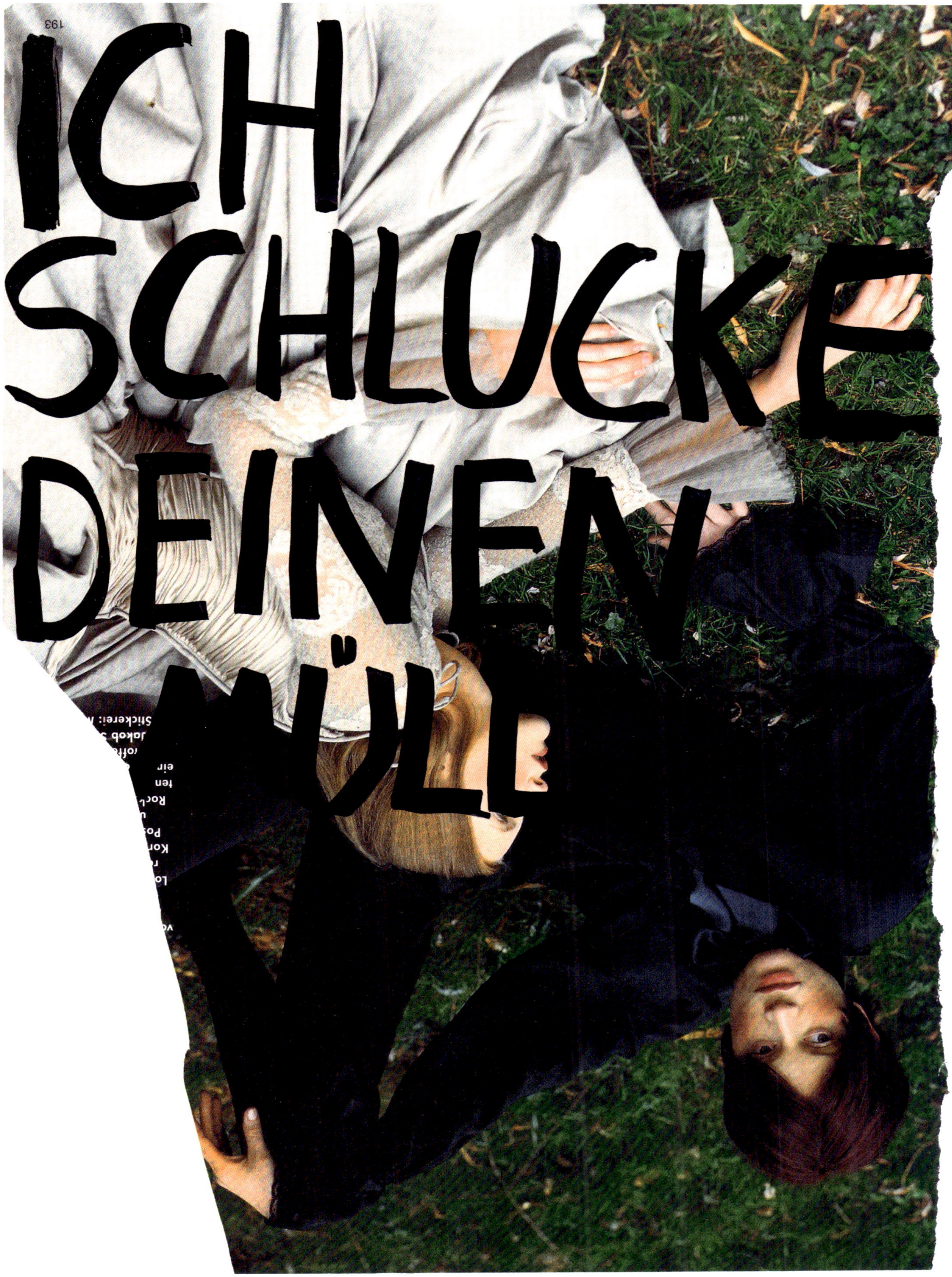
ICH
SCHLUCKE
DEINEN

Untitled, 2011
Wood, metal
73 × 70 × 80.5 cm

Untitled, 2011
Paint on c-print
40.5 × 30.3 cm

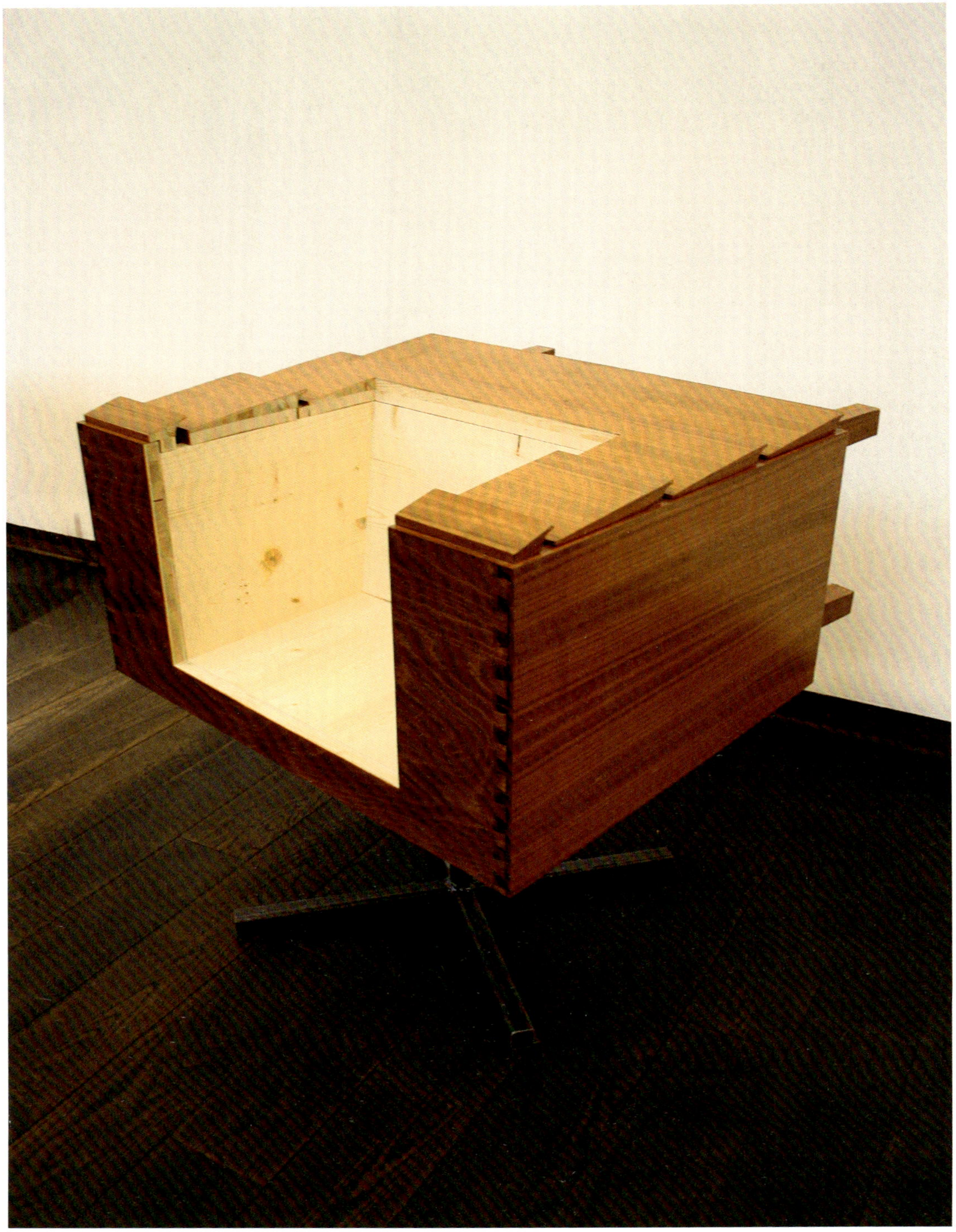

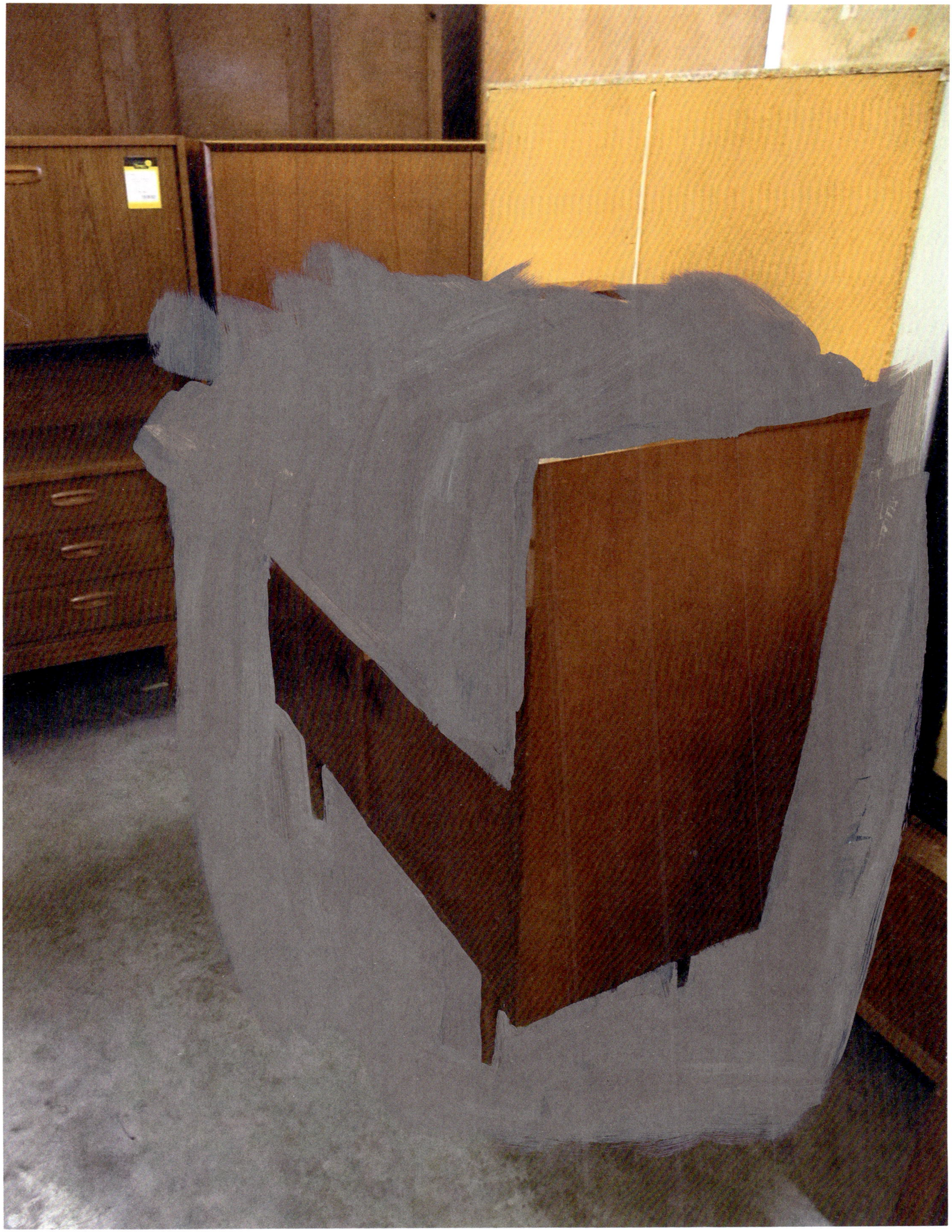

Untitled, 2011
Paint on c-print
21 × 29.6 cm

Untitled, 2011
Paint on c-print
30.3 × 40.5 cm

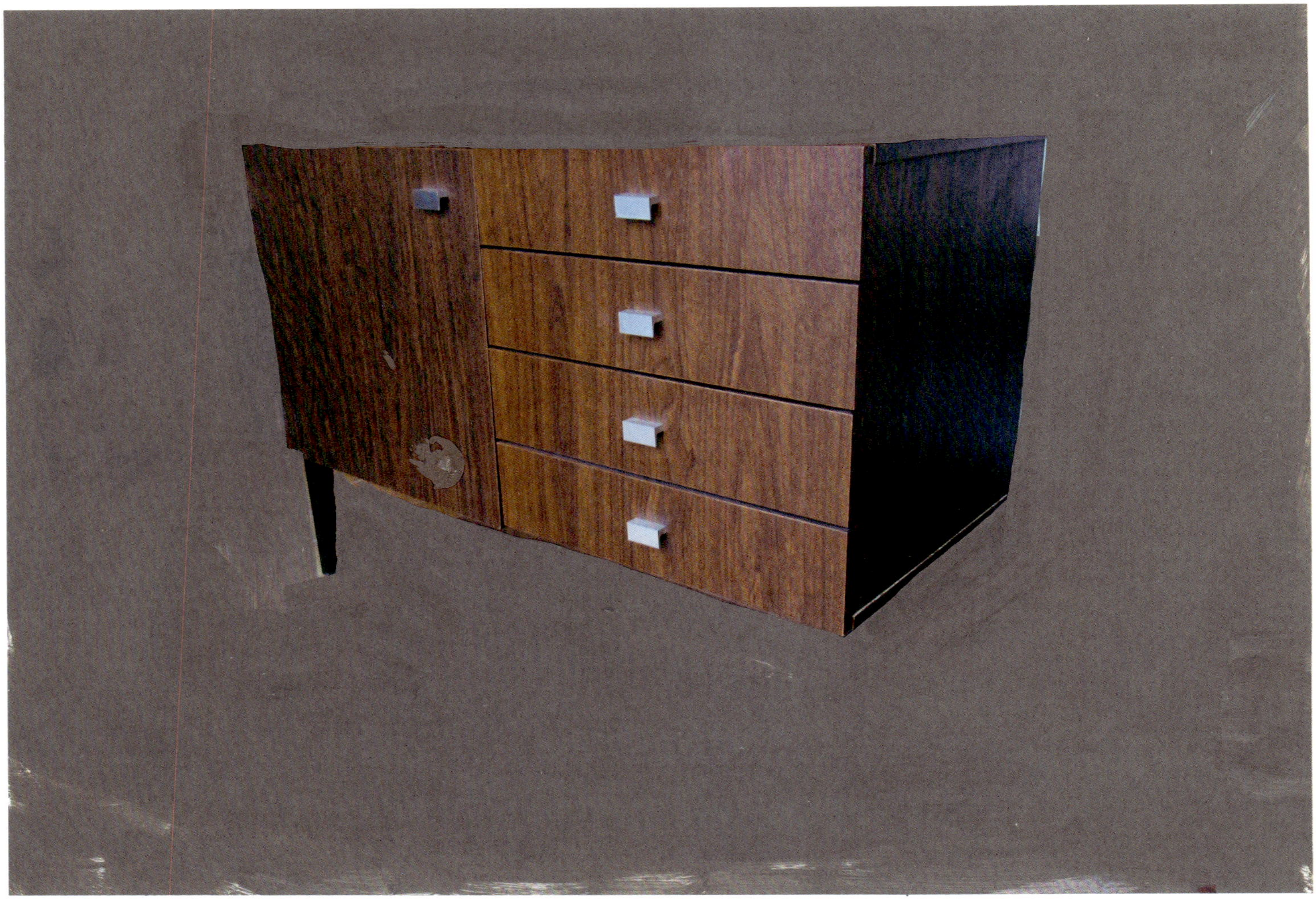

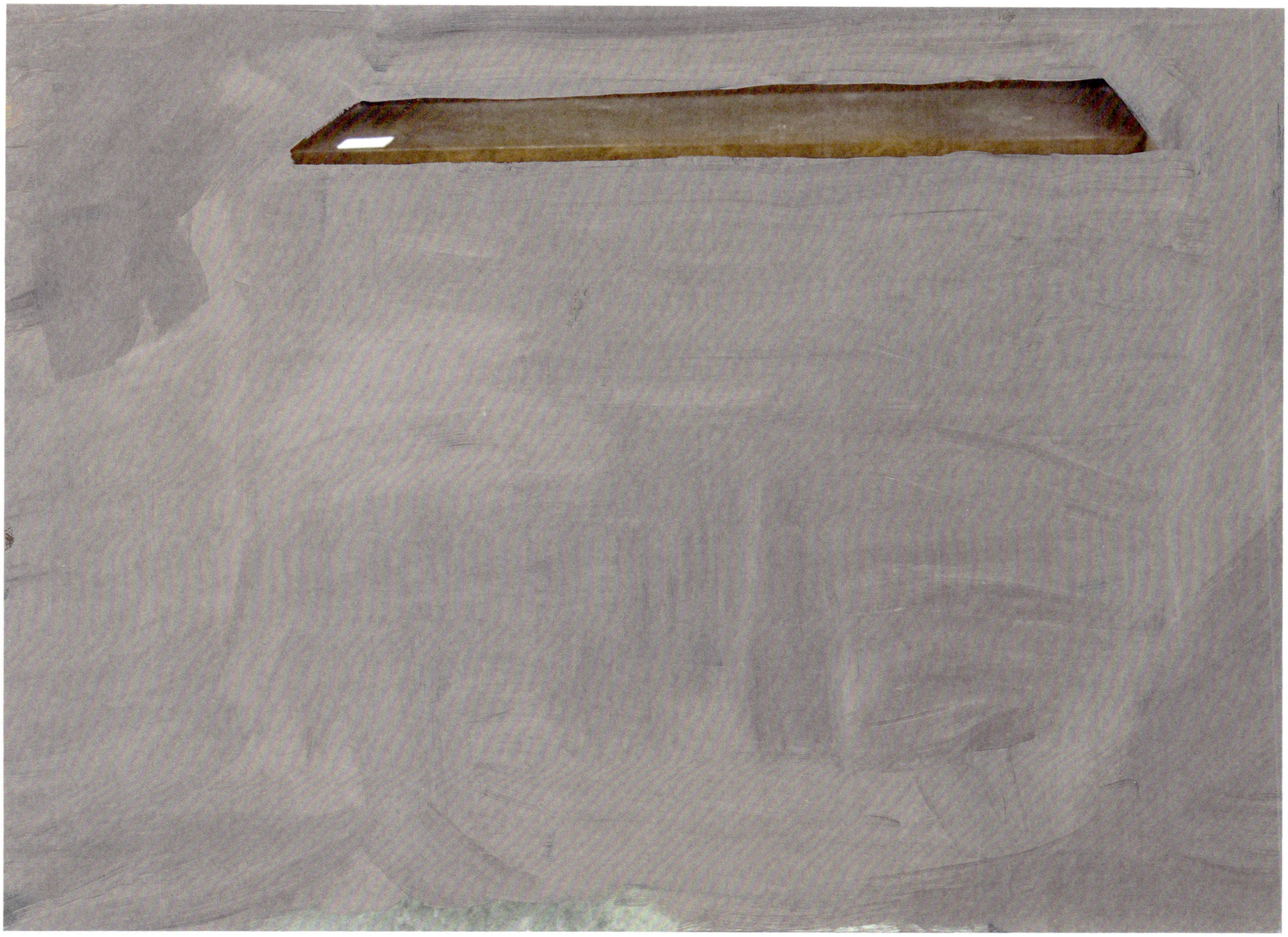

Möbel denkt, 2011
Paint, pen on catalogue
30 × 23.9 cm

Furniture hypnosis, 2011
Paint, pen on catalogue
30 × 23.9 cm

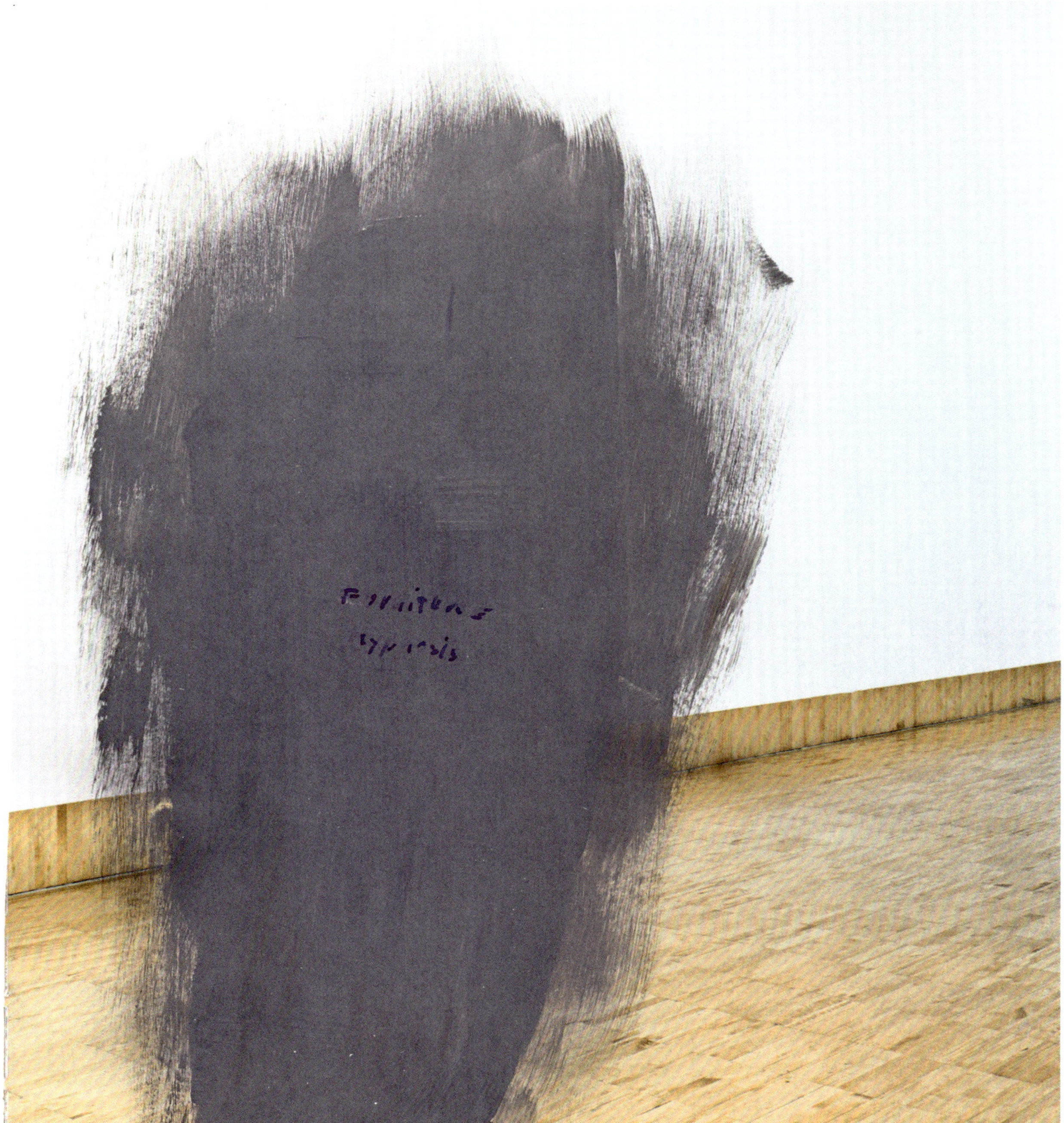

Ost, 1991
Felt-marker, paint
on catalogue
21 × 25.4 cm

Untitled, 2011
Paint on catalogue
30 × 23.7 cm

The untouchable, 2011
Wood, metal, lacquer
117 × 181 × 52 cm

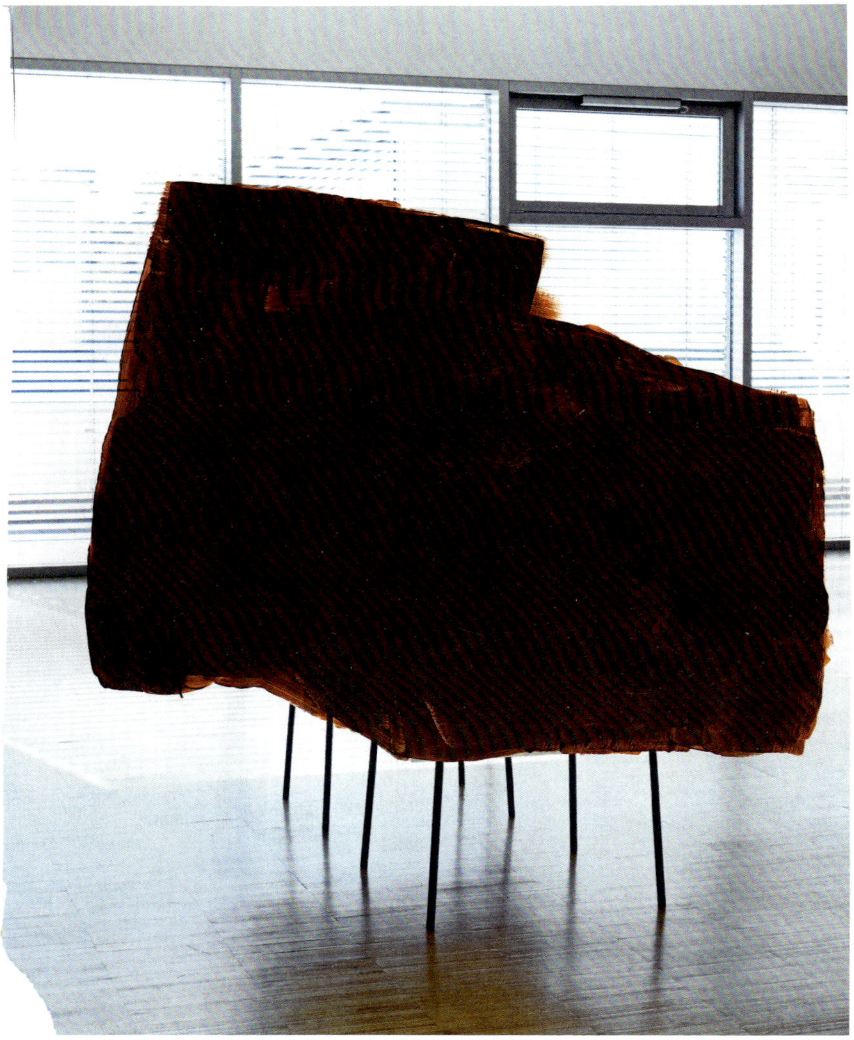

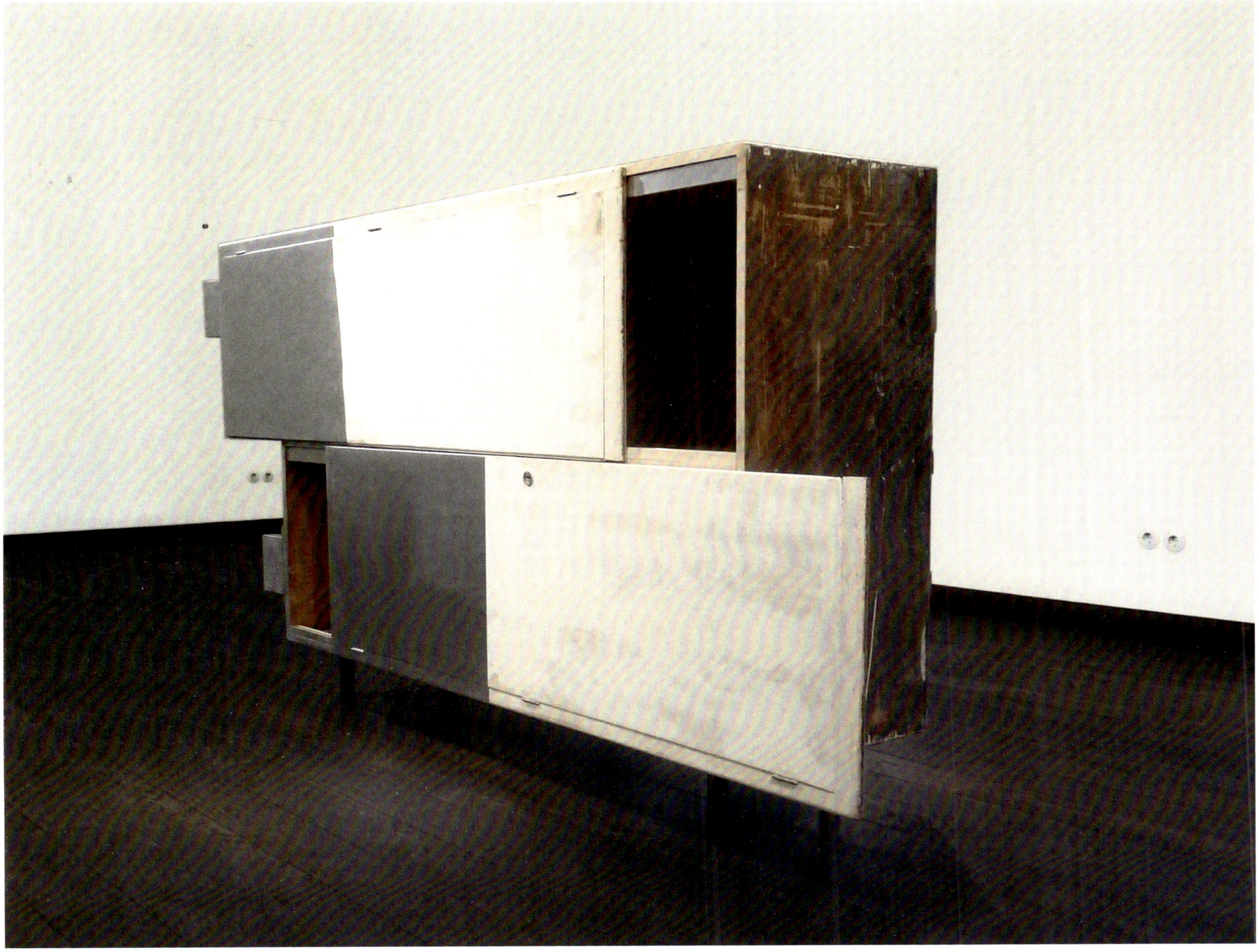

A near miss, 1987
Felt-marker on catalogue
26.8 × 21.7 cm

Untitled, 1991
Felt-marker on catalogue
25.5 × 20.9 cm

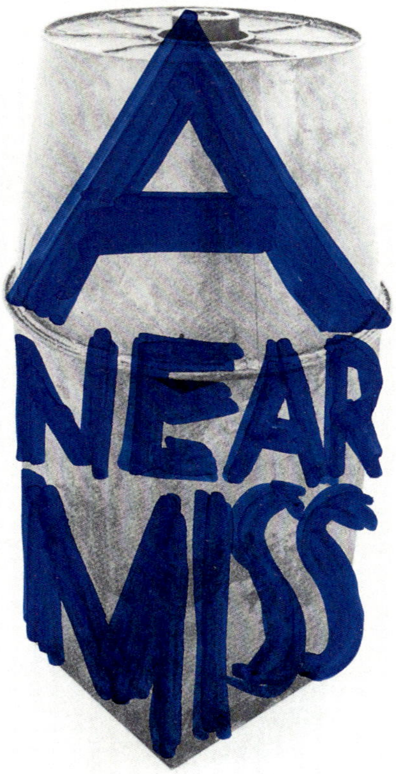

O. T., 1987
Holz, Plastik, Blech, Blei, 150 x 80 x 80 cm

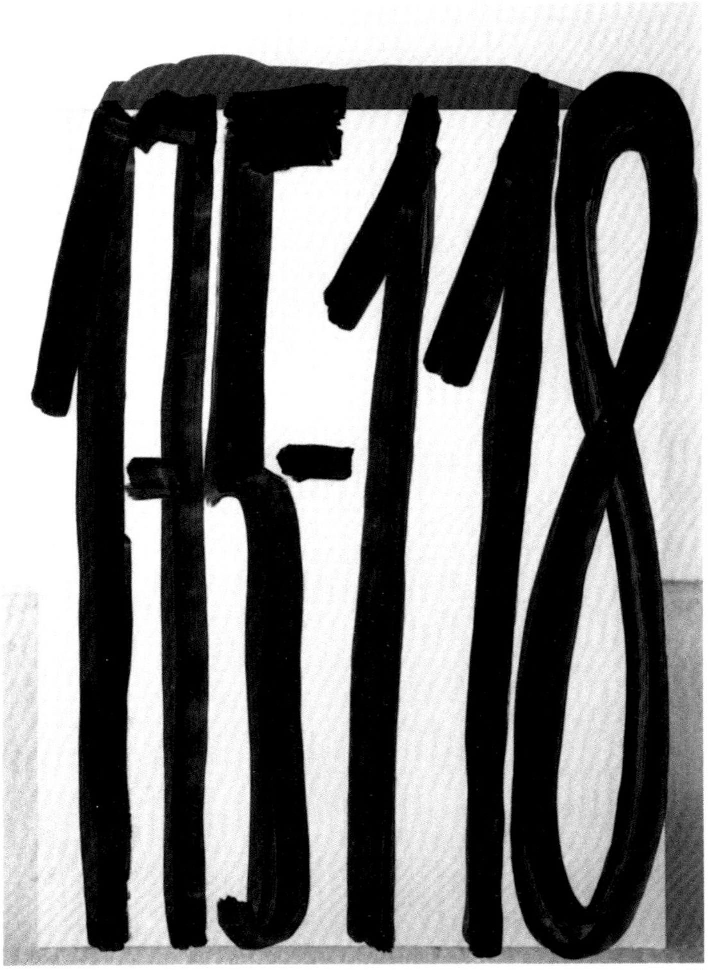
15-118

Nord Nord Ost, 1991
Felt-marker on catalogue
28 × 24.5 cm

Gestern-Heute, 1991
Paint, pen on catalogue
23.8 × 17.6 cm

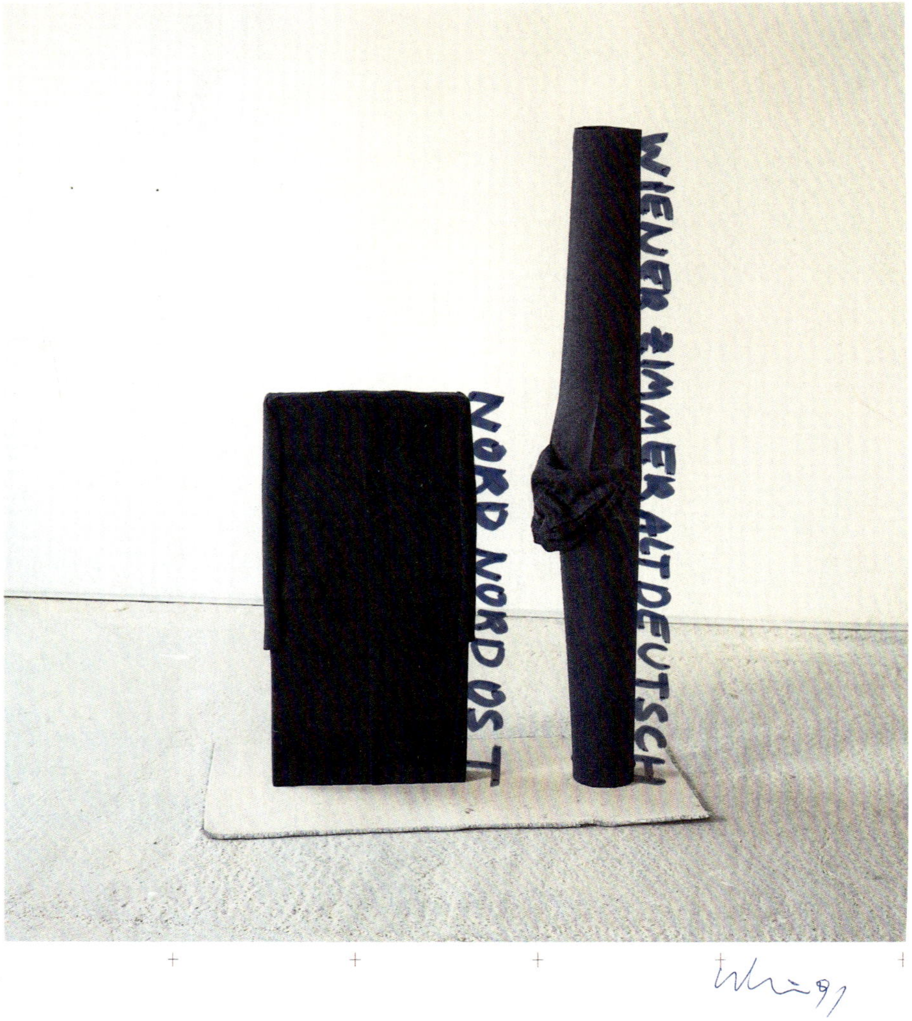

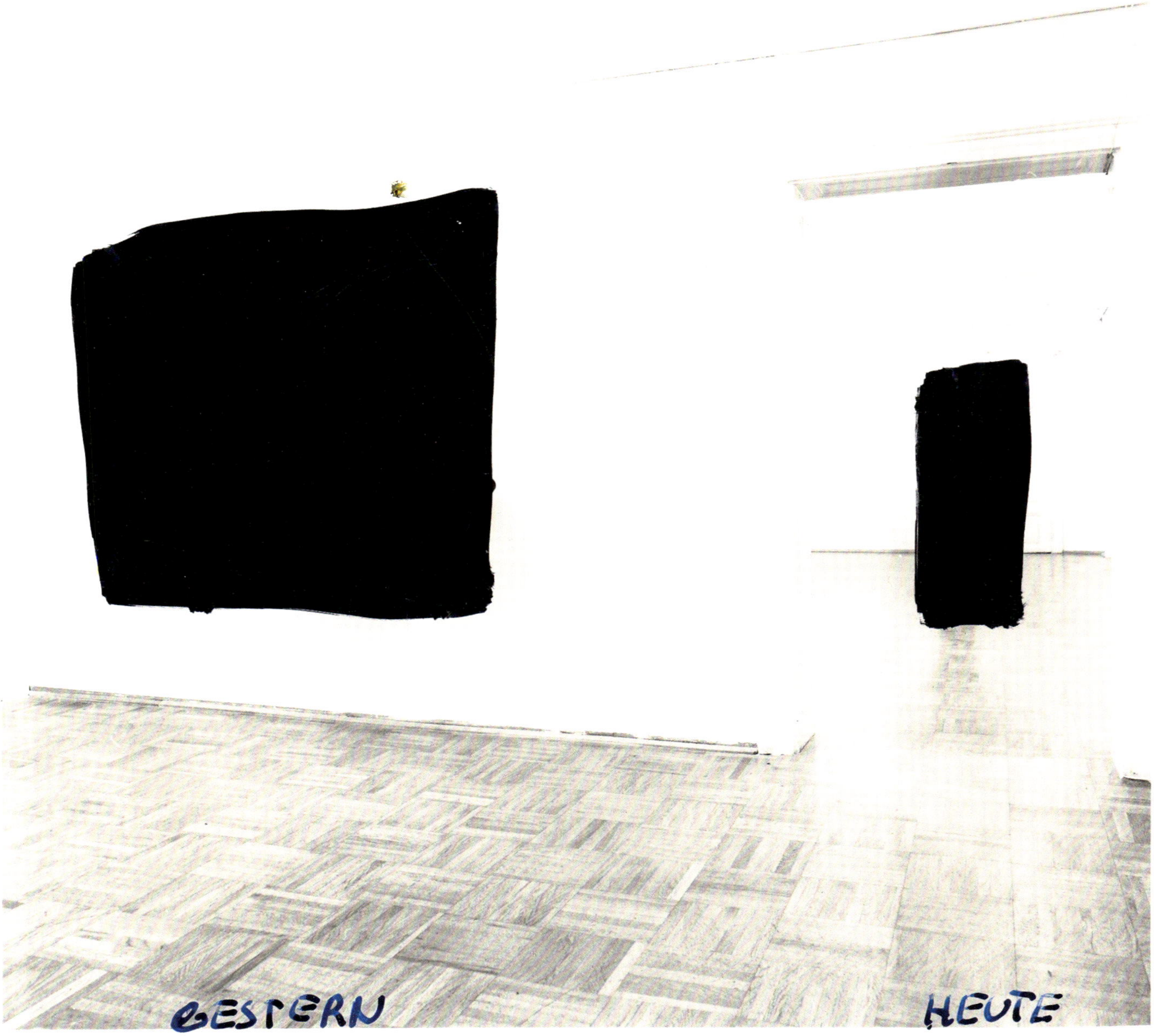
GESTERN
HEUTE

Ich schlucke deinen Müll, 1995
Felt-marker on magazine
29.9 × 14-17.6 cm

Mittagsschlaf, 1995
Felt-marker on magazine
19.5-20.5 × 21.5-22.1 cm

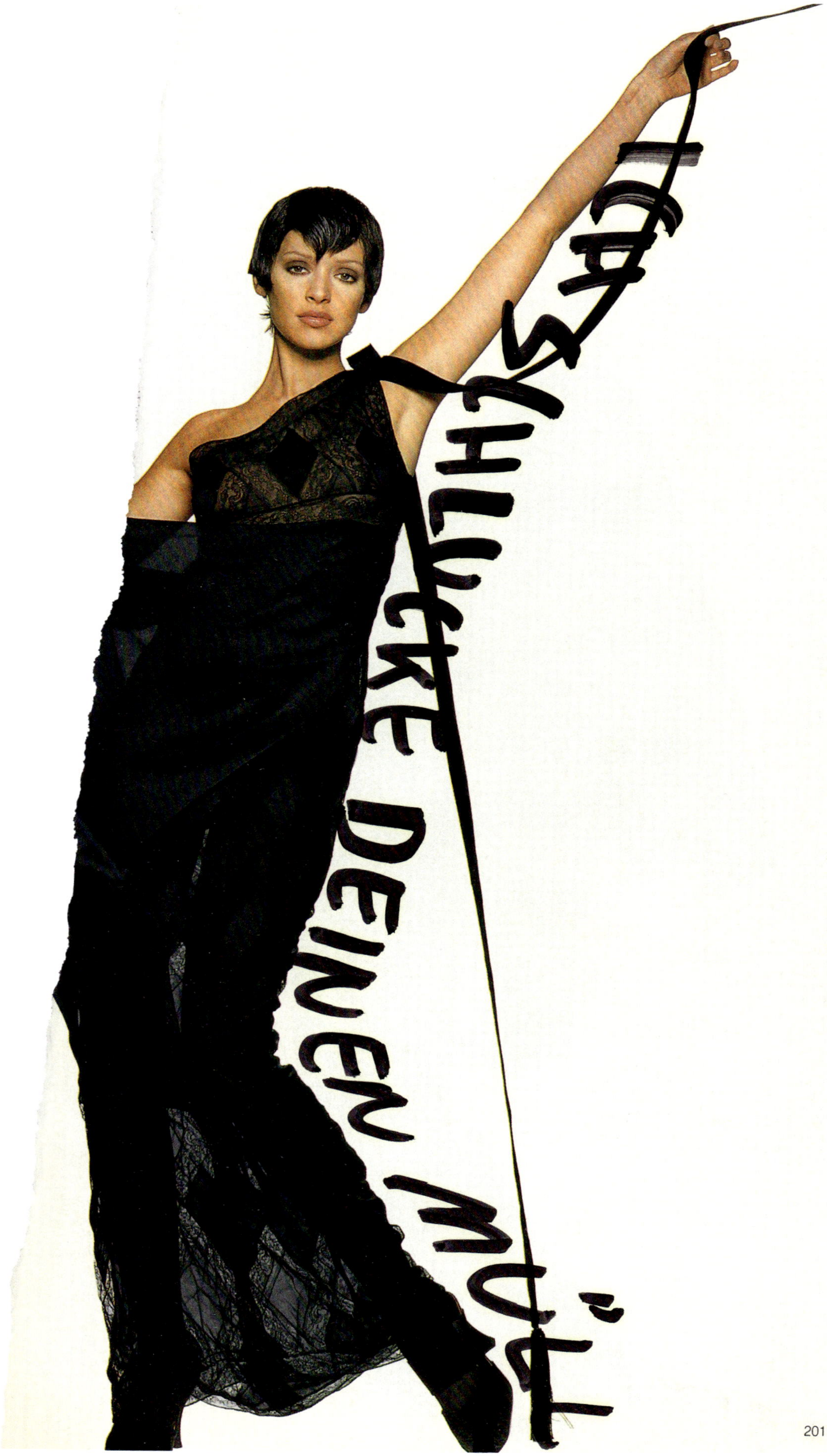

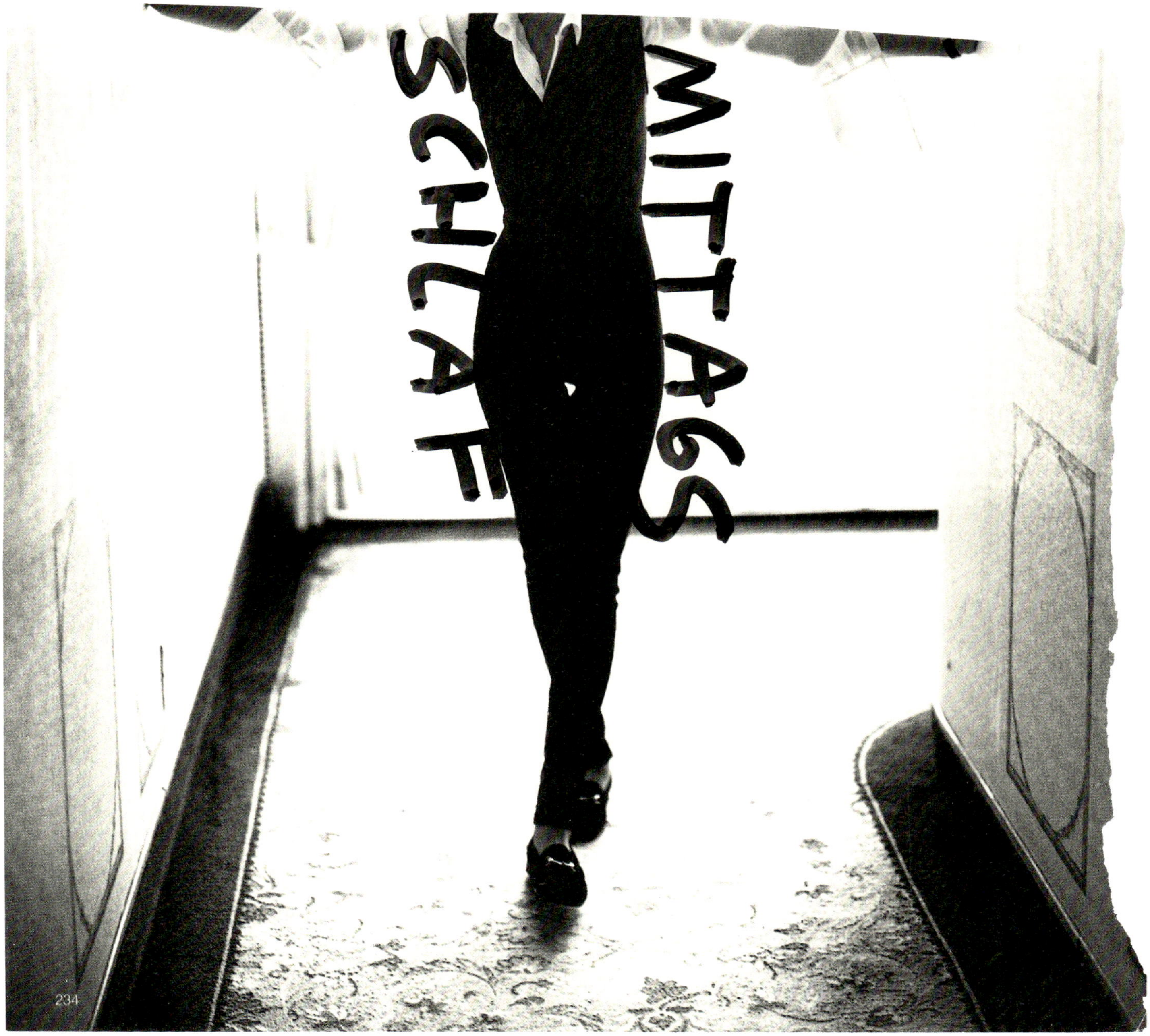
MITTAGS
SCHLAF

Untitled, 1985
Paint, pen, pencil
on paper
37 × 24.9 cm

Cloth hypnosis, 2011
Paint, pen on magazine
33 × 21.6-25.5 cm

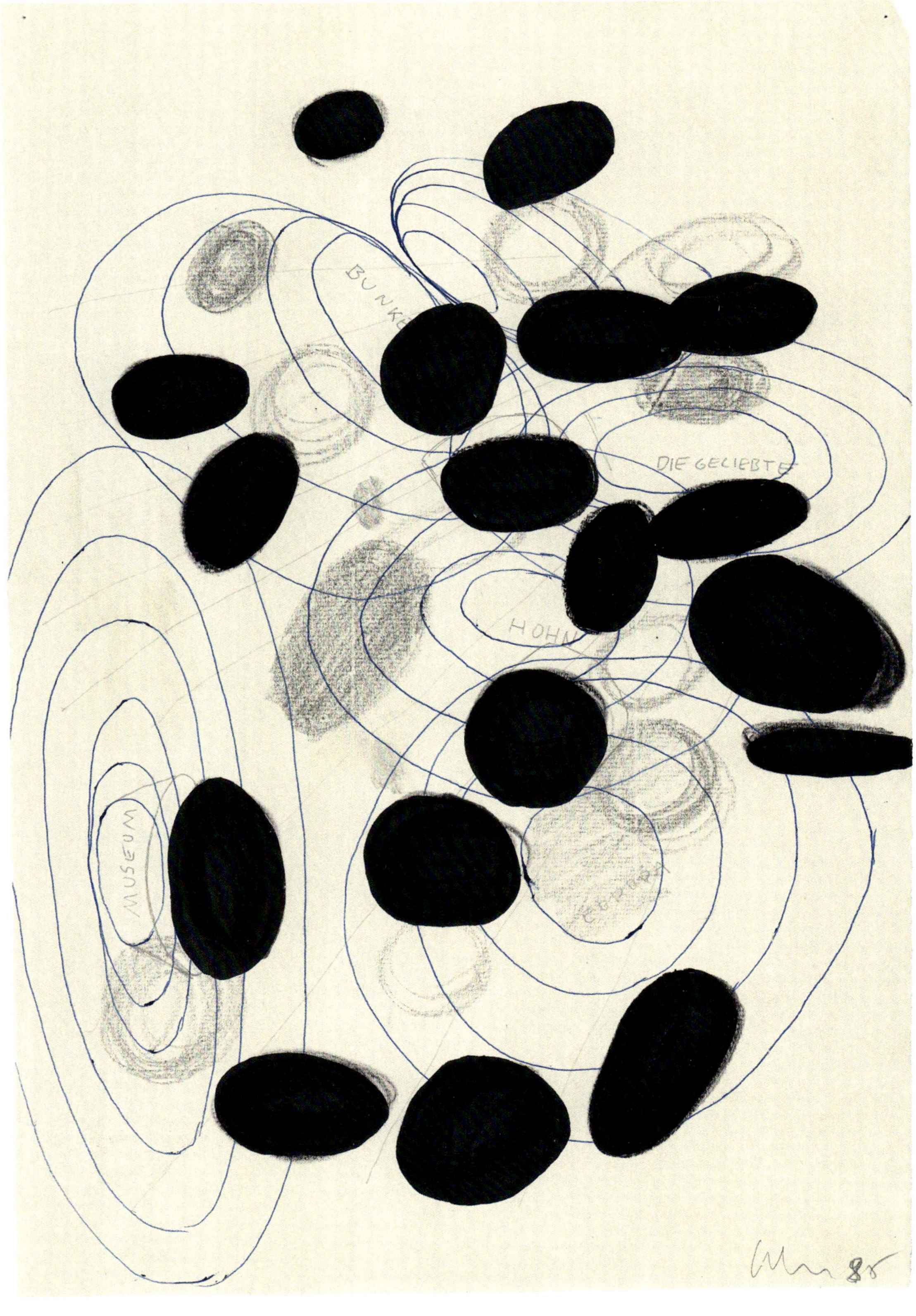

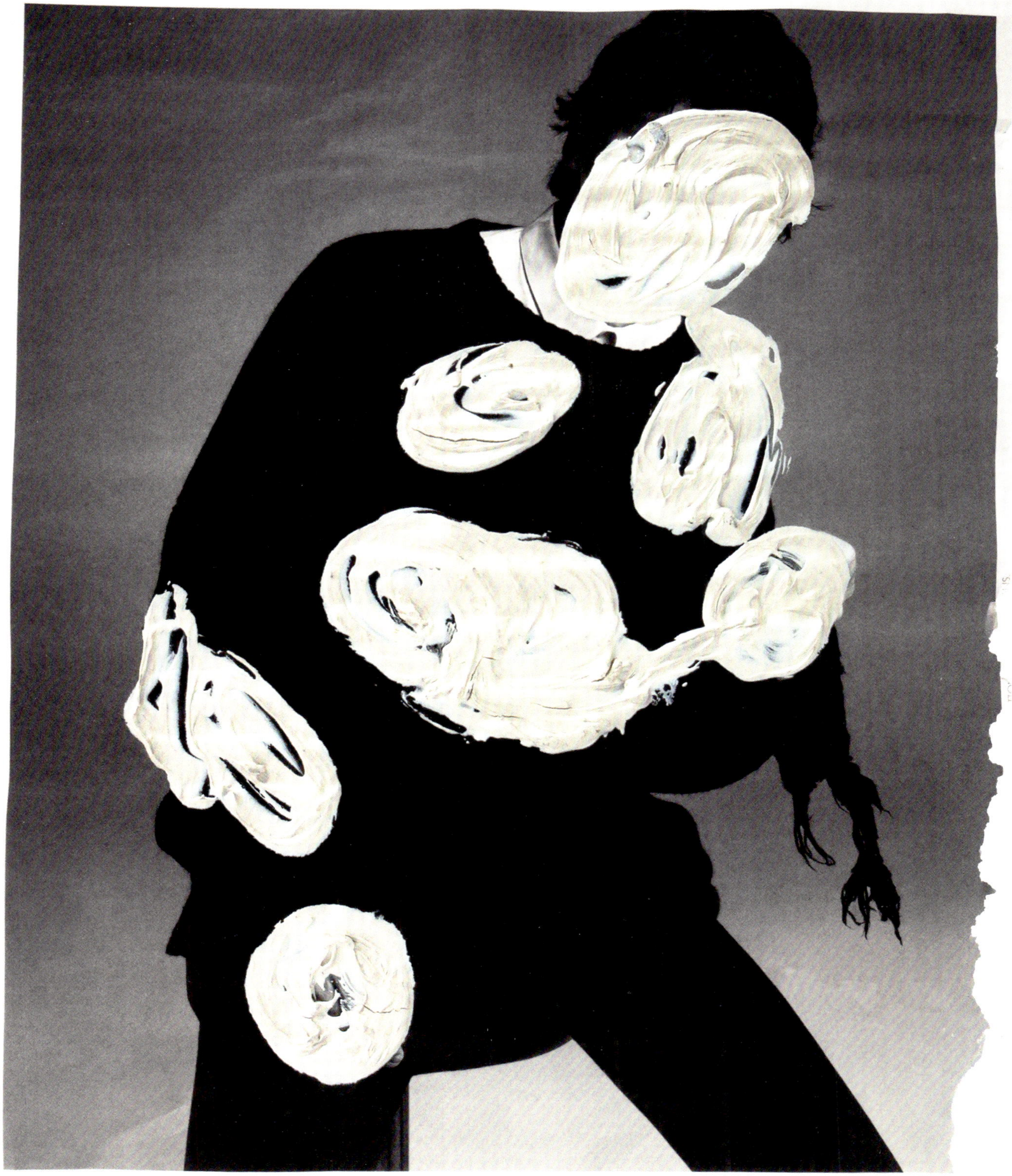

CLOTH hypnosis

JESSE EISENBERG

IN "THE SOCIAL NETWORK"

"I started acting to be included in a group, because I felt excluded in school. The final product was out of my control, so it didn't really matter to me. I just liked being in a group of people that didn't kick my shin."

Untitled, 2011
Paint, pen on magazine
33 × 21.6–25.5 cm

Hypnose, 2011
Pen on magazine
33 × 22.5–25.3 cm

Ort, 1995
Pen on catalogue
32.9 × 22.9 cm

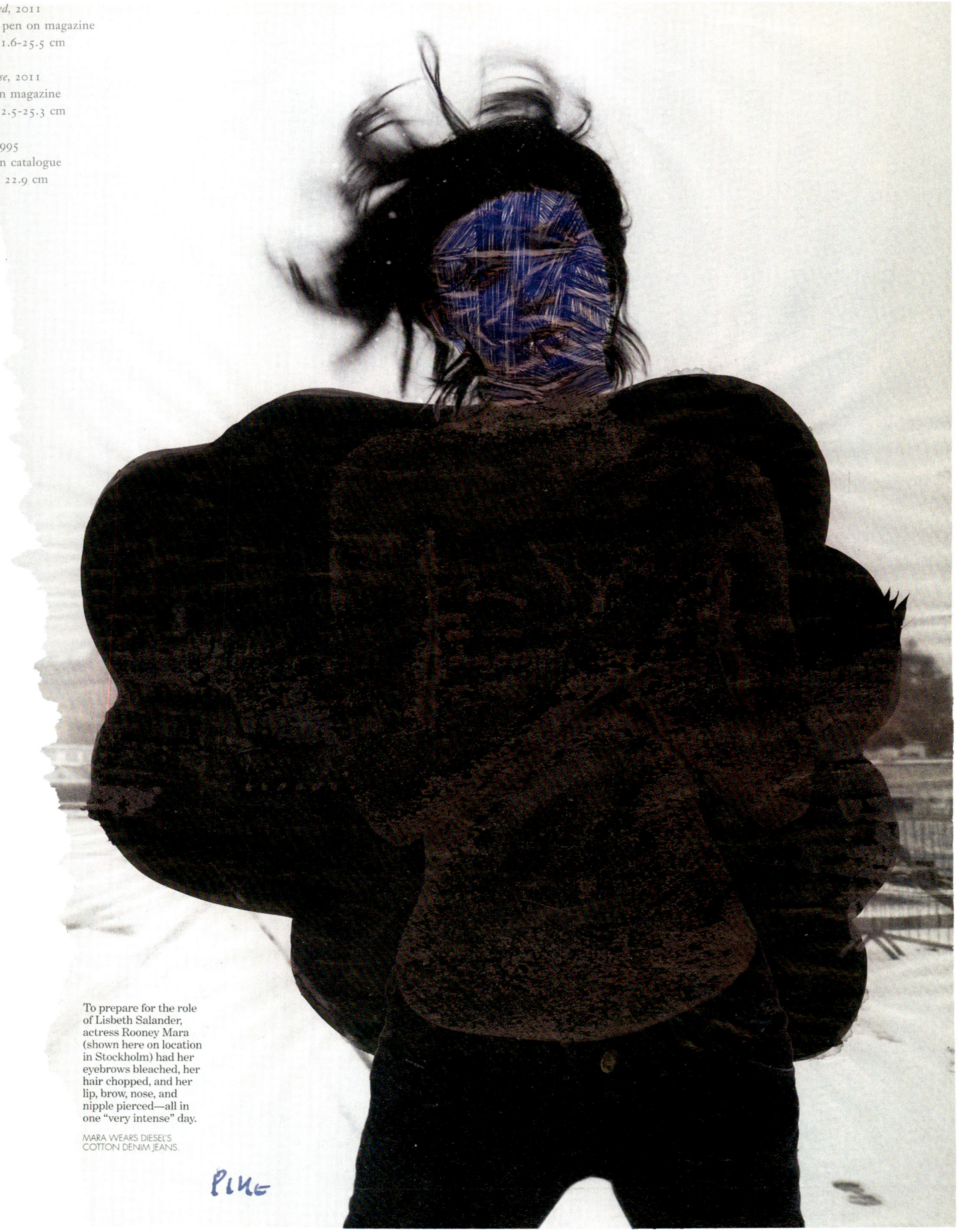

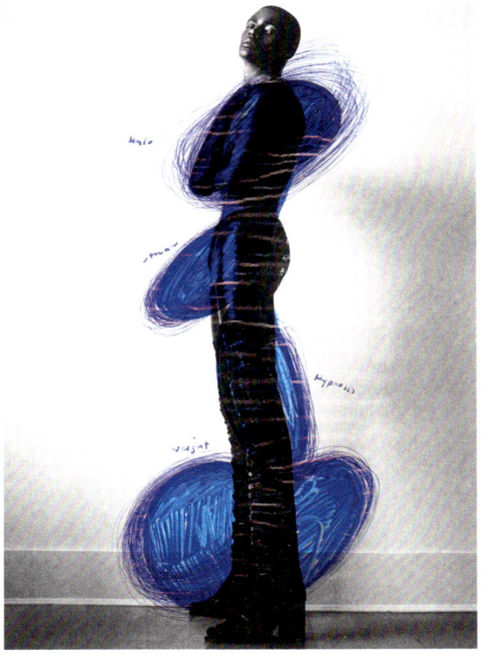
halo
hypnosis

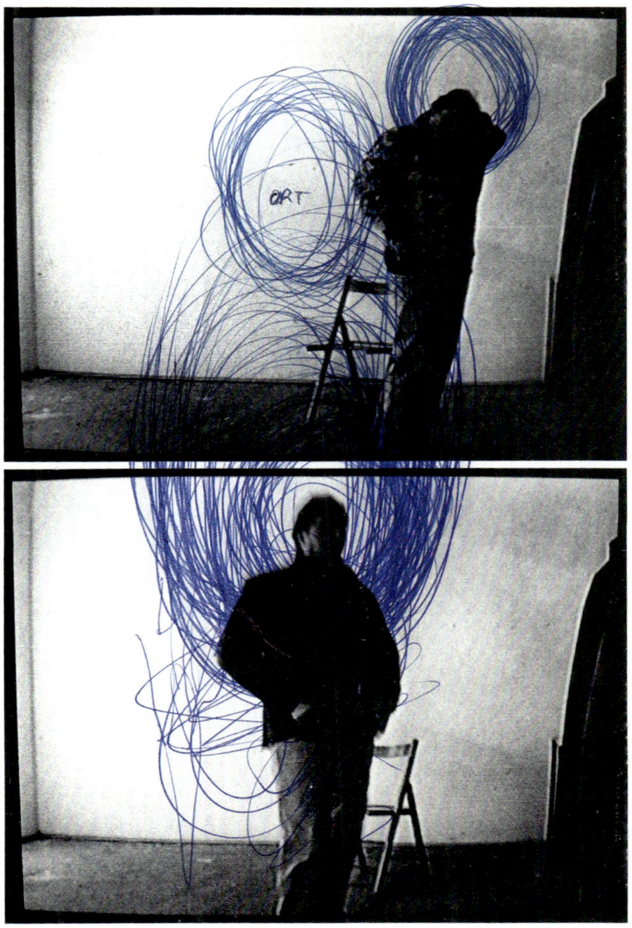
ART

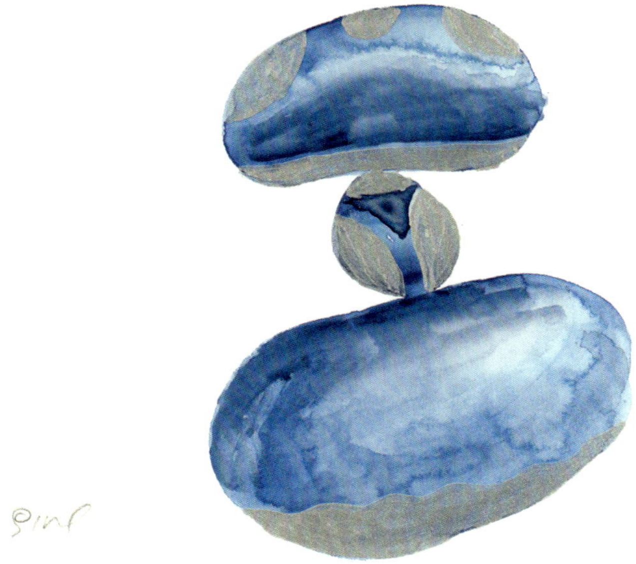

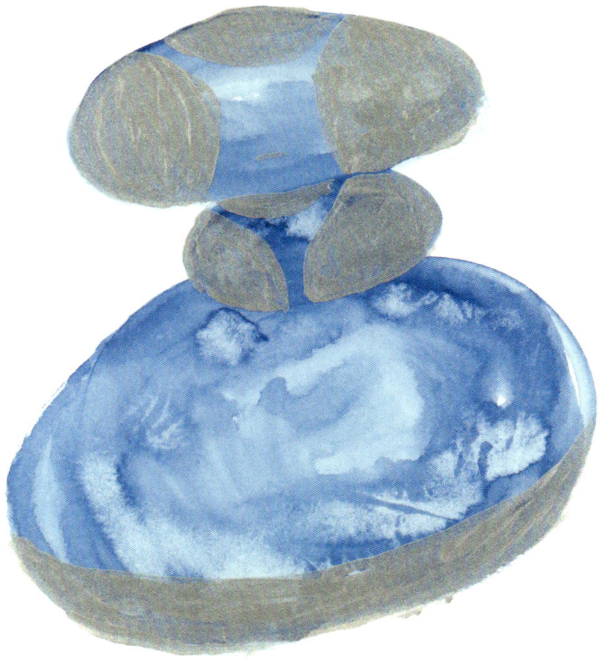

Untitled, 2007
Watercolor on paper
31 × 41 cm

Furniture dress, 2011
Paint, pen on magazine
33 × 22.3–25.2

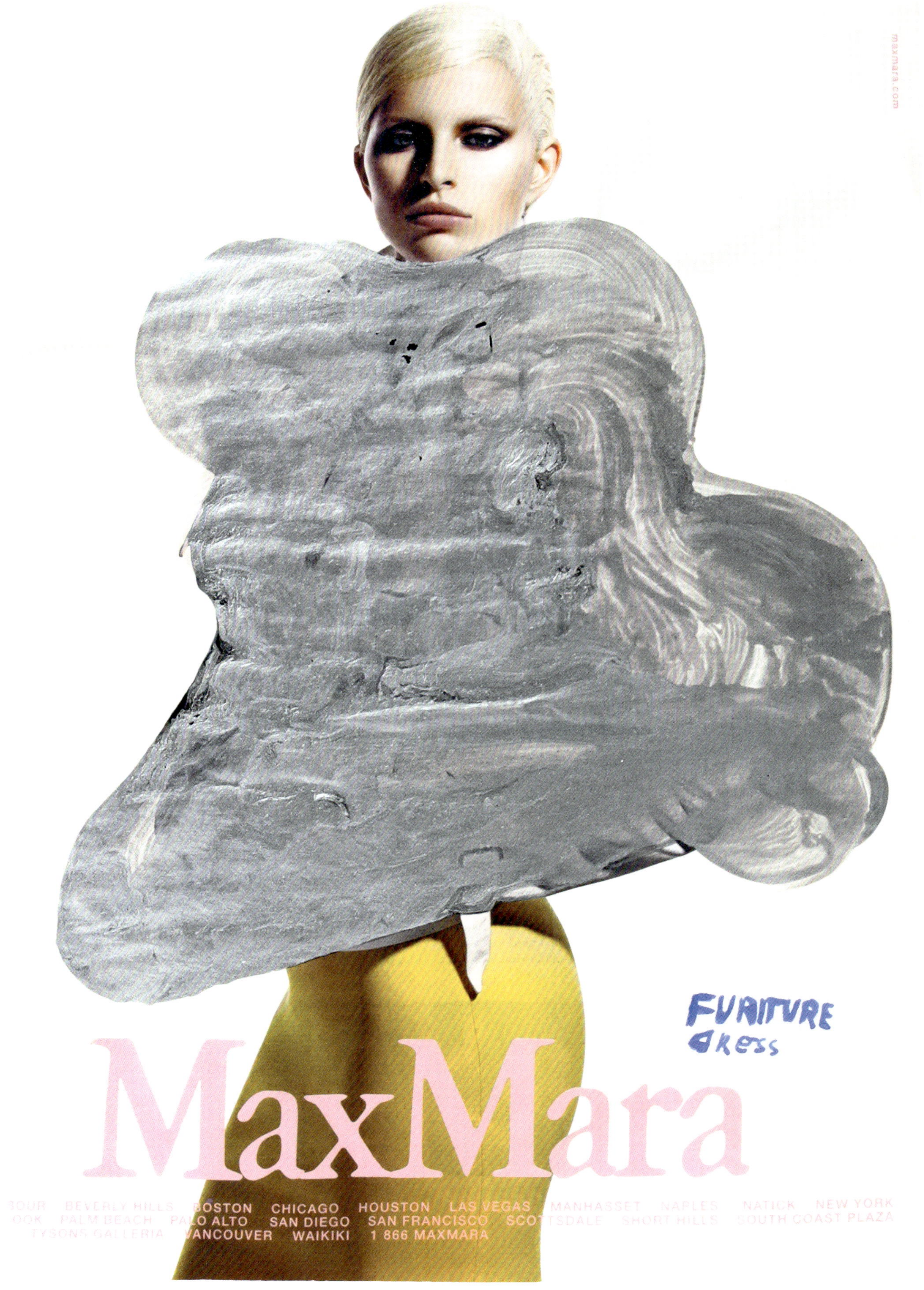
maxmara.com
FURITURE
dress
MaxMara
BOUR BEVERLY HILLS BOSTON CHICAGO HOUSTON LAS VEGAS MANHASSET NAPLES NATICK NEW YORK
OOK PALM BEACH PALO ALTO SAN DIEGO SAN FRANCISCO SCOTTSDALE SHORT HILLS SOUTH COAST PLAZA
TYSONS GALLERIA VANCOUVER WAIKIKI 1 866 MAXMARA

Hypnosis, 2011
Paint, pen on magazine
32.8 × 20-22.9 cm

Next page:
Psychos: Big psycho 8, 2010
Aluminum, paint
300 × 170 × 110 cm

Untitled, 2011
Knitted wall
550 × 1400 cm
Installation view, 2011
Galerie Thaddaeus
Ropac, Paris

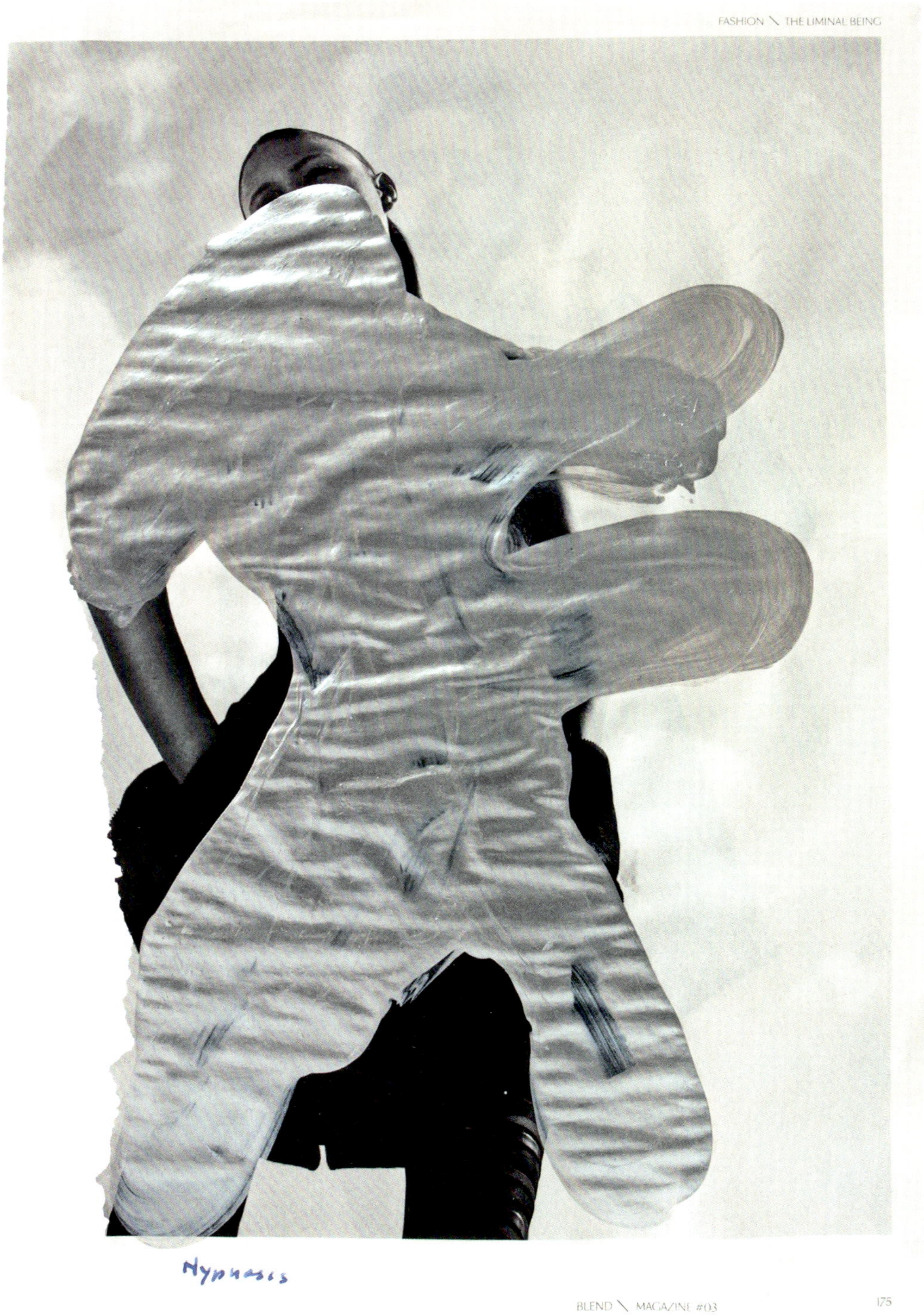

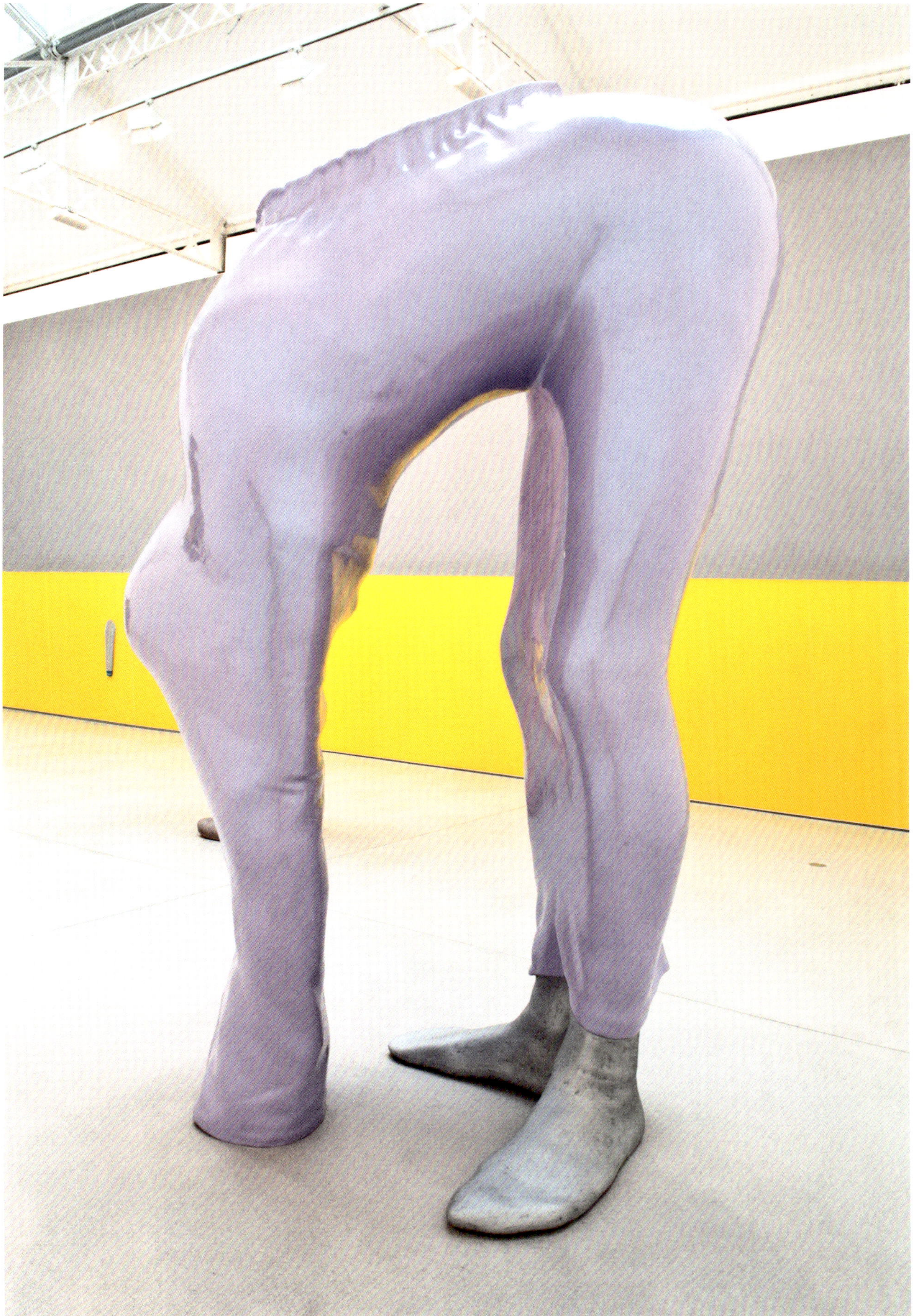

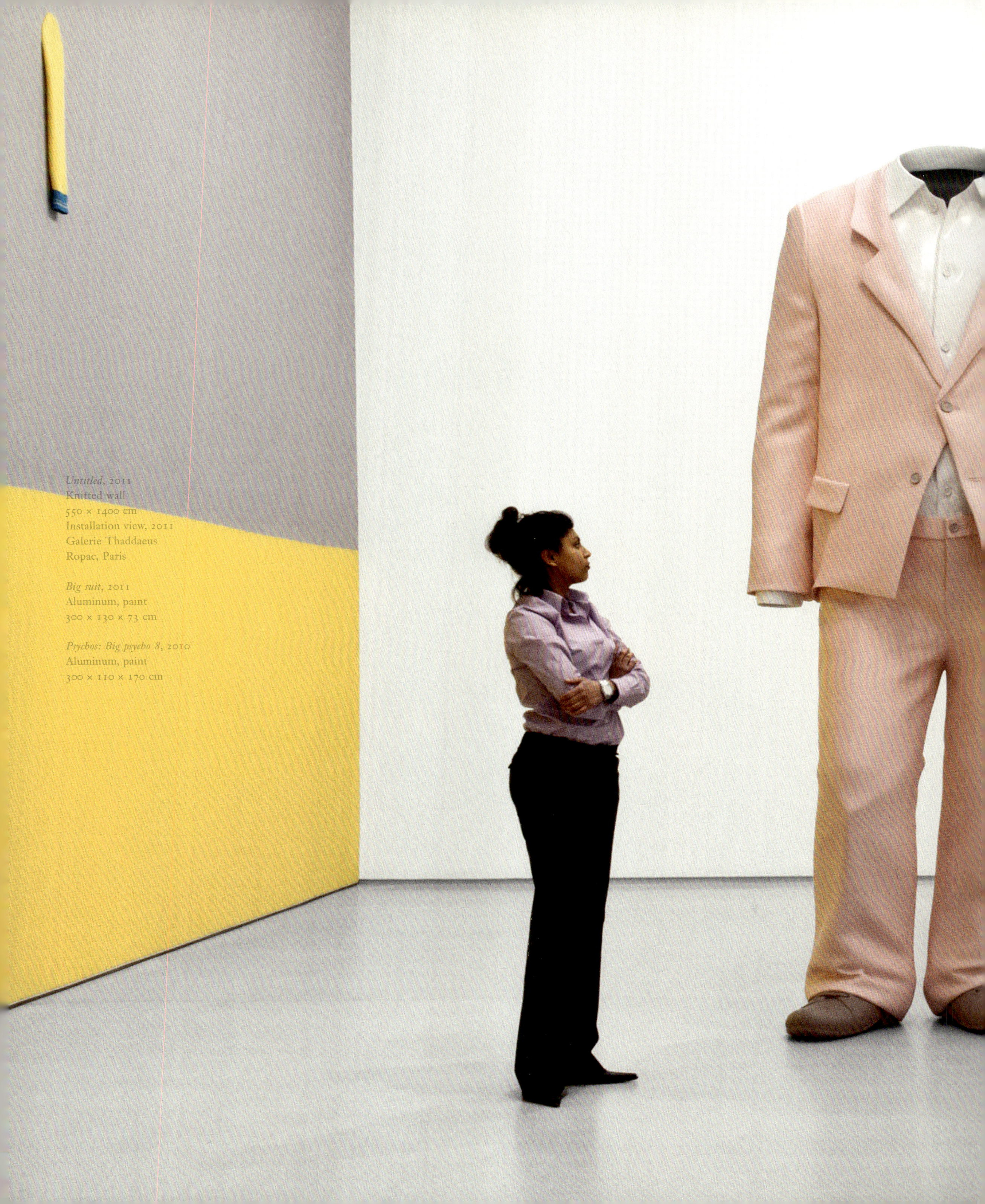

Untitled, 2011
Knitted wall
550 × 1400 cm
Installation view, 2011
Galerie Thaddaeus
Ropac, Paris

Big suit, 2011
Aluminum, paint
300 × 130 × 73 cm

Psychos: Big psycho 8, 2010
Aluminum, paint
300 × 110 × 170 cm

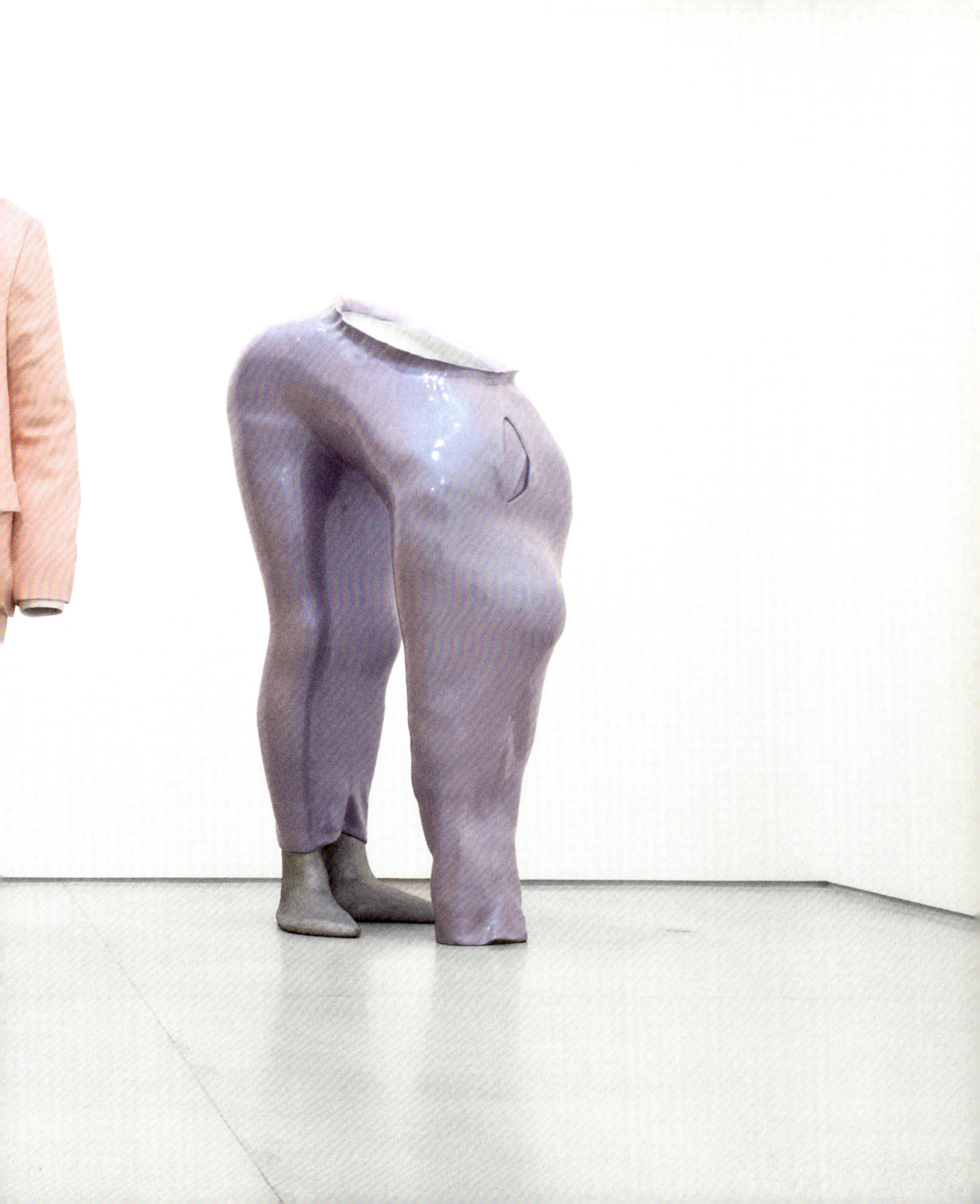

Psychos: psycho 7, 2010
Aluminum, paint
120 × 107 × 39 cm

Philosophers: suit, 2009
Acrylic, cloth
48 × 20 × 12 cm
Photo: Elsa Okazaki

Untitled, 2010
Acrylic, paint
57 × 18 × 11 cm
Photo: Galerie
Thaddaeus Ropac, Paris,
Ulrich Ghezzi

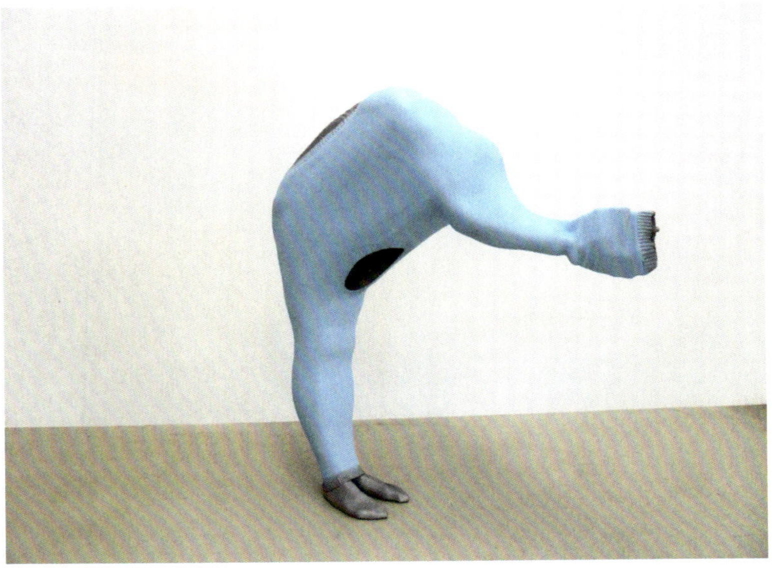

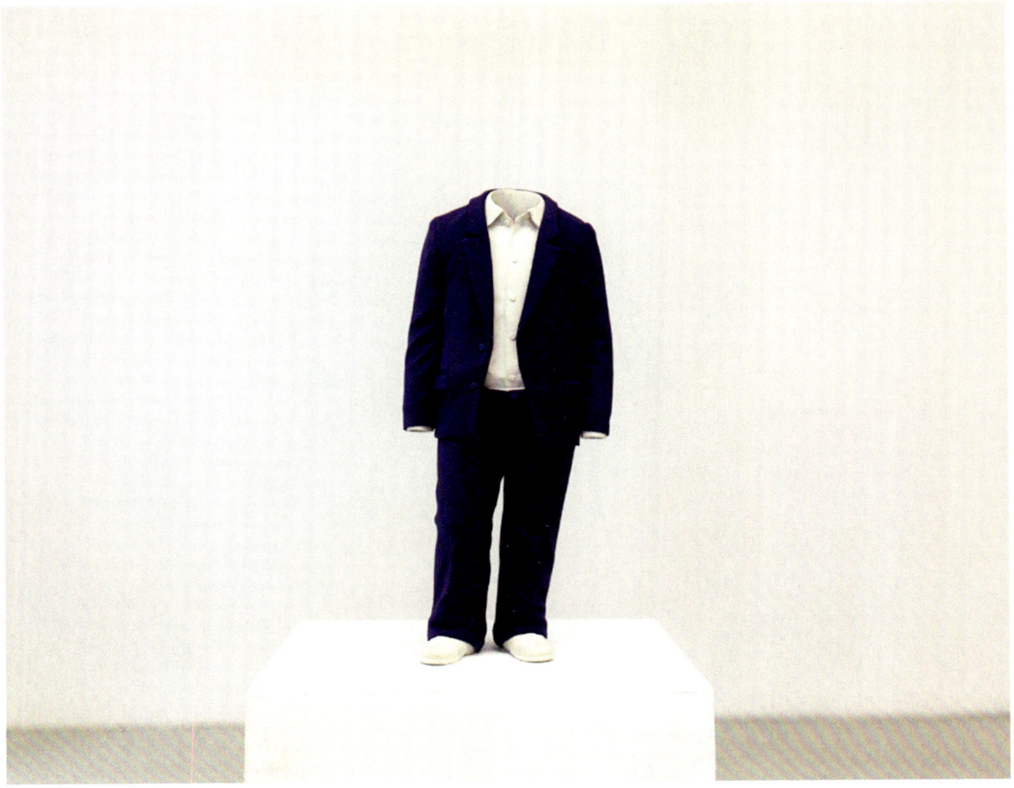

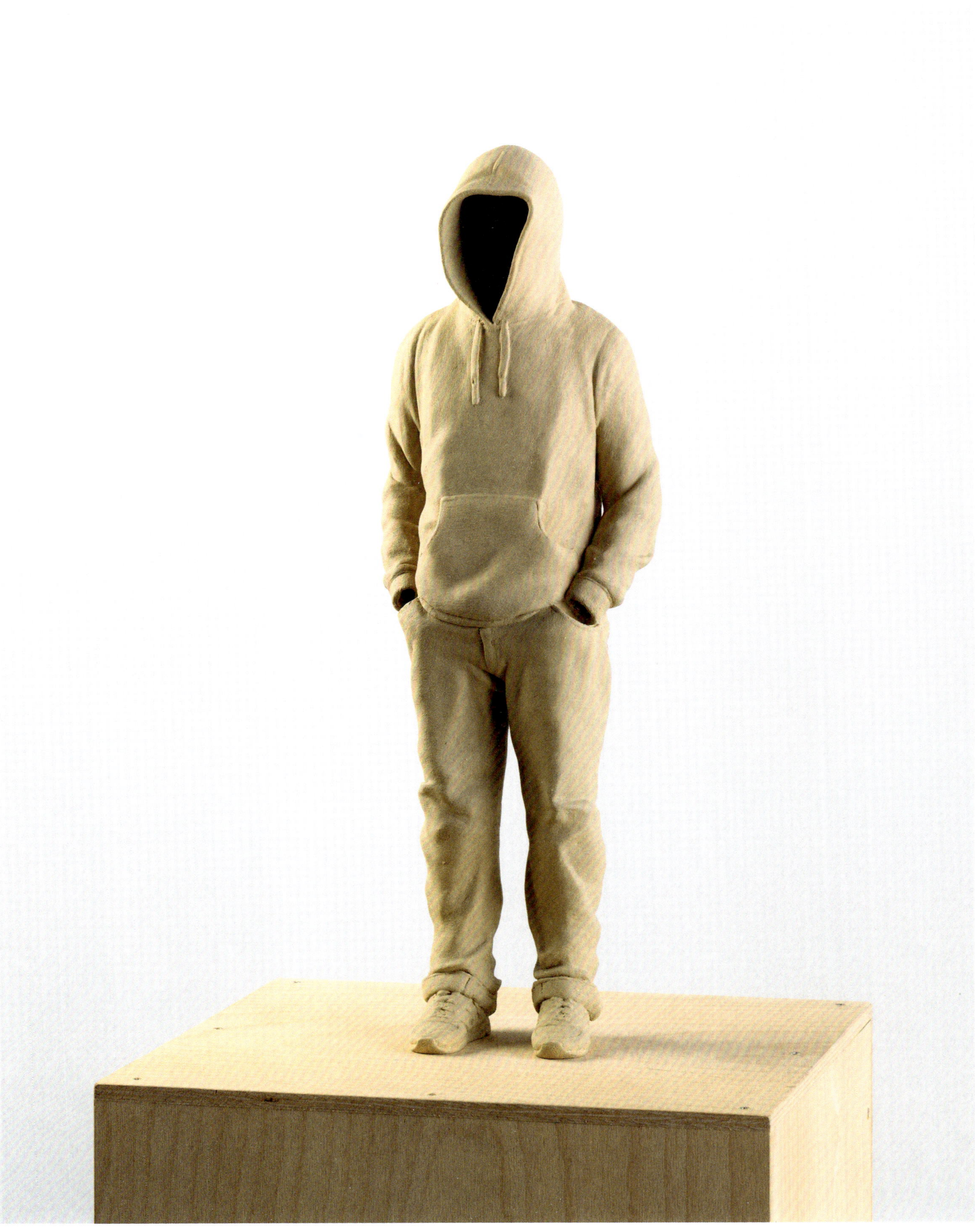

Small Psychos, 2010
Acrylic, paint
Installation view, 2011
Galerie Thaddaeus
Ropac, Paris

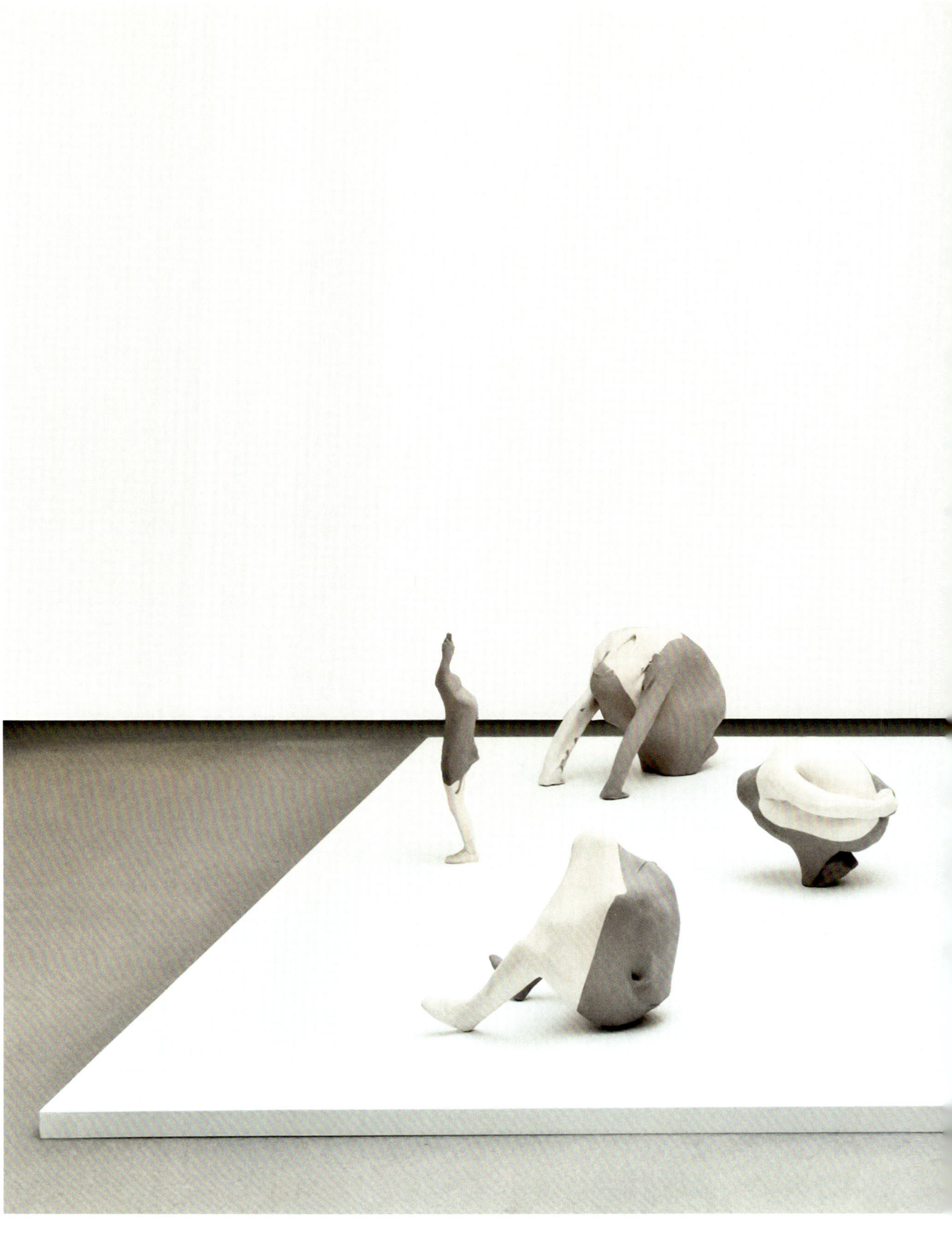

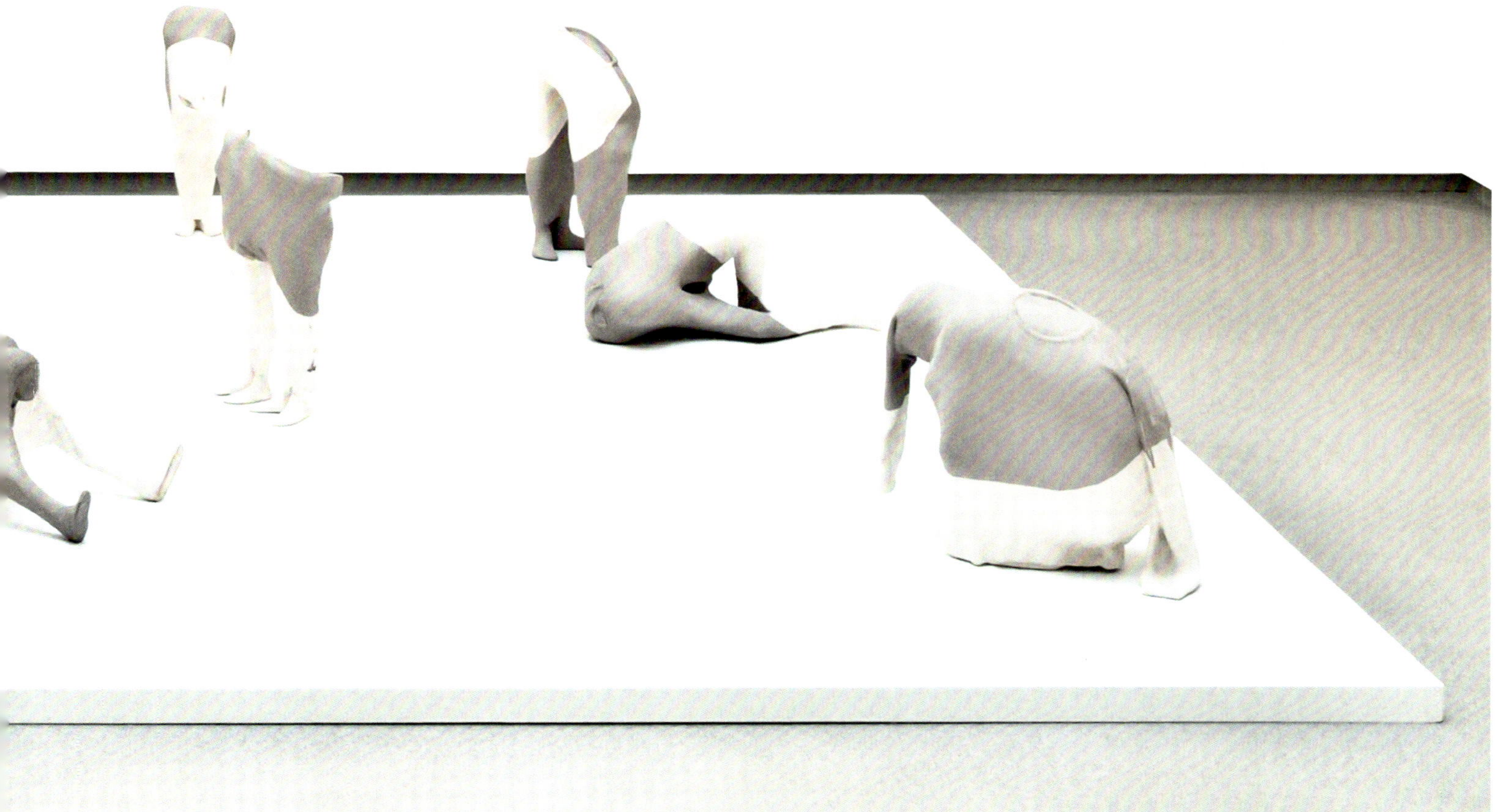

Dress me up, 2011
Paint, pen on magazine
32.9 × 21.6-22.9 cm

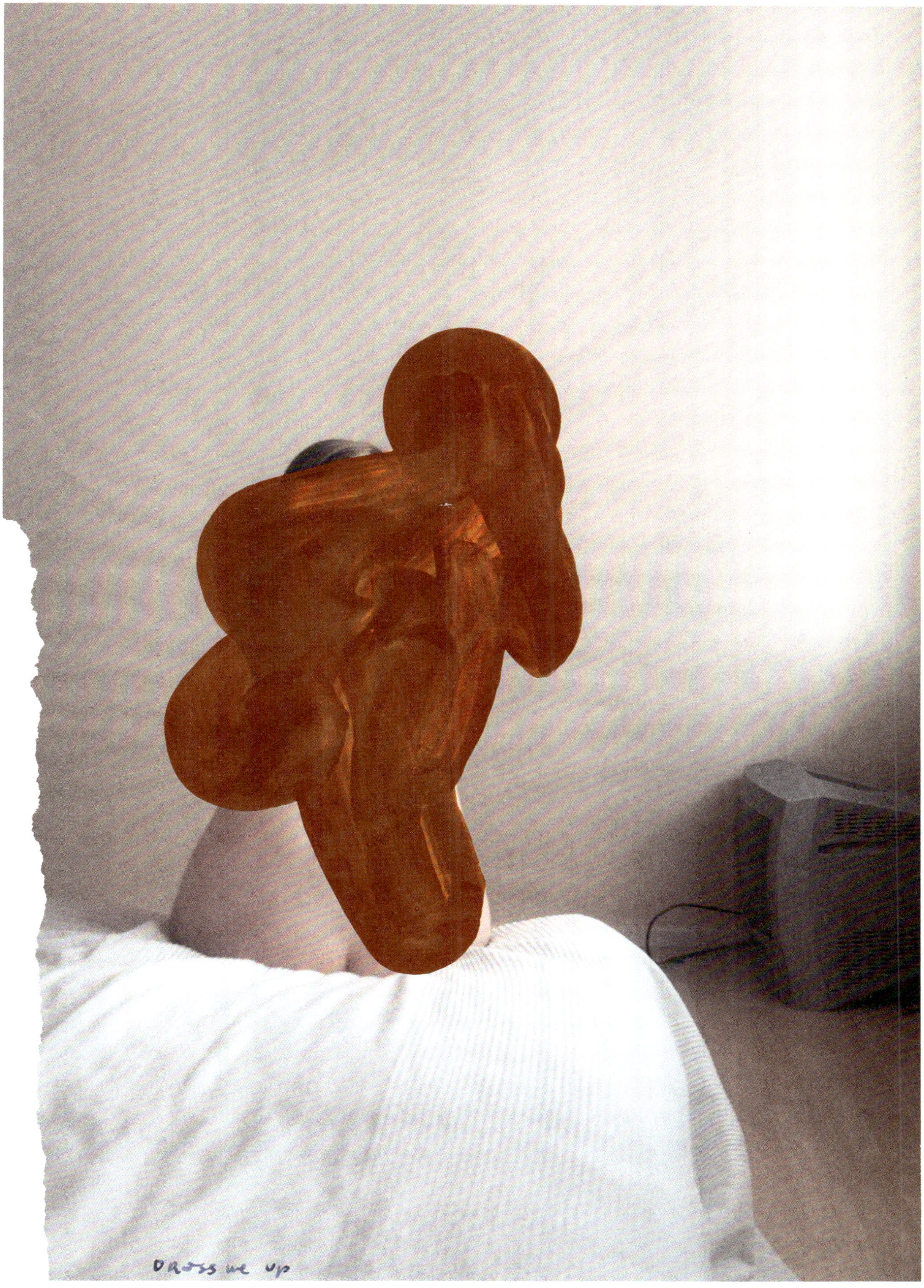
DRESS me up

Untitled, 2007
Watercolor on paper
31 × 41 cm

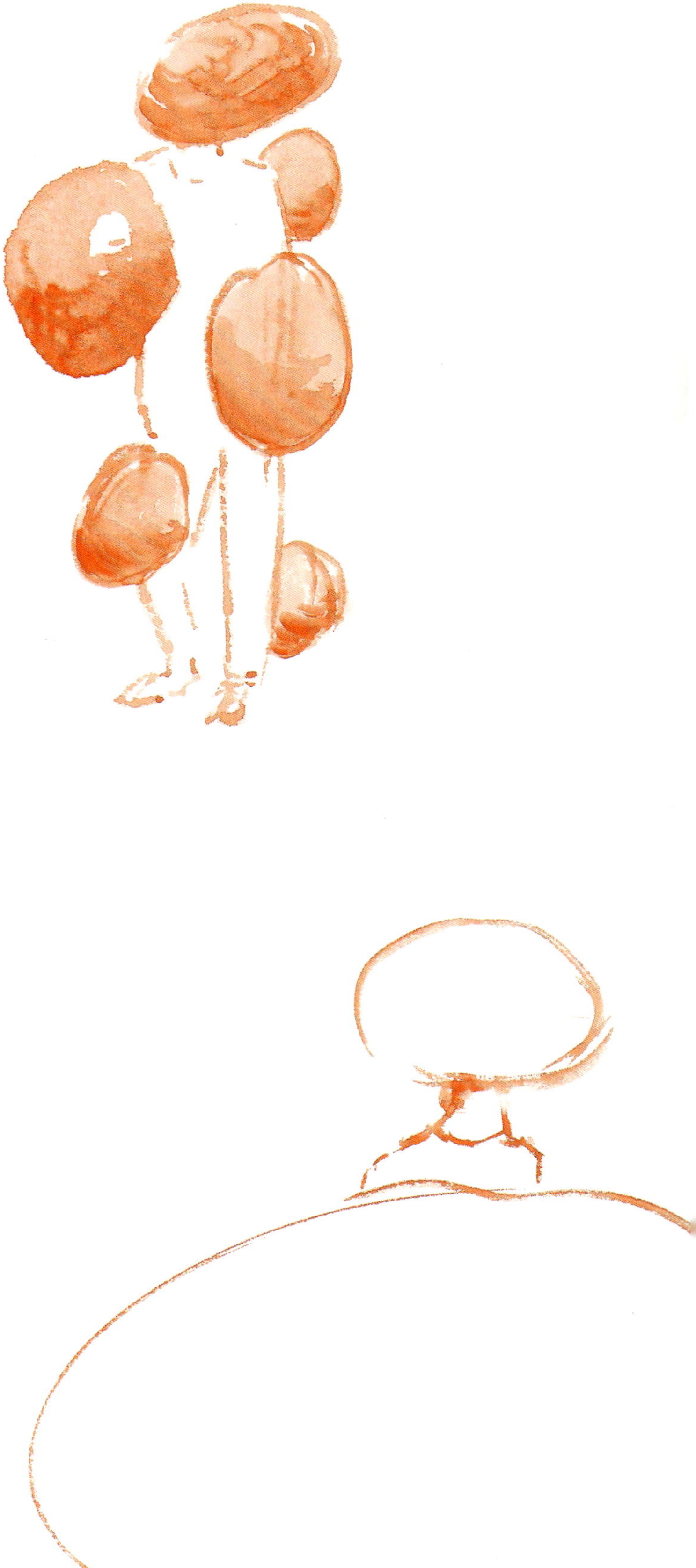

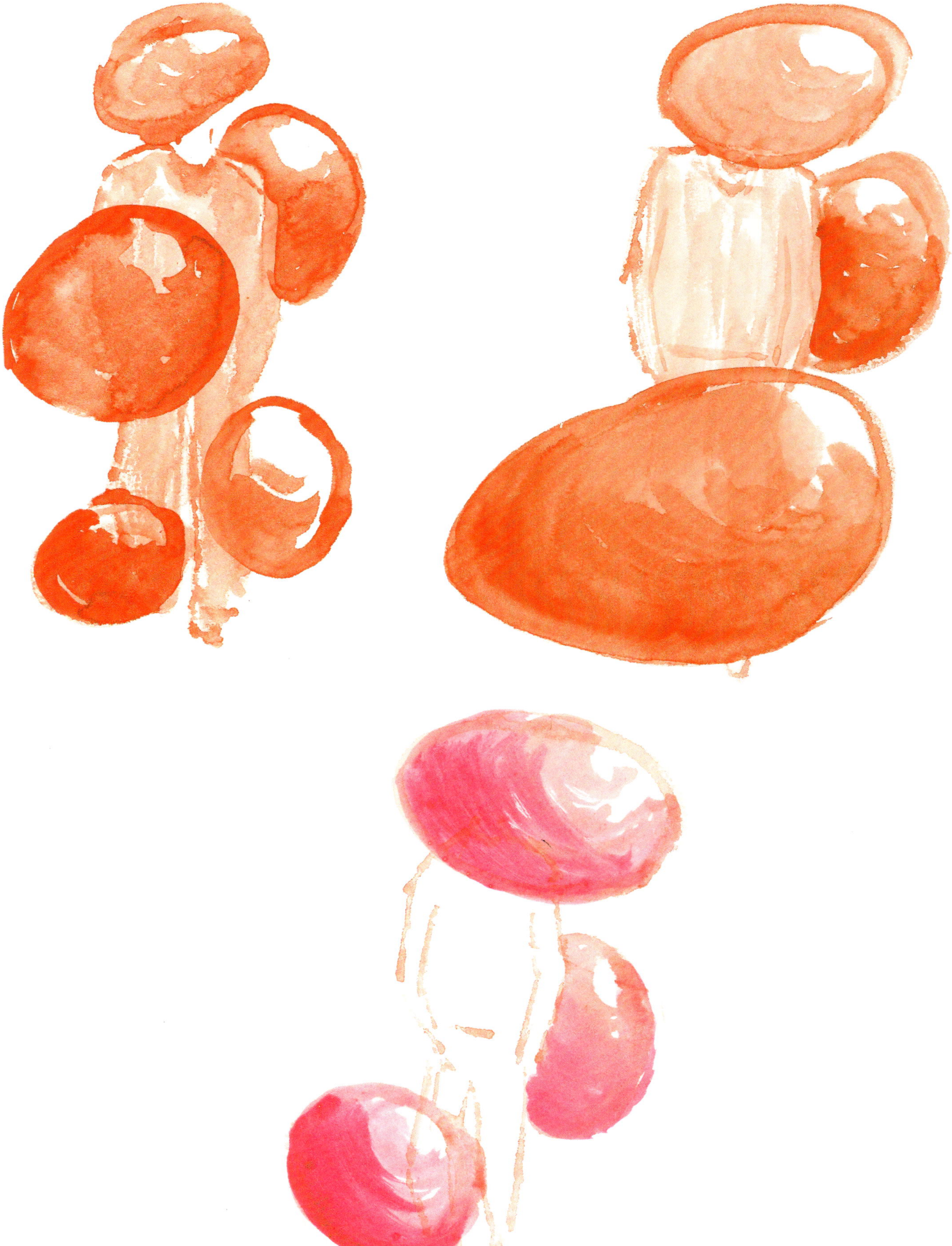

Untitled, 2011
Paint on magazine
33 × 20.6-22.9 cm

Untitled, 2007
Watercolor on paper
31 × 41 cm

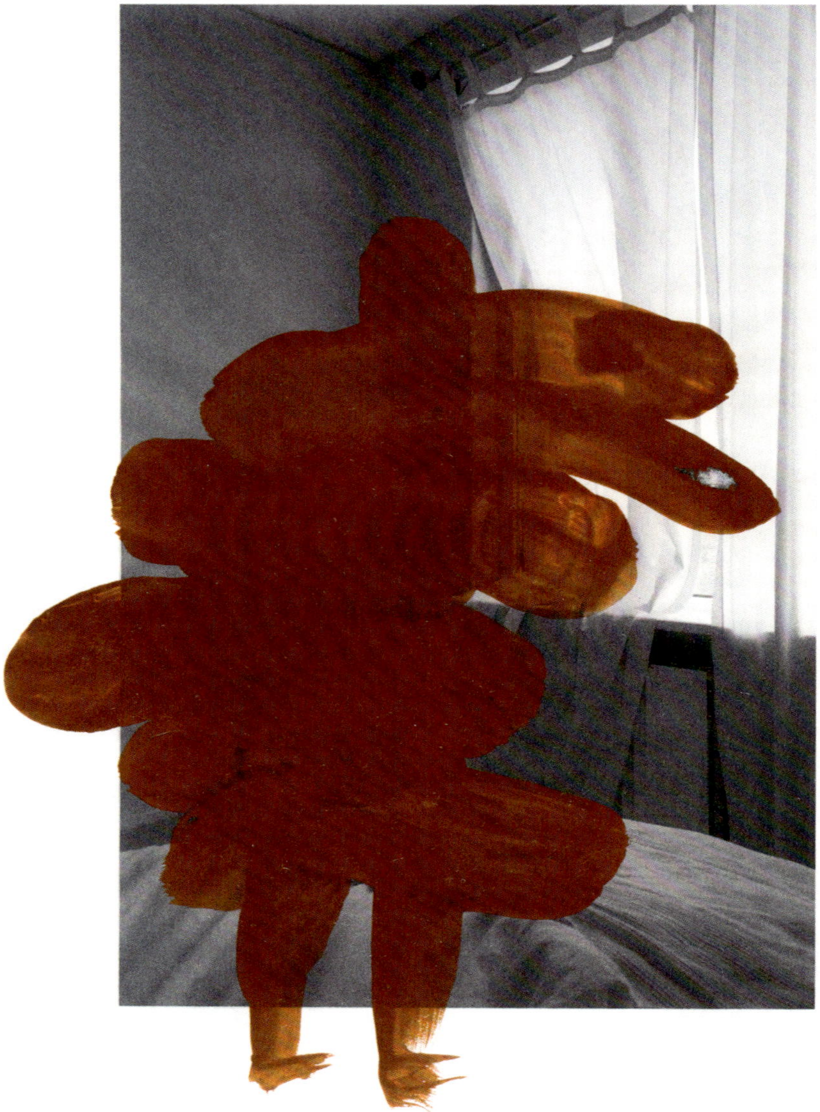

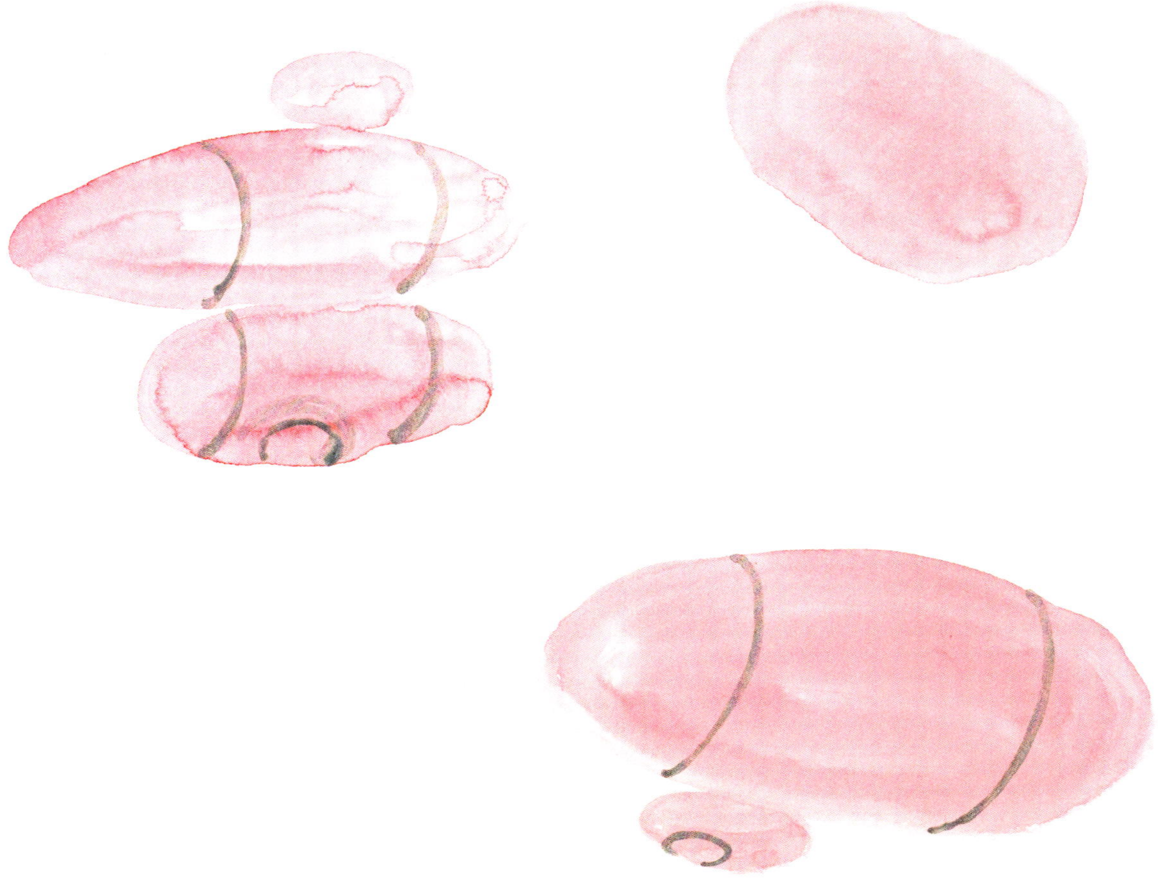

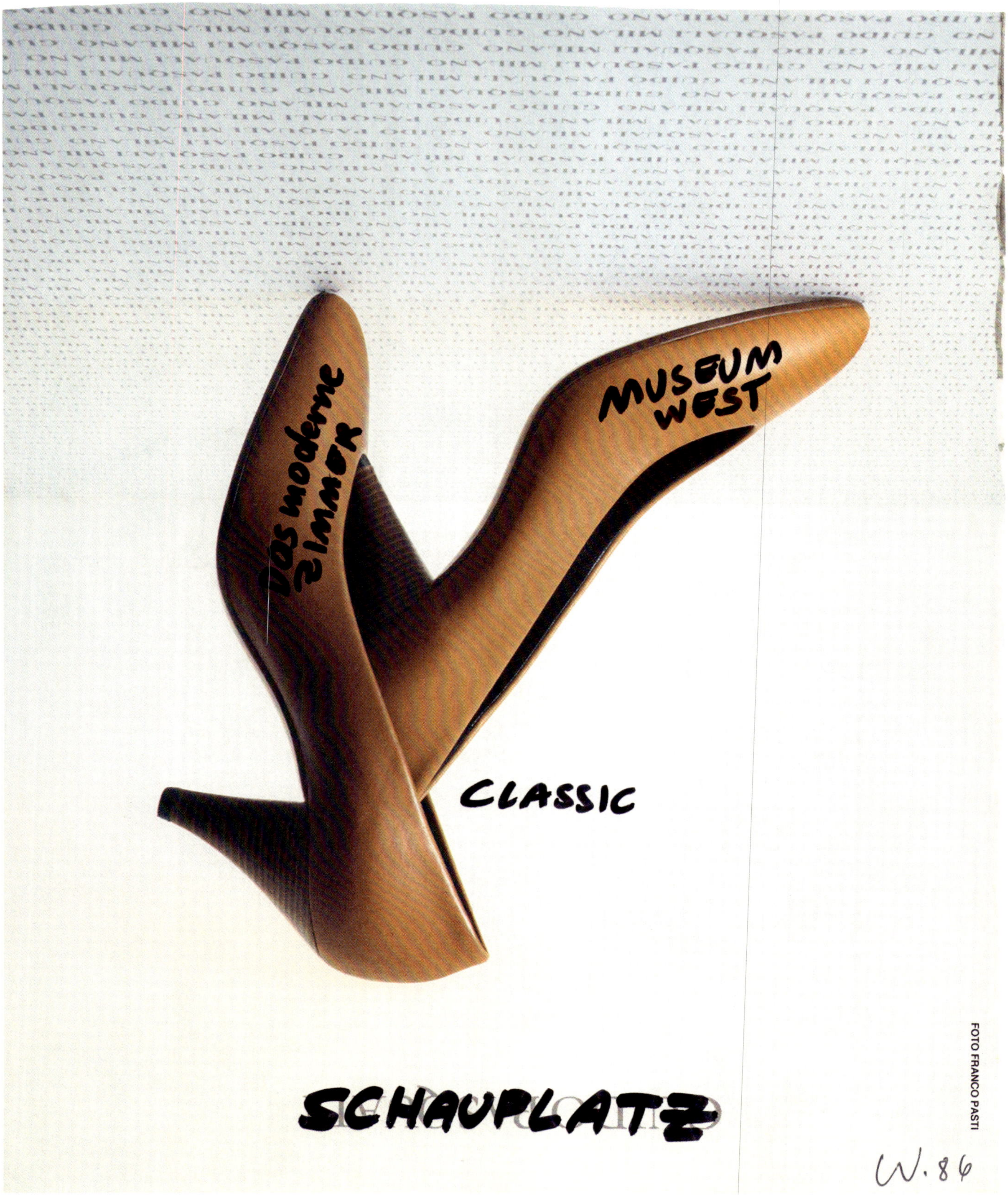

Schauplatz, 1986
Felt-marker on magazine
26 × 21.7 cm

Installation view, 2011
MAK, Vienna

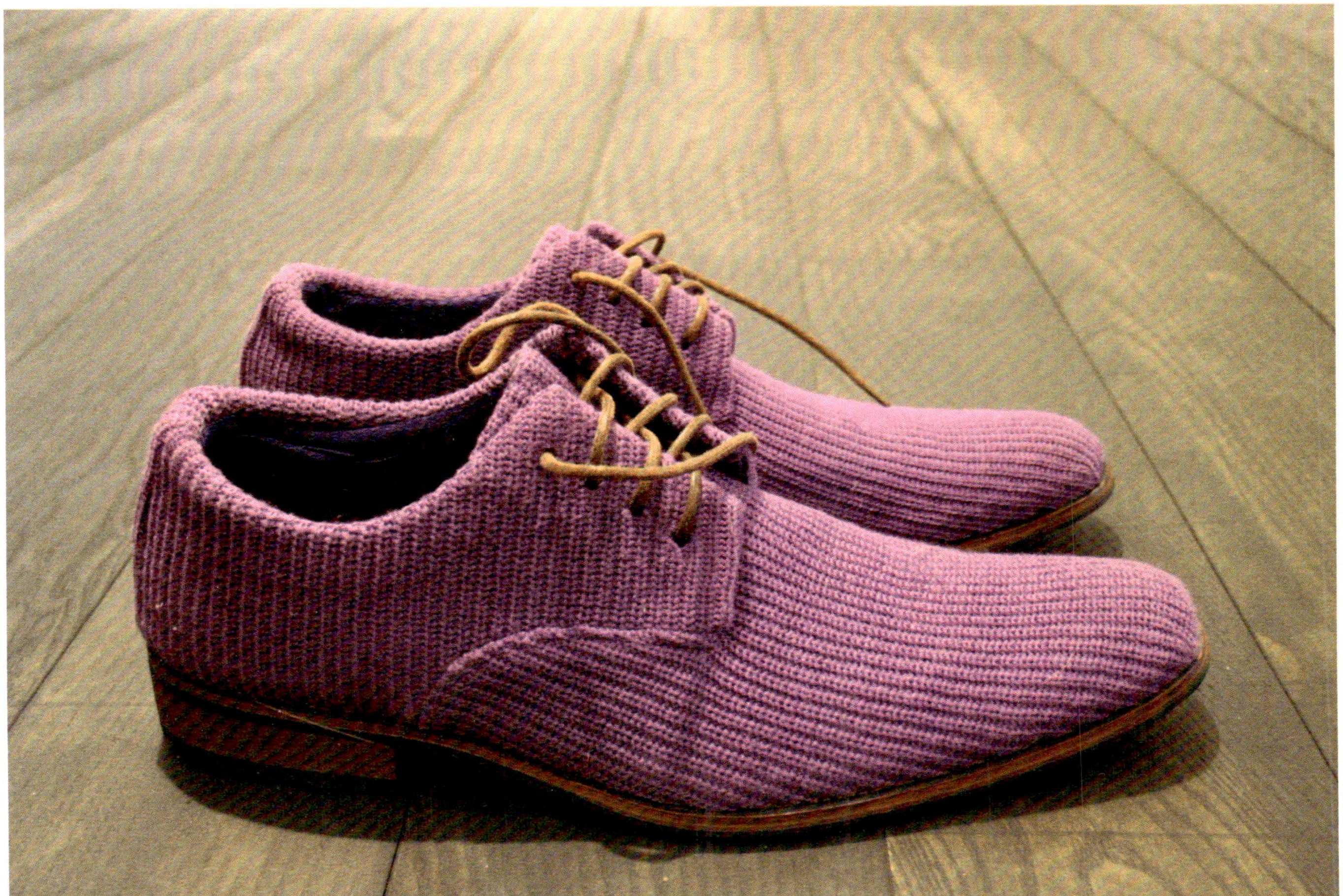

Wallhouse #2, 2009
Installation view (detail), 2009
Groningen, The Netherlands

Wallhouse #2, 2009
Installation view, 2009
Groningen, The Netherlands

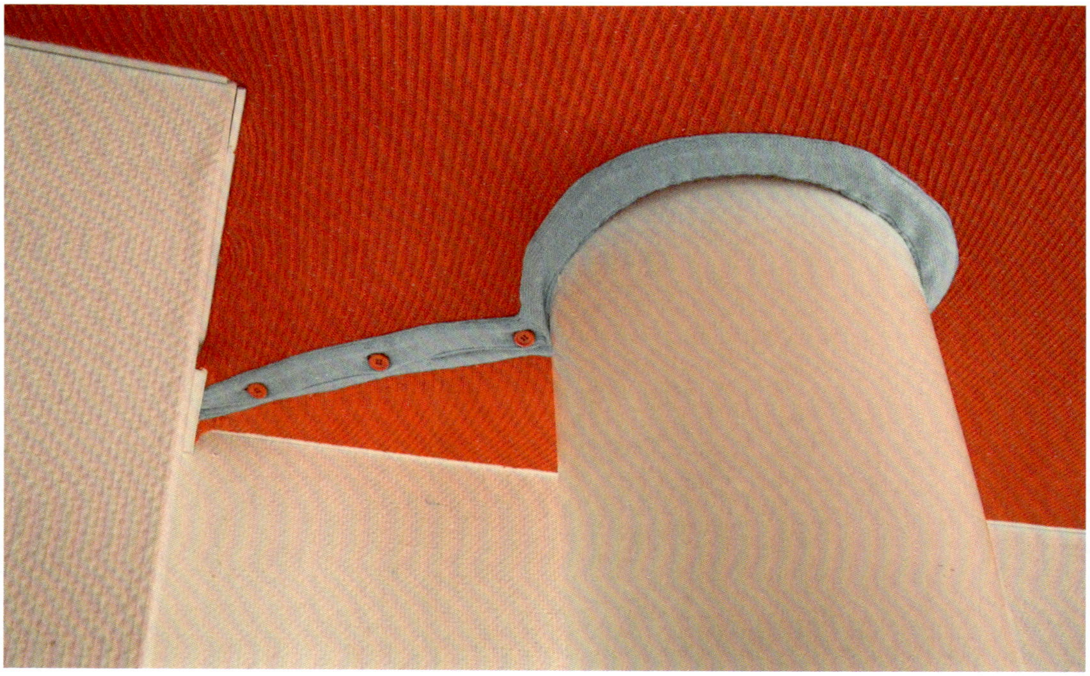

Next page
Middelheim ceiling, 2011
Middelheim Museum,
Antwerp
Photo: Ottomura

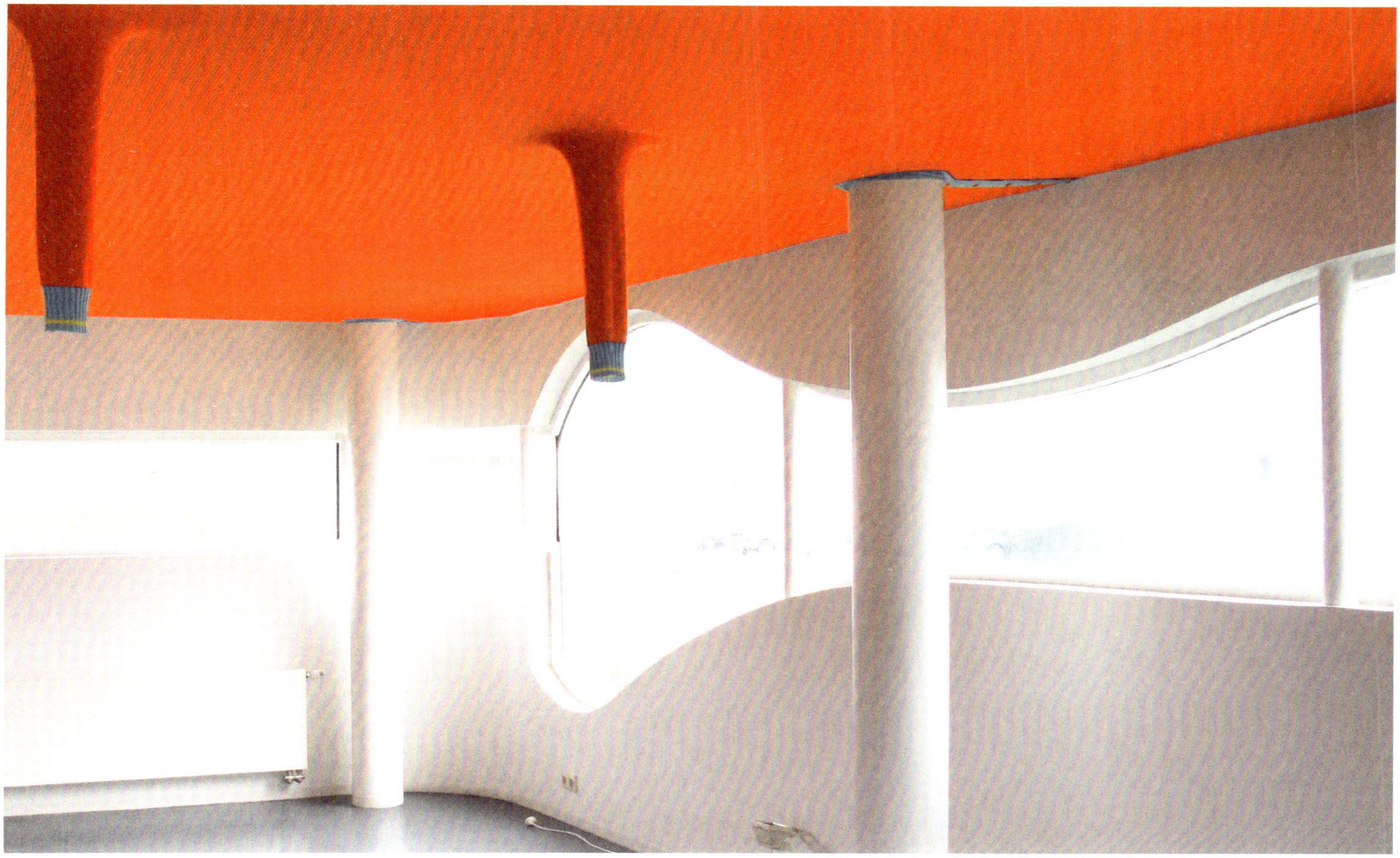

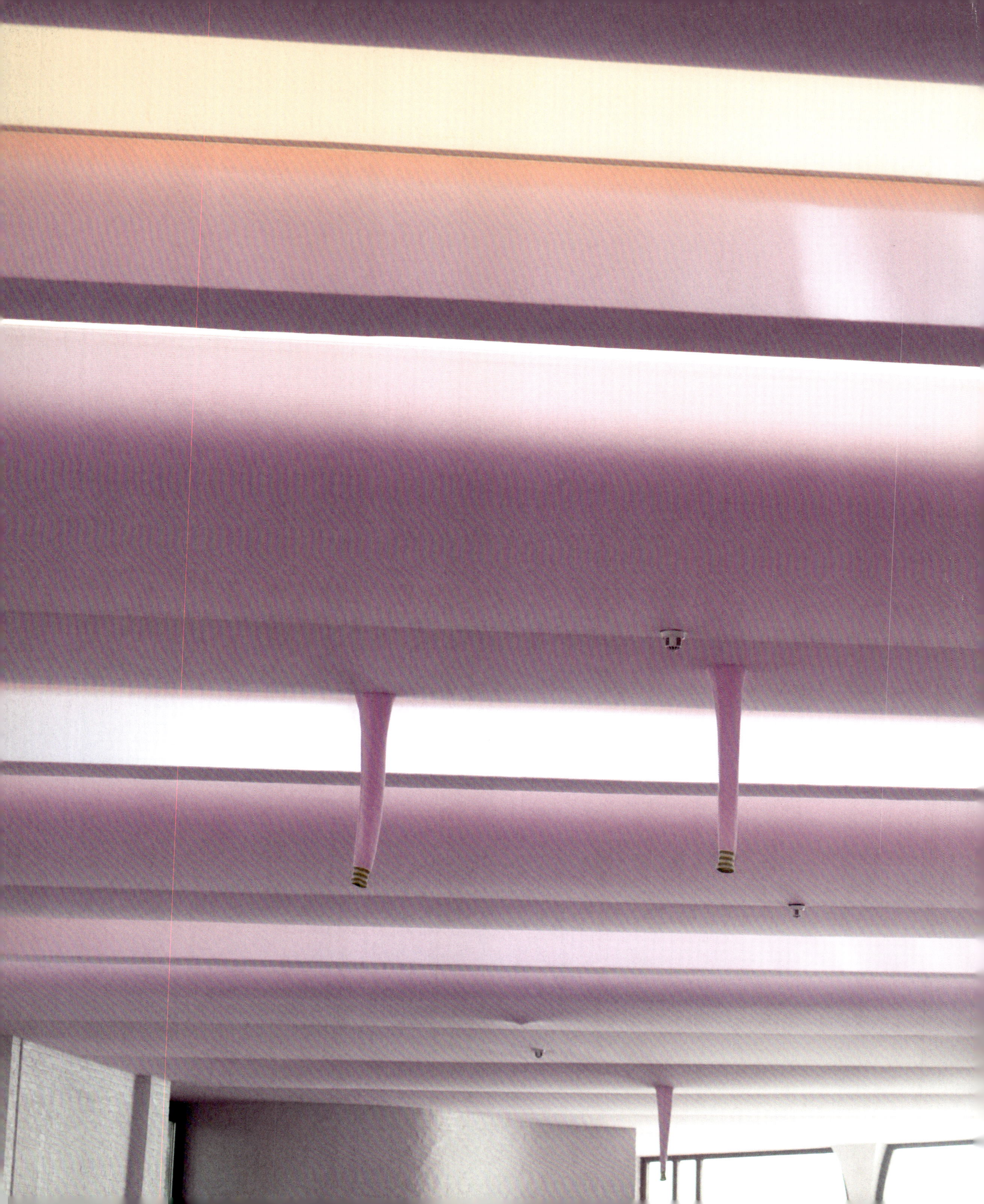

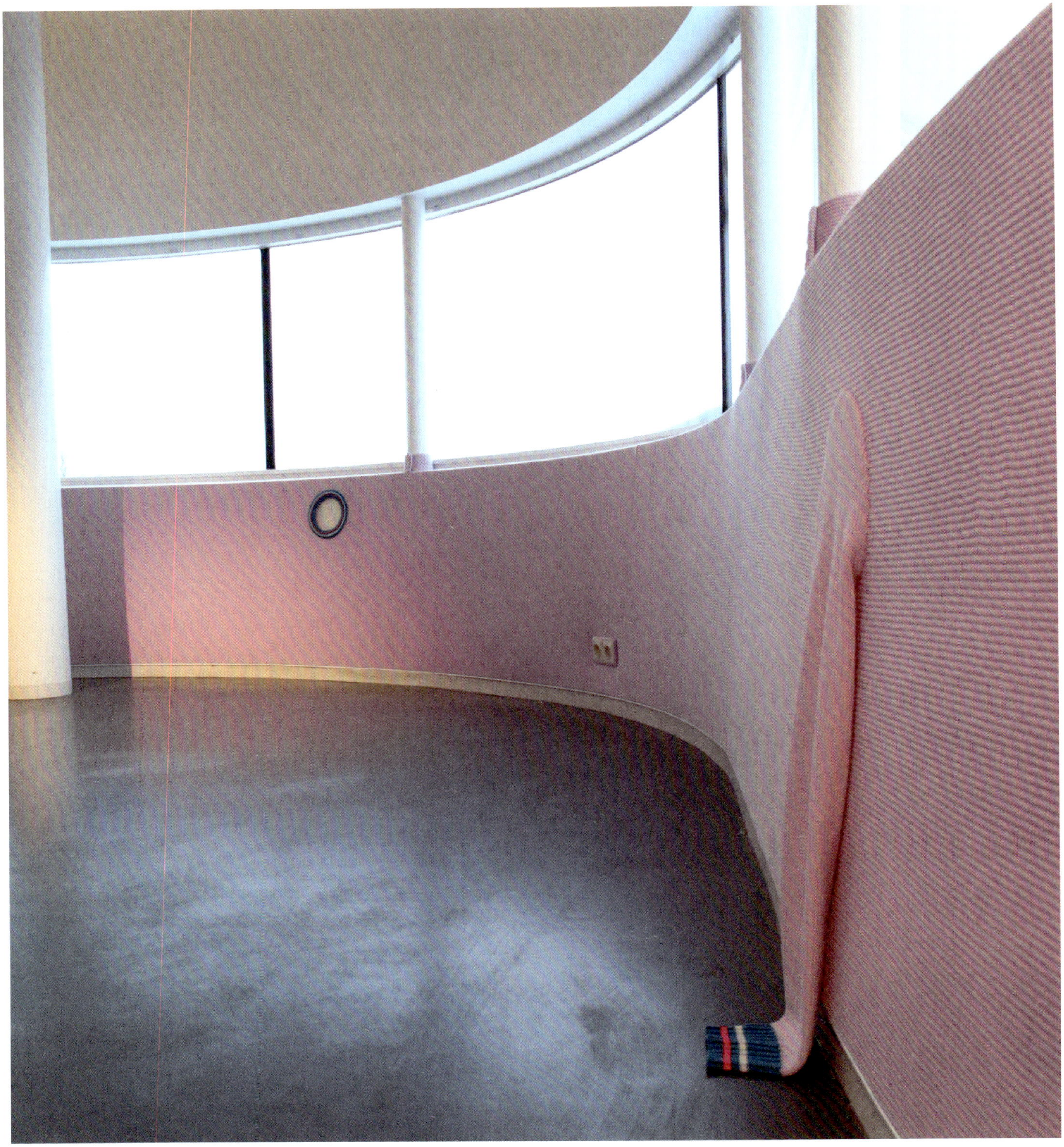

Wallhouse #2, 2009
Installation view (detail), 2009
Groningen, The Netherlands

Wallhouse #2, 2009
Installation view (detail), 2009
Groningen, The Netherlands

Hypnoseblasen, 2007
Watercolor on paper
31 × 41 cm

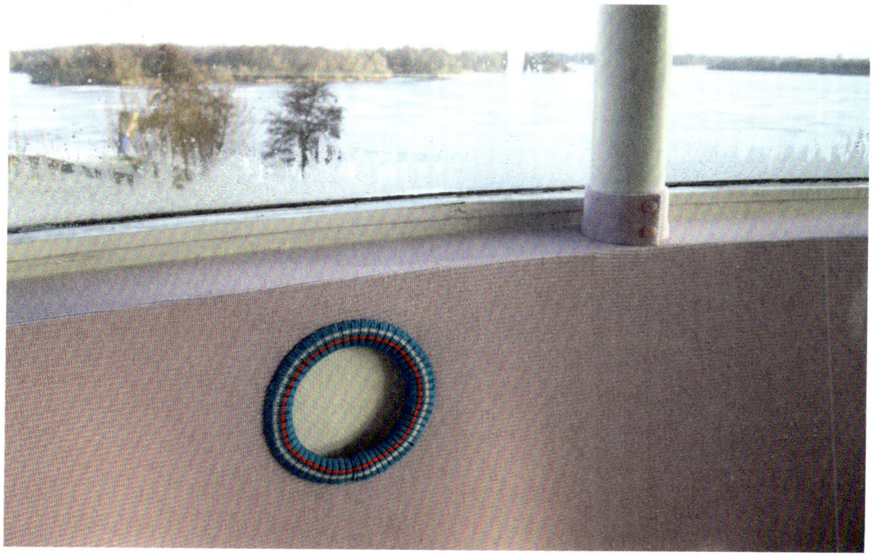

Hypnose blasen

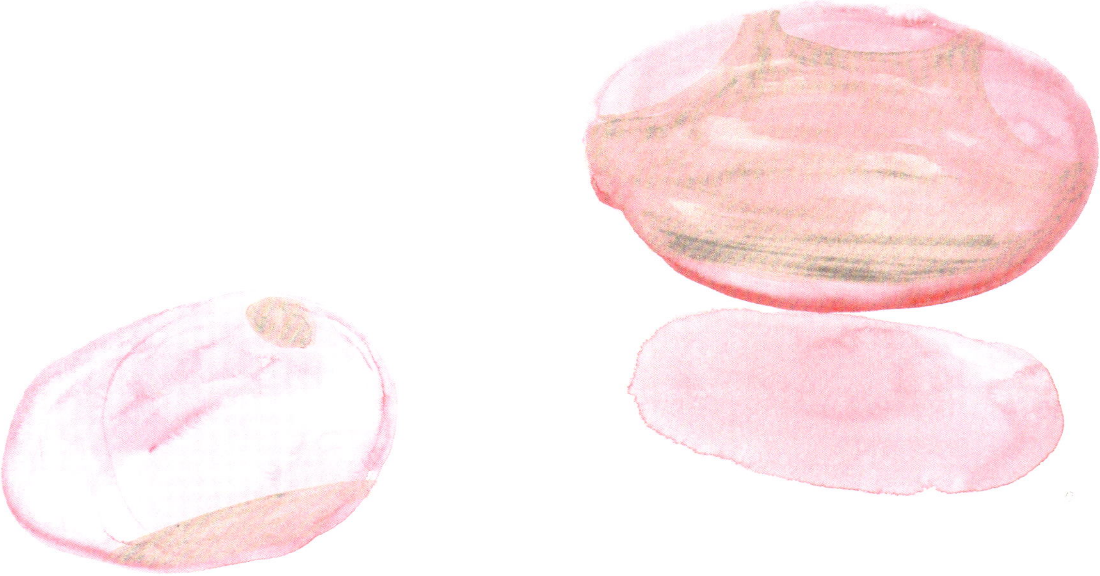

Untitled, 2010
Wool
320 × 800 cm
Installation view, 2011
Kunsthallen Brandts,
Odense, Denmark
Photo: Torben Eskerod

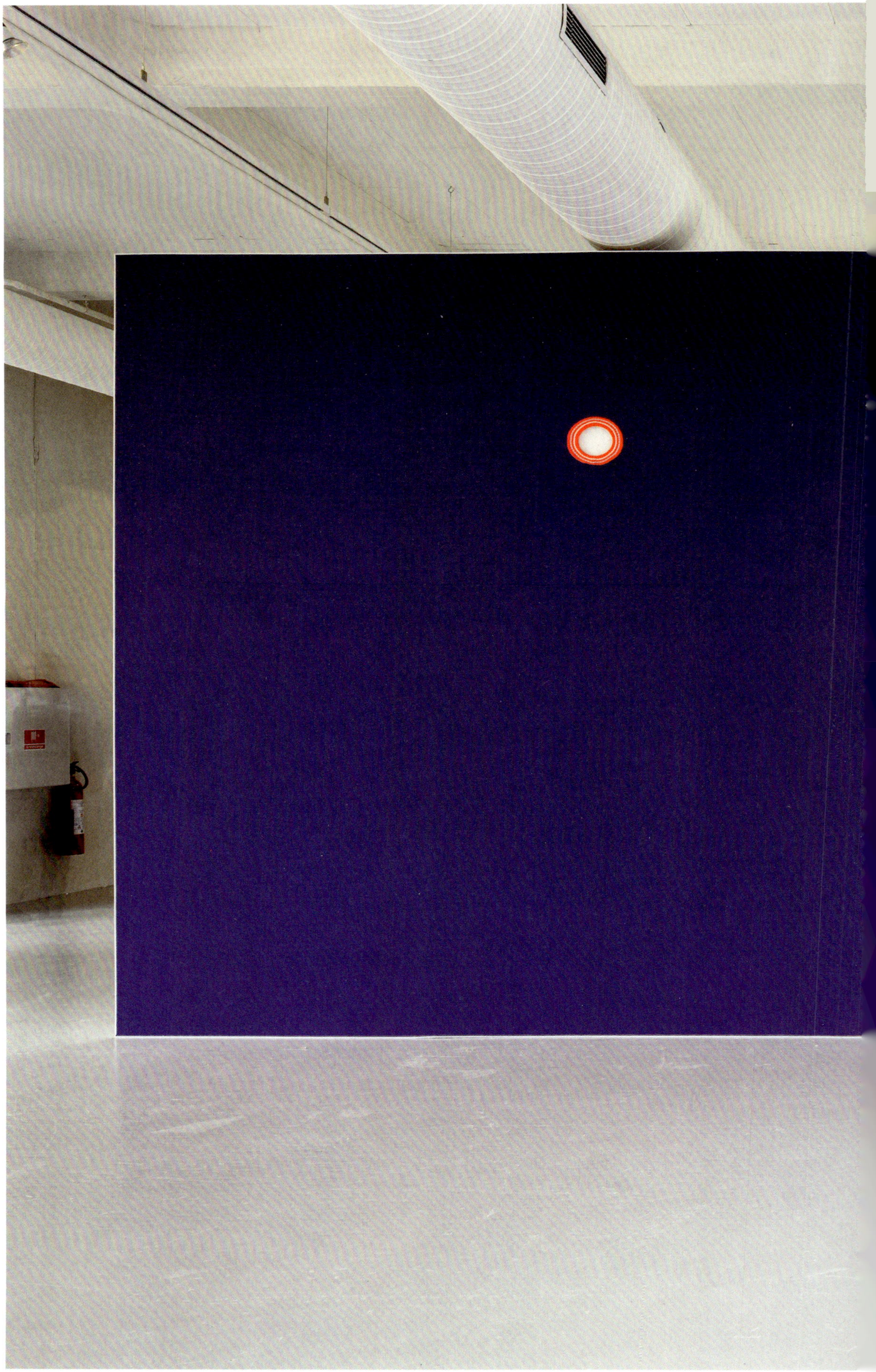

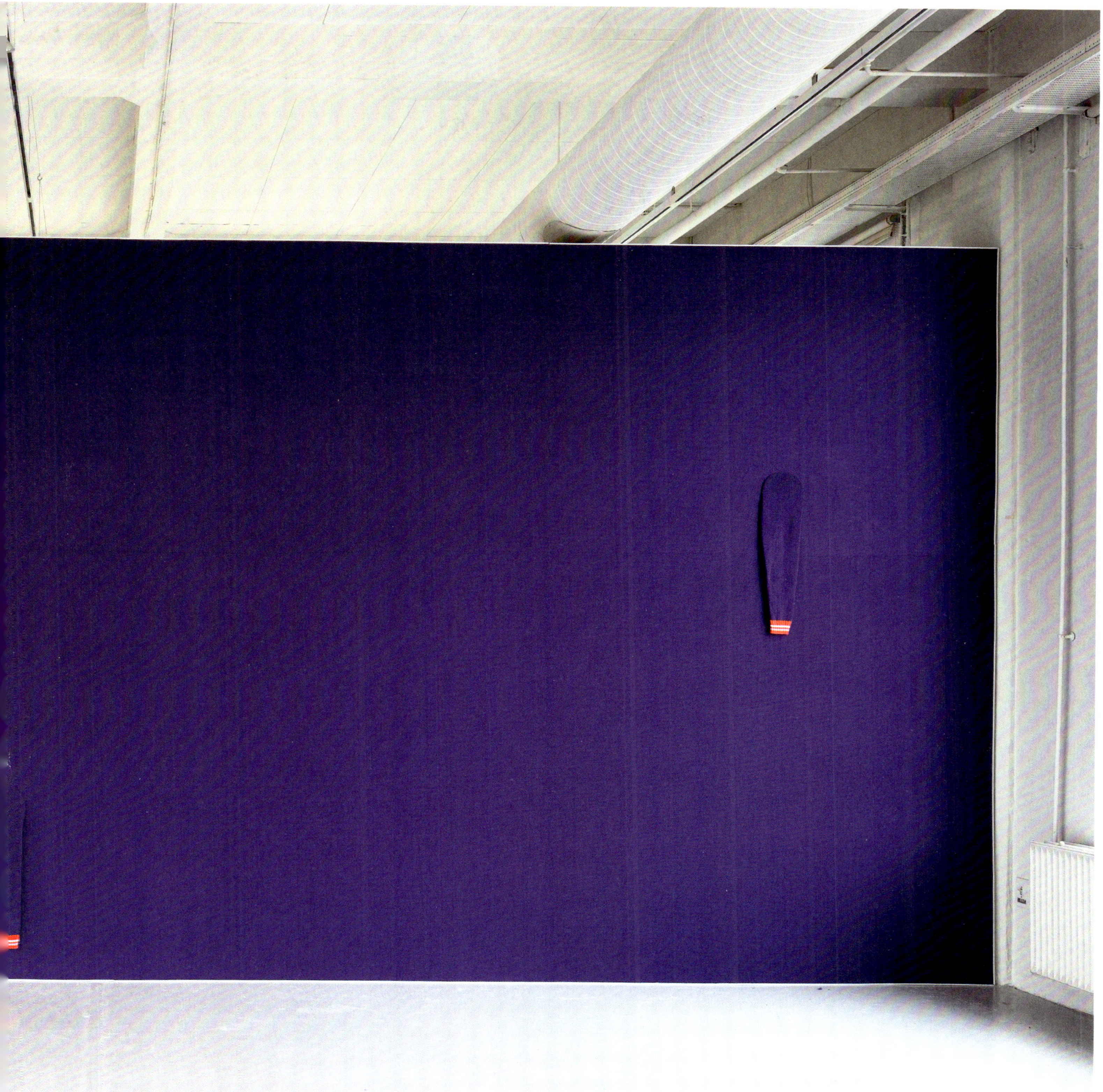

Untitled, 2011
Paint on magazine
37.8 × 26.5 cm

Telekinesis, 2011
Paint, pen on magazine
33 × 23.6-25.2 cm

Instruction Drawing
Do it at Park Avenue
Hotel at 8am, 2001
Pen on paper
33 × 23.6-25.2 cm

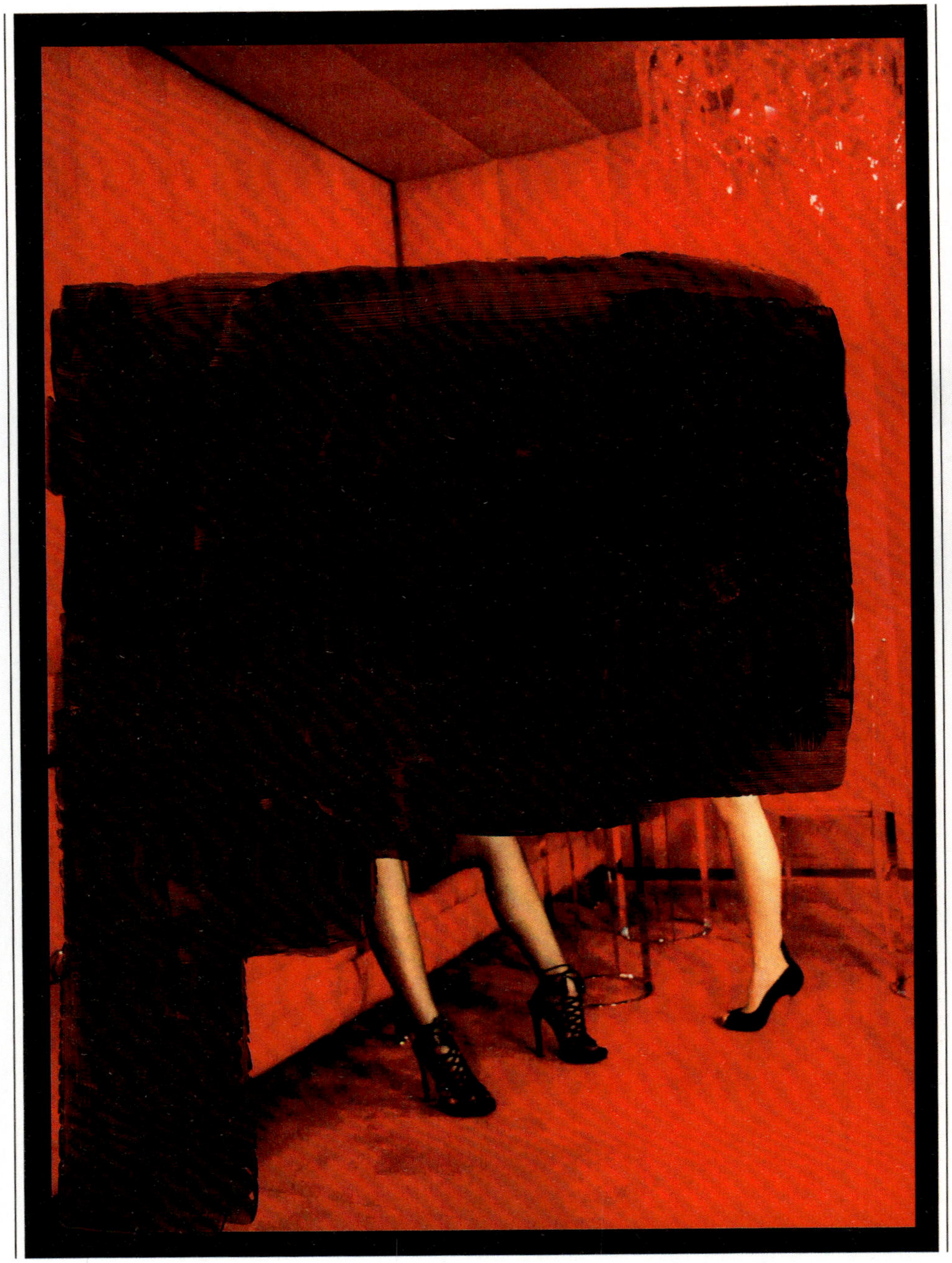

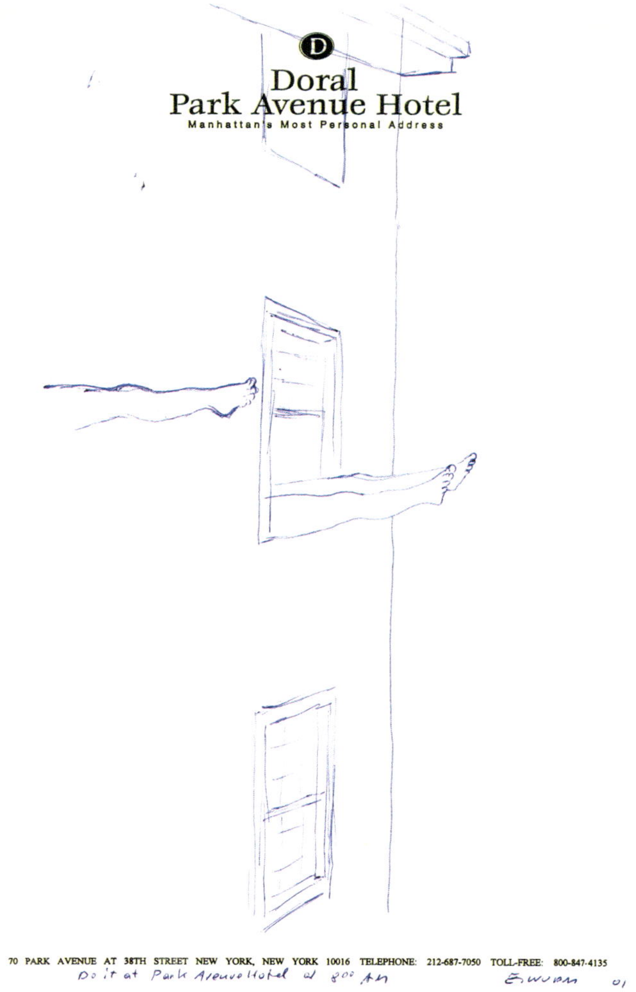
Doral
Park Avenue Hotel
Manhattan's Most Personal Address
70 PARK AVENUE AT 38TH STREET NEW YORK, NEW YORK 10016 TELEPHONE: 212-687-7050 TOLL-FREE: 800-847-4135

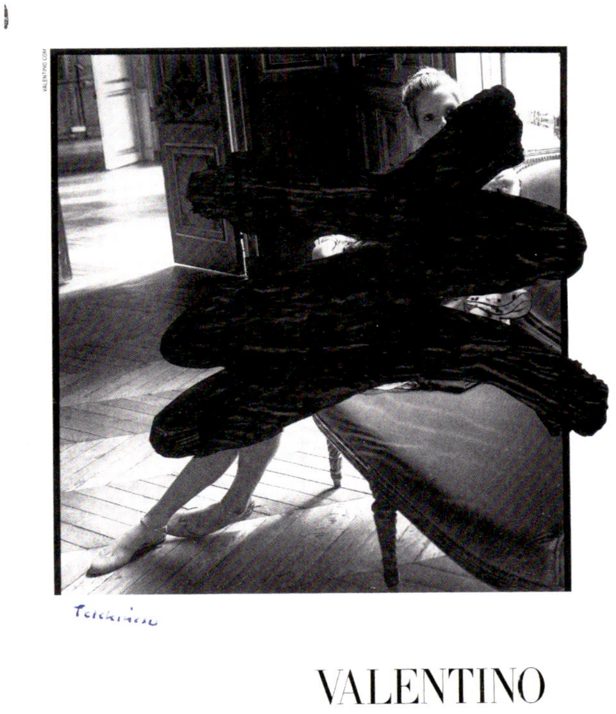
VALENTINO.COM
VALENTINO

O.T., 1987
Felt-marker on catalogue
26.8 × 21.7 cm

Holz, 1987
Felt-marker on catalogue
26.8 × 21.7 cm

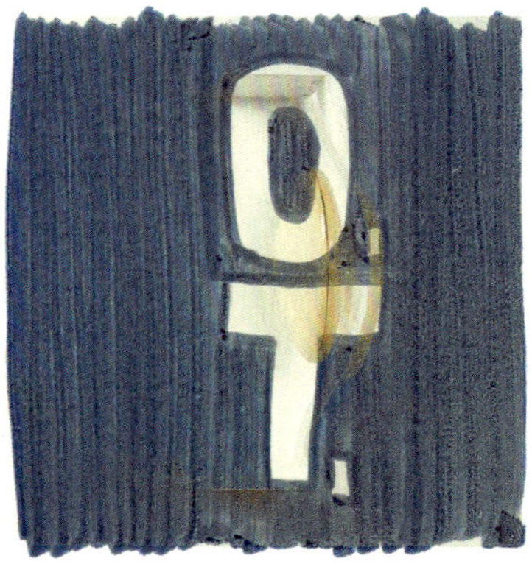

O. T., 1987
Holz, Glas, Öl, 70 x 31 x 36 cm

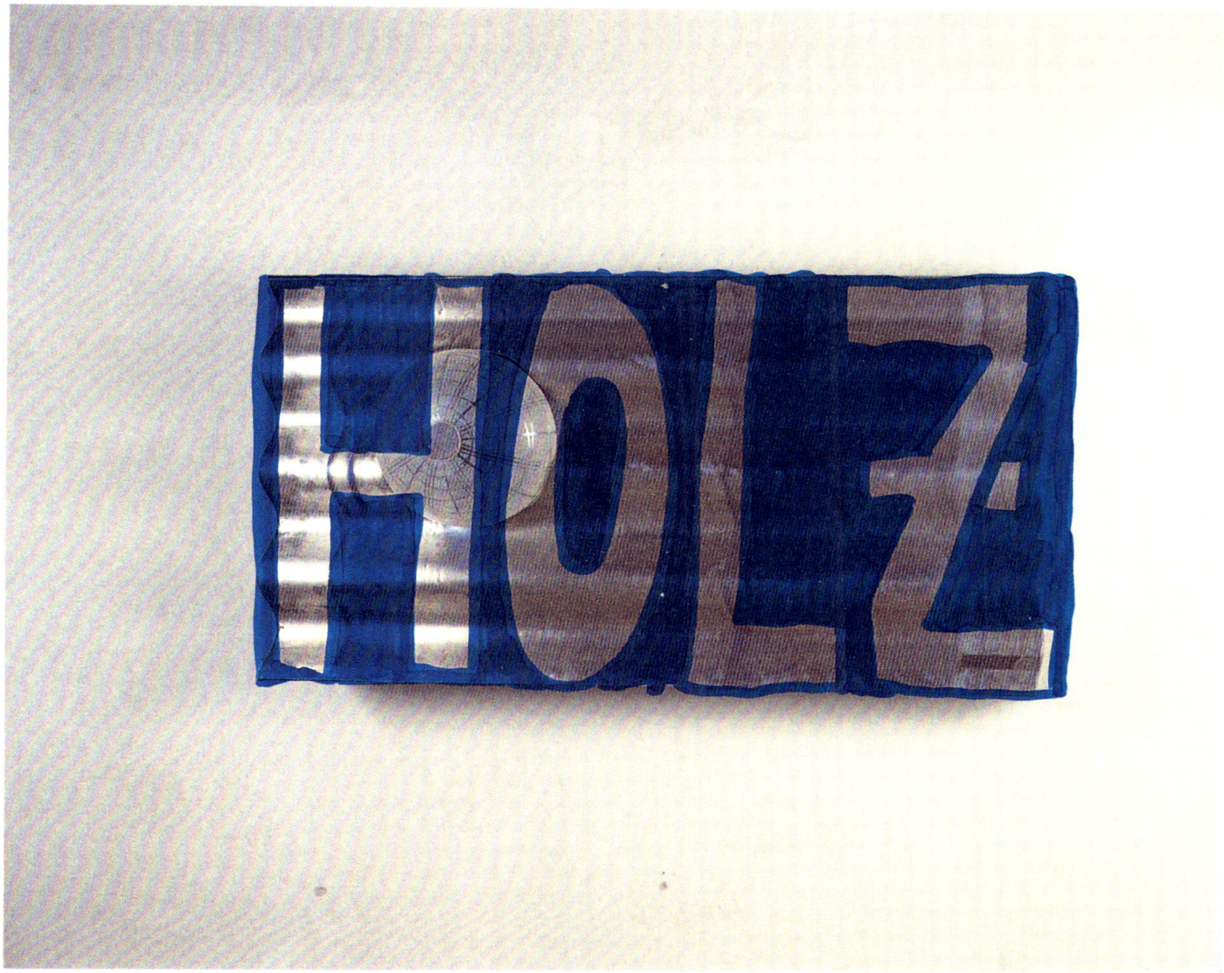

O. T., 1987
Holz, Eternit, Glas, Blei, 68 x 128 x 27 cm

Skulptur, 1987
Pen on catalogue
28 × 21.3-22 cm

Untitled, 1987
Pen on catalogue
26.8 × 21.7 cm

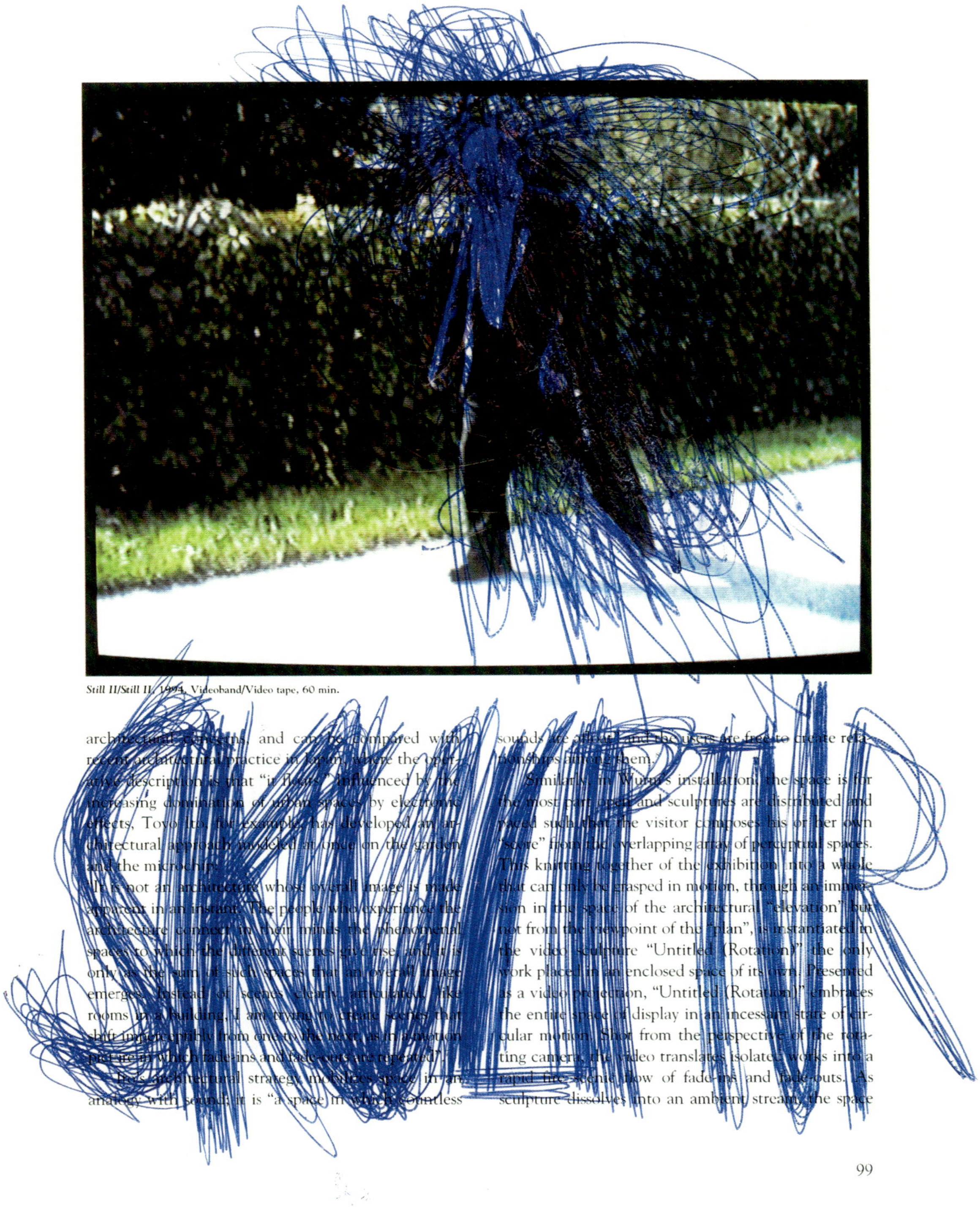

Still II/Still II, 1994, Videoband/Video tape, 60 min.

architectural concerns, and can be compared with recent architectural practice in Japan, where the operative description is that "it floats." Influenced by the increasing domination of urban spaces by electronic effects, Toyo Ito, for example, has developed an architectural approach modeled at once on the garden and the microchip:

"It is not an architecture whose overall image is made apparent in an instant. The people who experience the architecture connect in their minds the phenomenal spaces to which the different scenes give rise, and it is only as the sum of such spaces that an overall image emerges. Instead of scenes clearly articulated, like rooms in a building, I am trying to create scenes that shift imperceptibly from one to the next, as in a motion picture in which fade-ins and fade-outs are repeated".

Ito's architectural strategy mobilizes space in an analogy with sound; it is "a space in which countless sounds are afloat and the users are free to create relationships among them."

Similarly, in Wurm's installation, the space is for the most part open and sculptures are distributed and paced such that the visitor composes his or her own "score" from the overlapping array of perceptual spaces. This knitting together of the exhibition into a whole that can only be grasped in motion, through an immersion in the space of the architectural "elevation" but not from the viewpoint of the "plan", is instantiated in the video sculpture "Untitled (Rotation)" the only work placed in an enclosed space of its own. Presented as a video projection, "Untitled (Rotation)" embraces the entire space of display in an incessant state of circular motion. Shot from the perspective of the rotating camera, the video translates isolated works into a rapid fire scenic flow of fade-ins and fade-outs. As sculpture dissolves into an ambient stream, the space

99

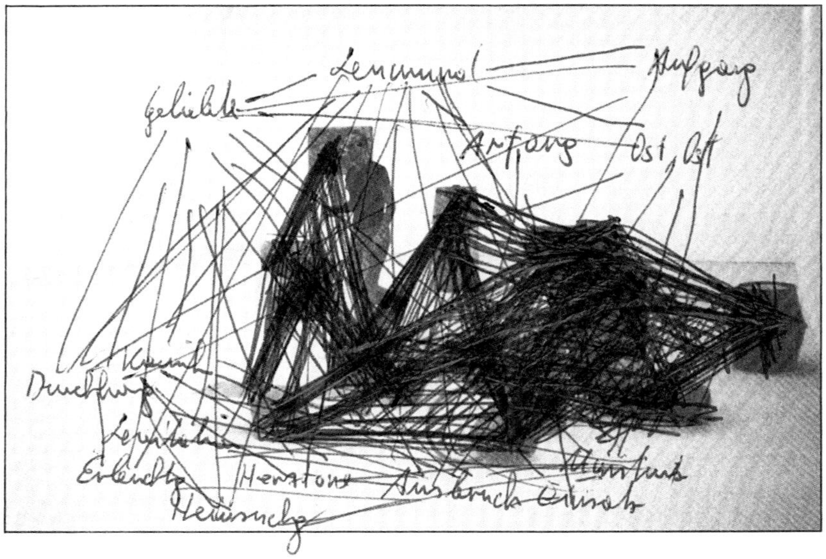

Biennale Sao Paolo, 1987

Lust—Last, 1995
Pen on magazine
26.8 × 21.7 cm

Uschi, 1987
Pen on catalogue
31.2 × 13.3-16 cm

Ort, 1995
Pen on catalogue
28 × 22 cm

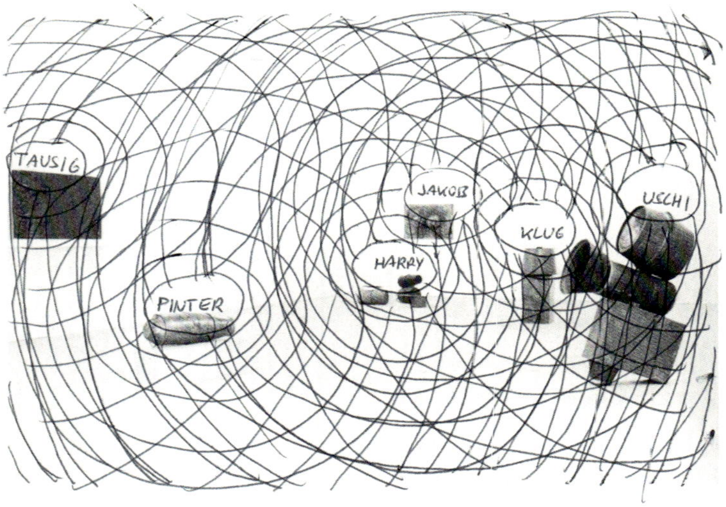

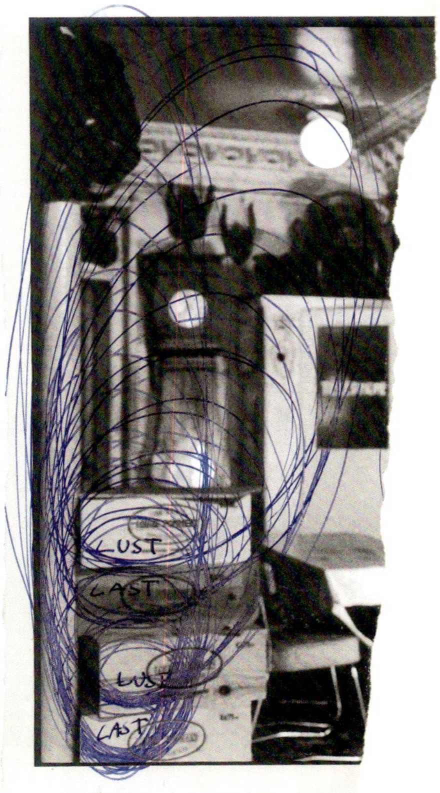

Biennale Sao Paolo, 1987

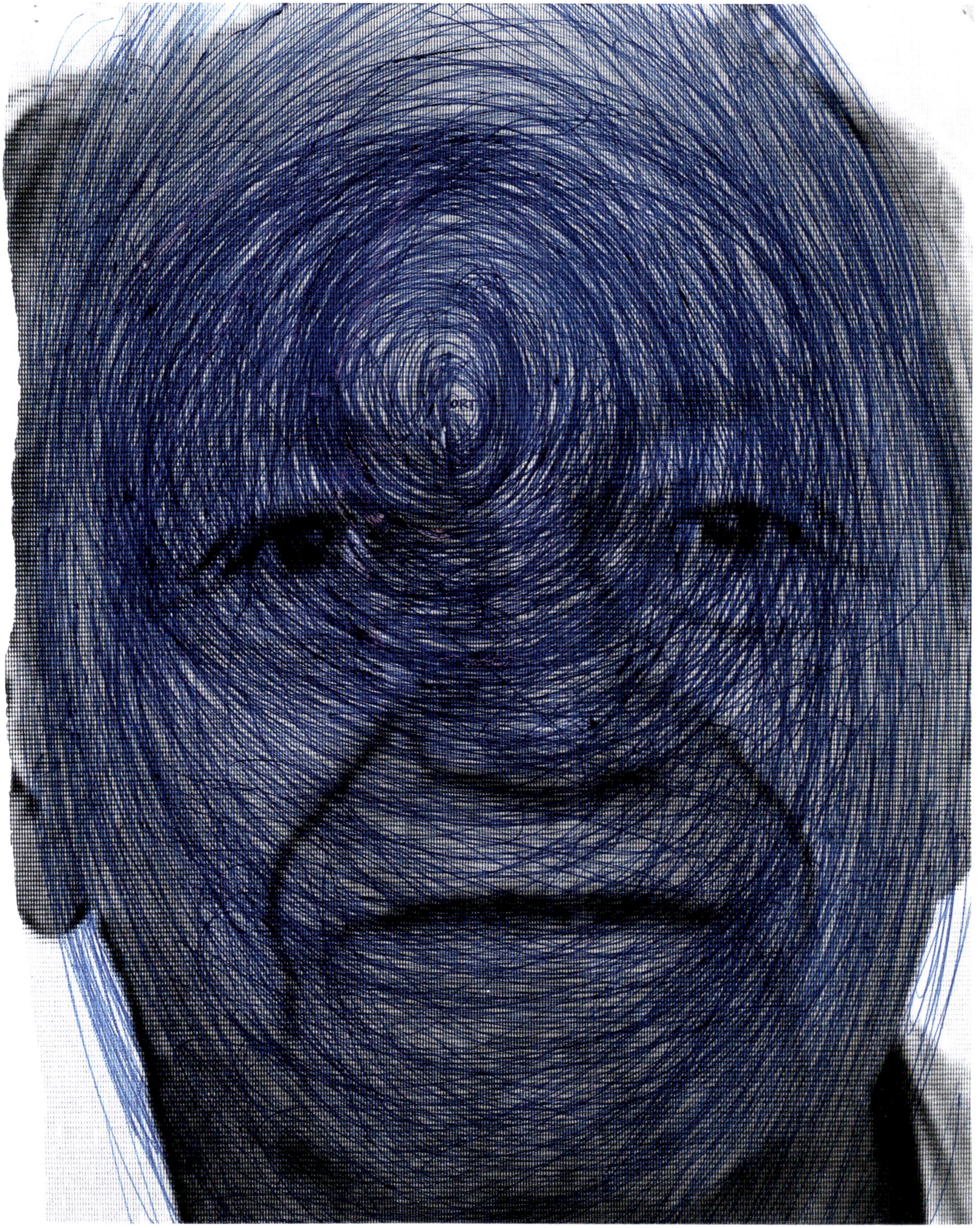

Anbau Wien, 1995
Paint, pen on catalogue
28 × 20.6-22 cm

Motivate — Motive, 1997
Pen on paper
27.8 × 38 cm

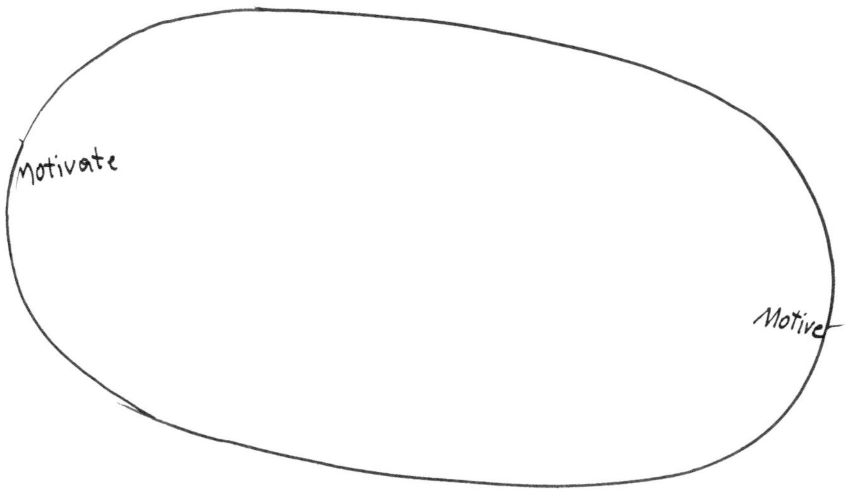
Motivate
Motive

Still, 1994
Felt-marker on magazine
24.5 × 50.5-52 cm

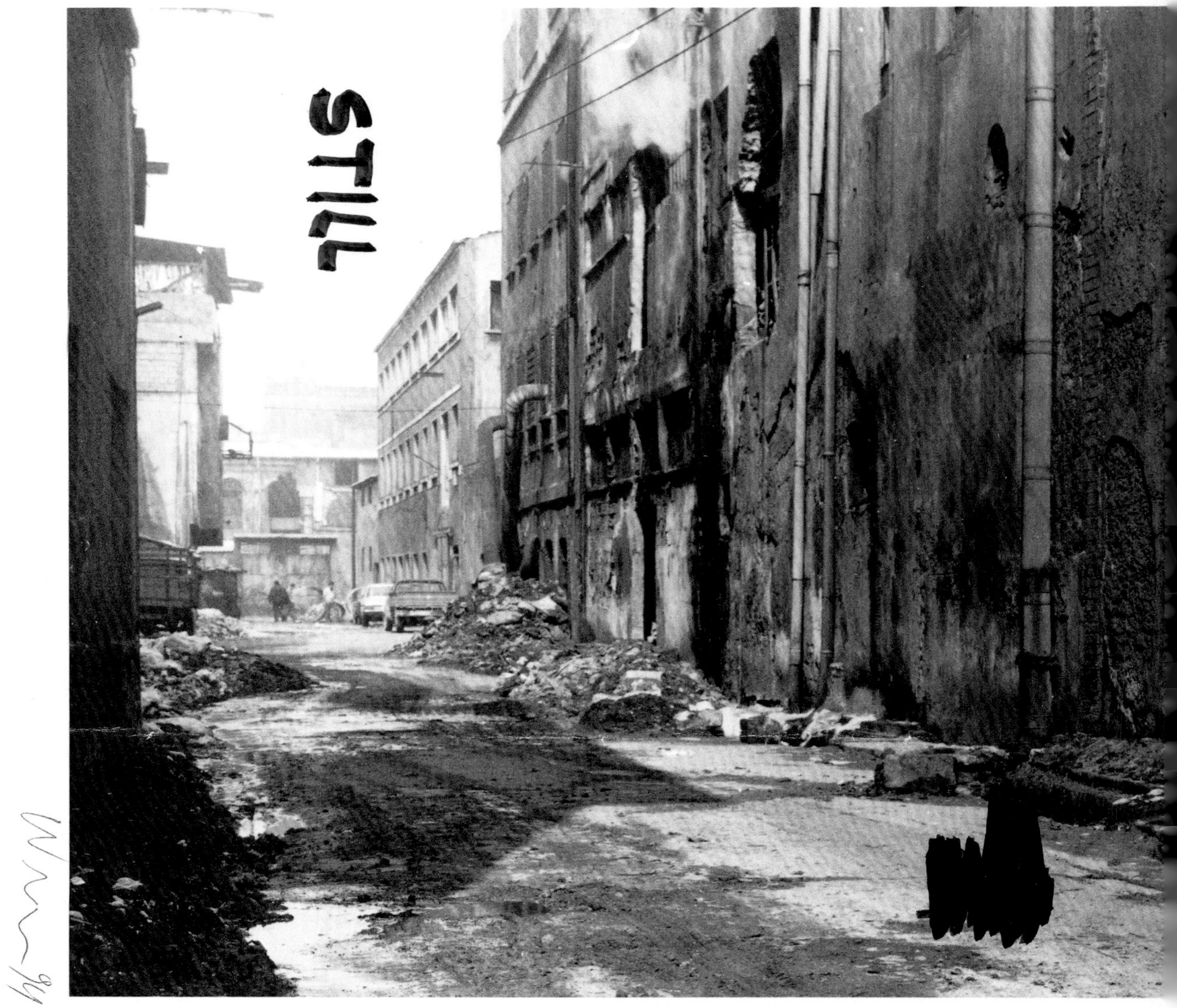

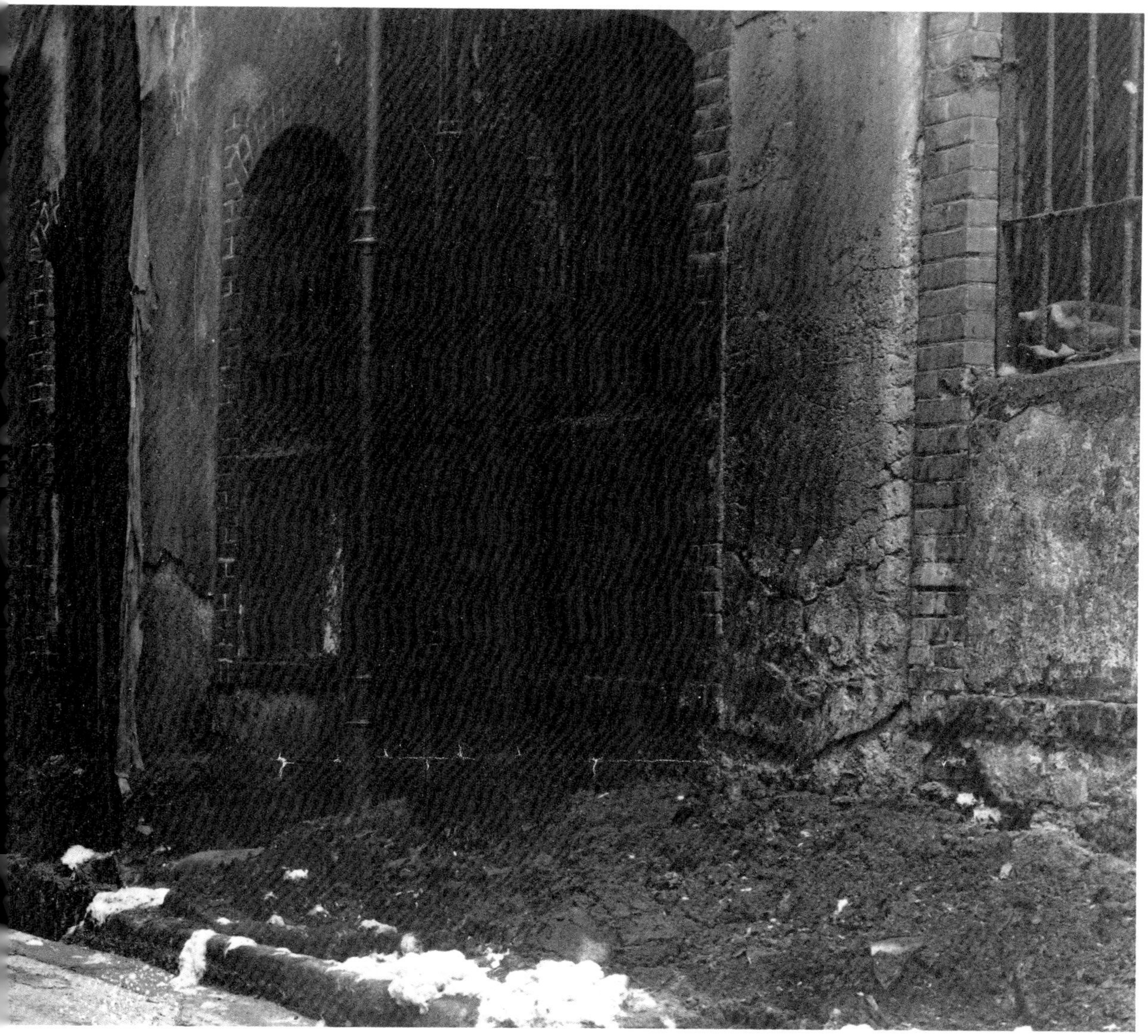

Der Grund des Reichtums, 1991
Felt-marker on catalogue
21 × 30 cm

Einzelhaft, 1991
Paint, pen on photocopy
29.6 × 42 cm

Metrische Systeme, 1986
Paint, pen on magazine
23.5-24.3 × 33.3 cm

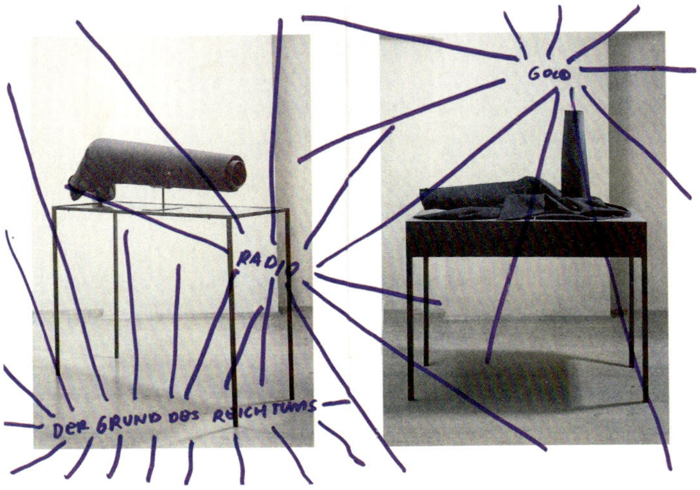

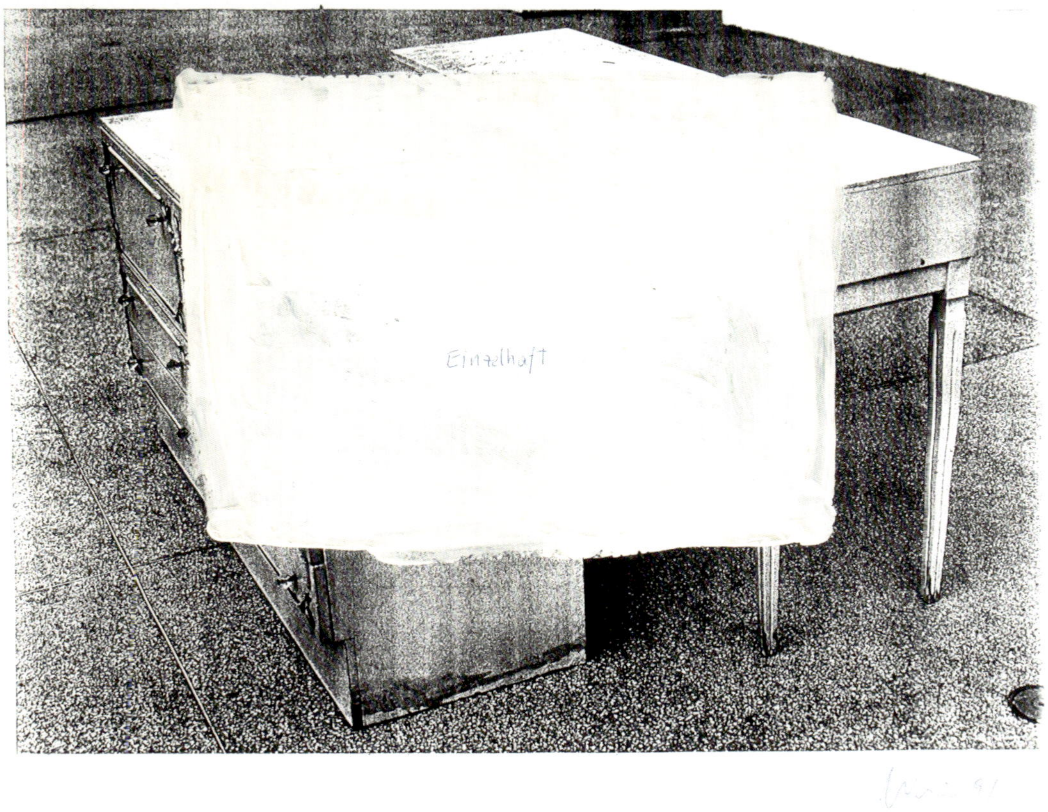

metrische Systeme
BLOCKADEN
WIENERIN

Möbel attack, 2011
Paint, pen on magazine
37.9 × 26.5 cm

Untitled, 2011
Paint on c-print
29.5 × 21 cm

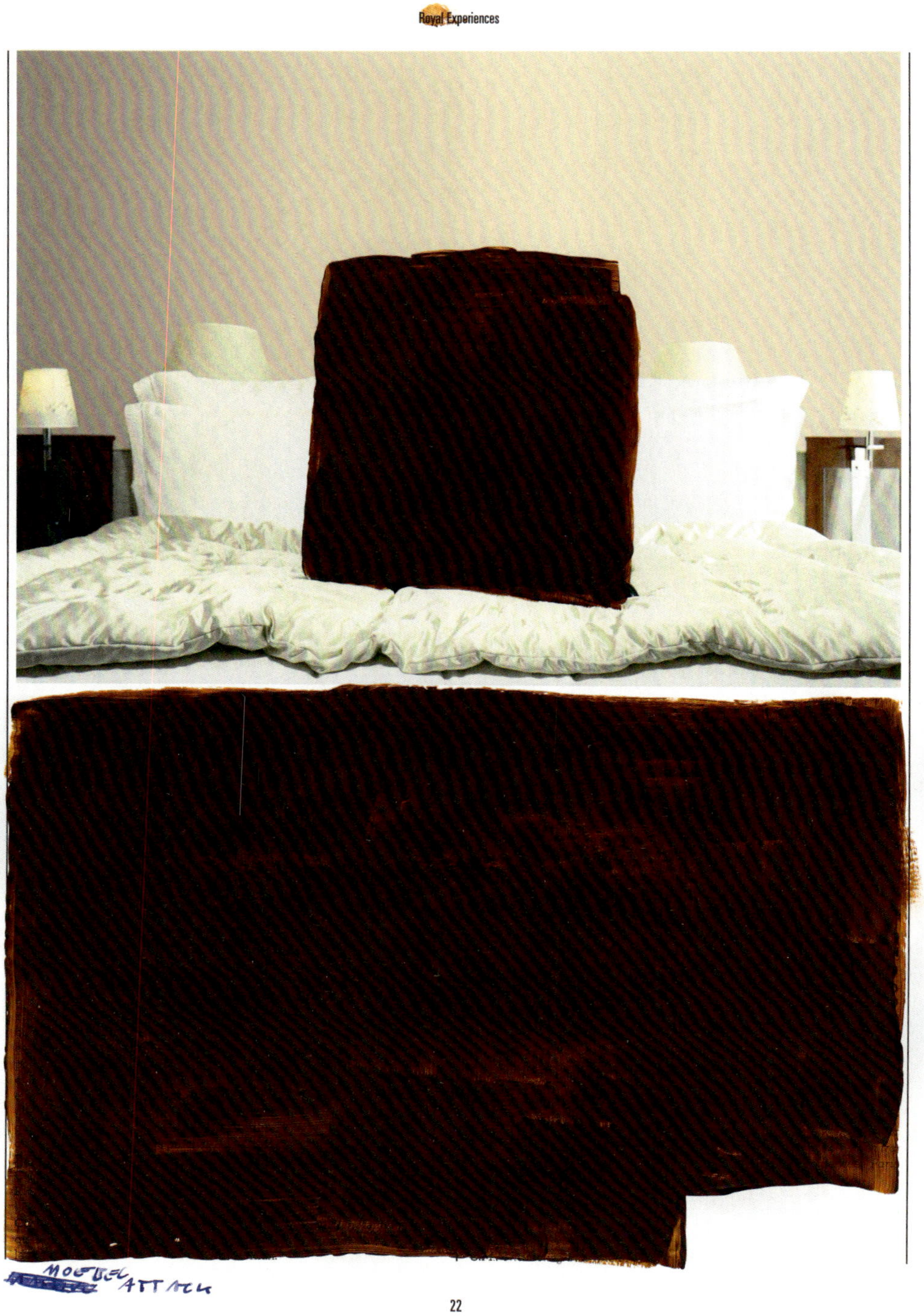

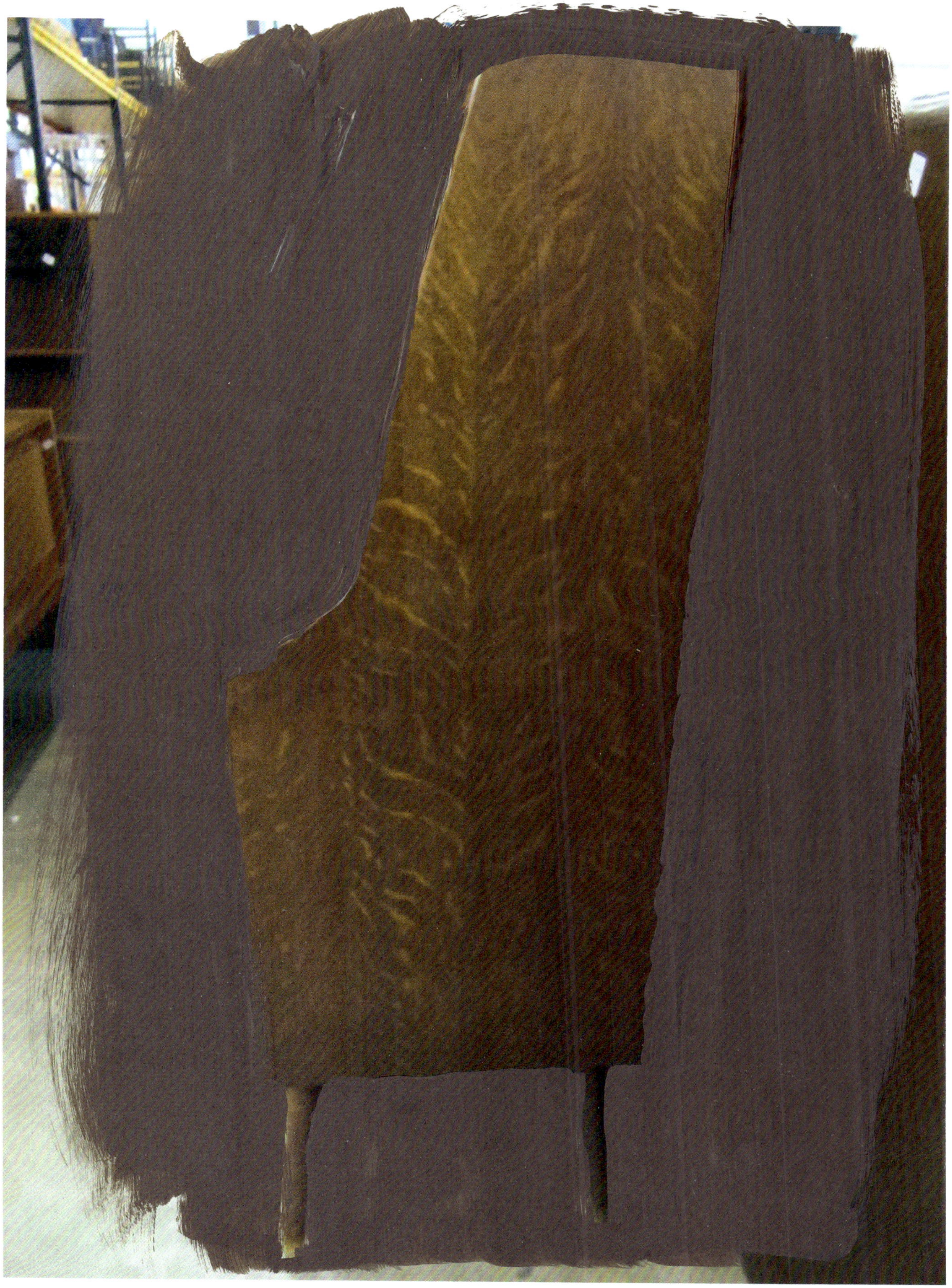

Versaille, 1995
Paint, pen on magazine
29.1–32.3 × 47.2 cm

2 Block Süd, 1995
Felt-marker,
paint on magazine
28.4 × 19.5–21.5 cm

Kästchen 1 and 2, 2010
Wood, metal, paint,
bottles
77 × 65 × 63 cm
76 × 80 × 50 cm

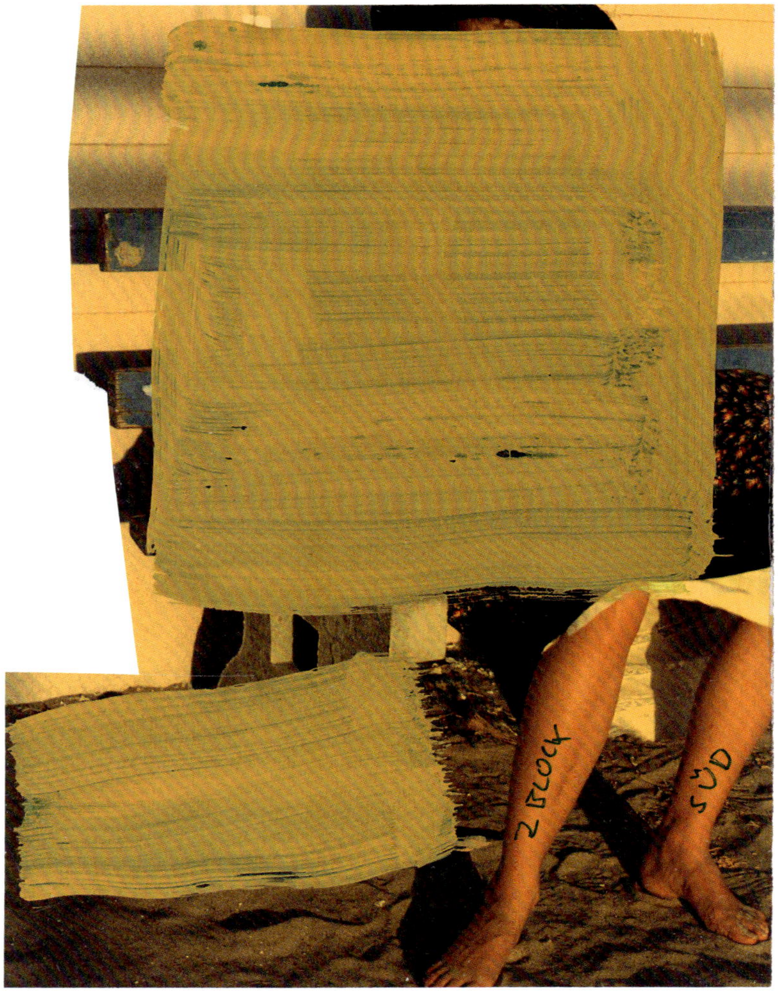

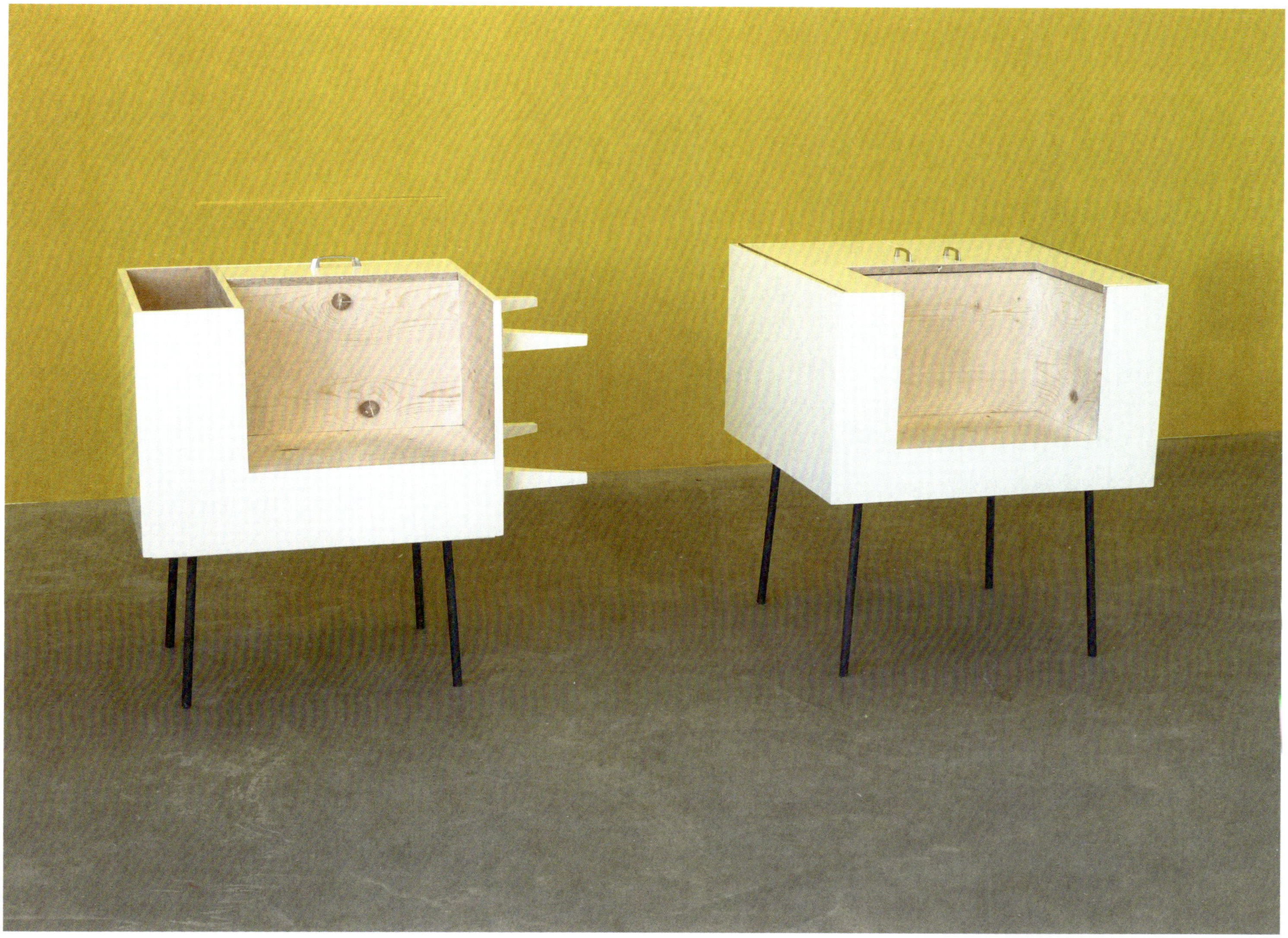

Strickslip #1, 2011
Wood, metal,
knitwear, foam
49 × 66 × 92 cm
Installation view, 2011
MAK, Vienna

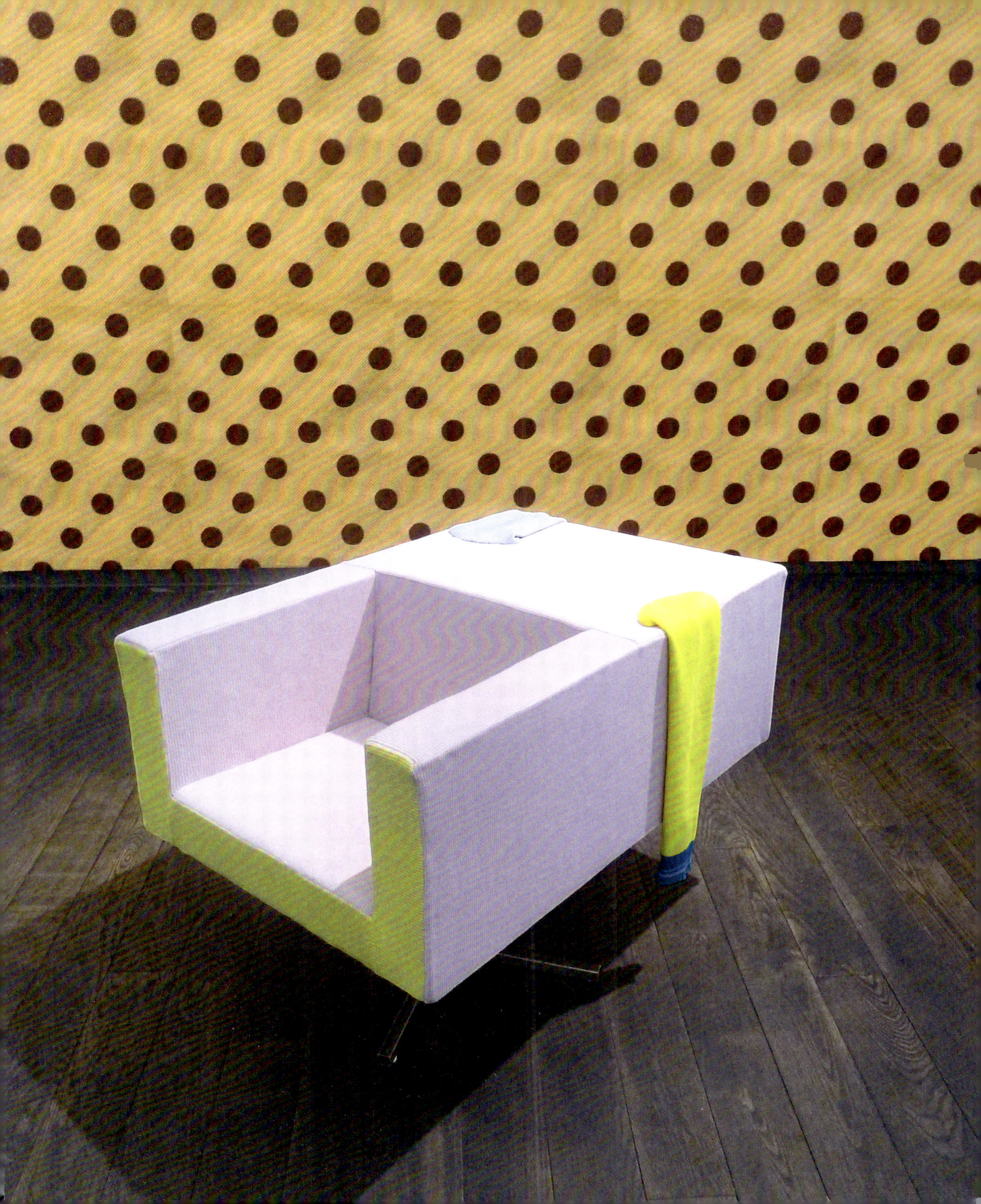

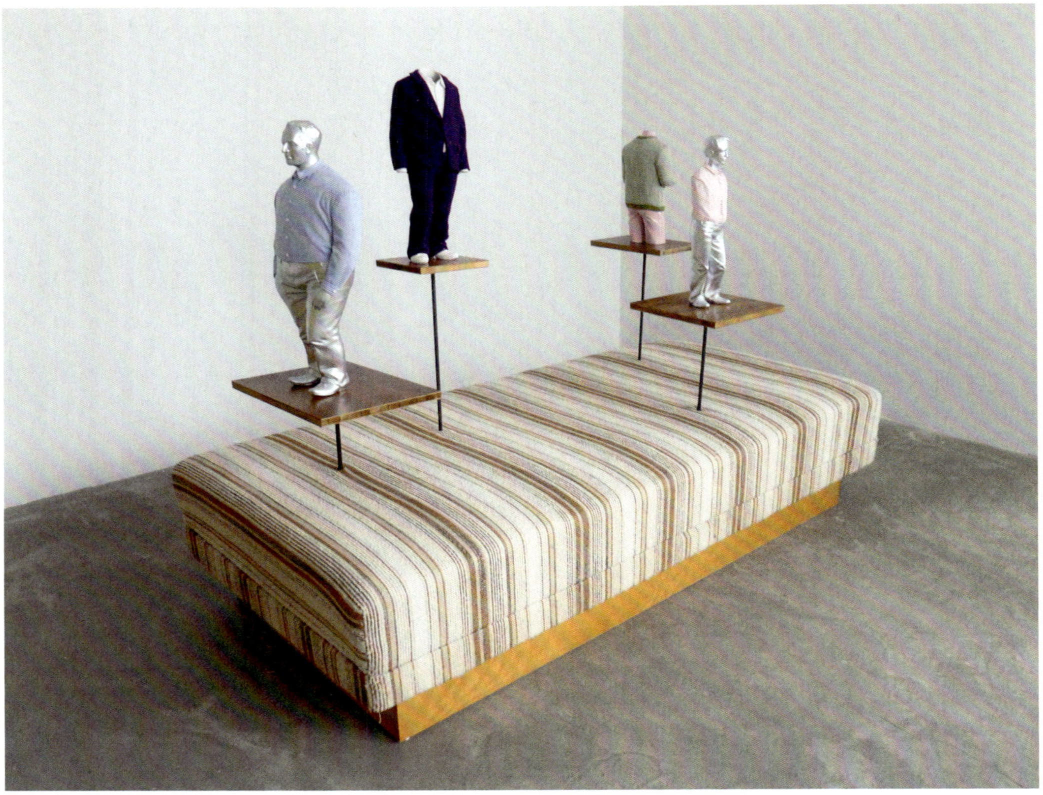

Bett, 2011
Wood, fabric, metal
100 × 200 × 100 cm

Tisch, 2011
Wood, metal
86 × 176 × 172.5 cm
Installation view, 2011
MAK, Vienna

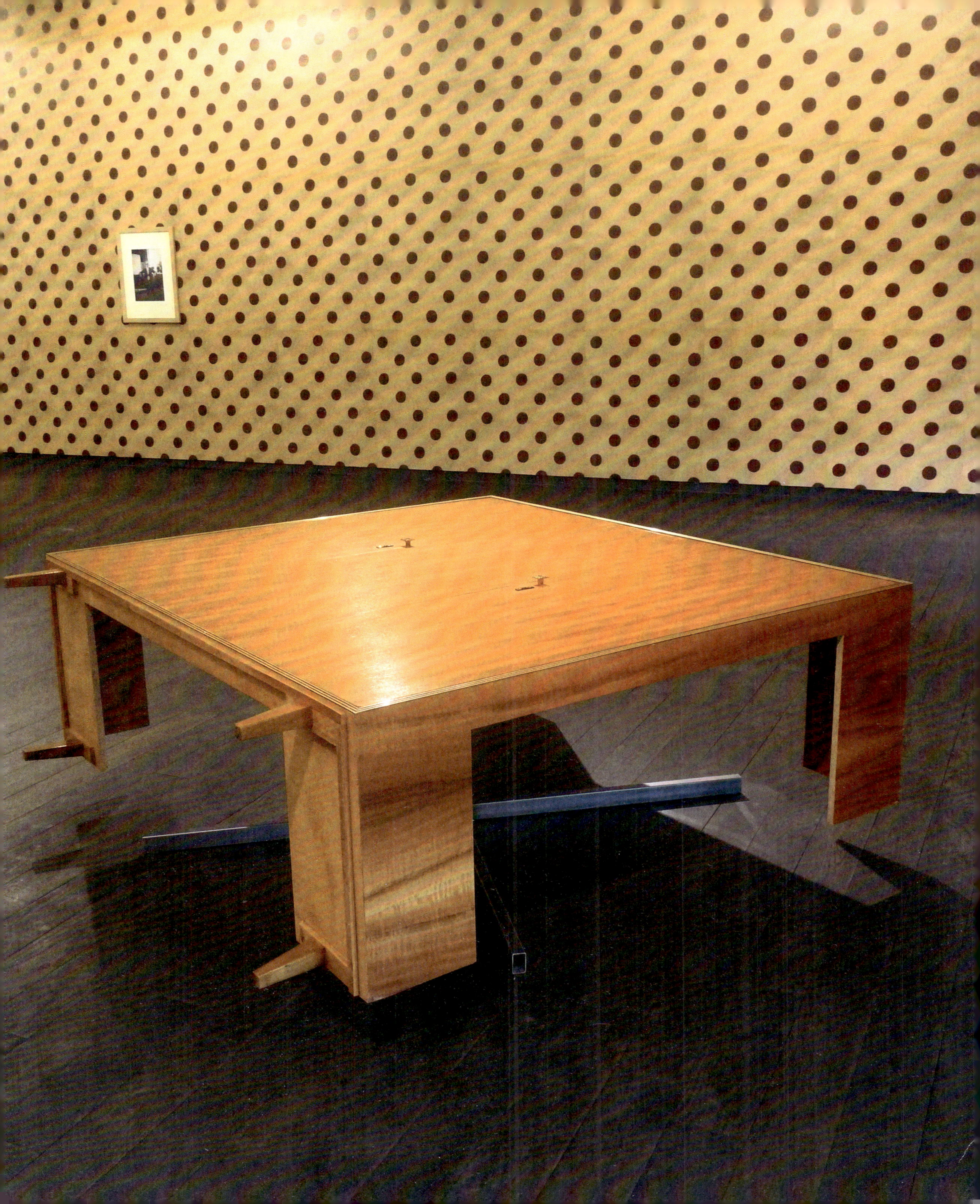

Untitled, 2007
Watercolor on paper
31 × 41 cm

Untitled, 2007
Watercolor on paper
31 × 41 cm

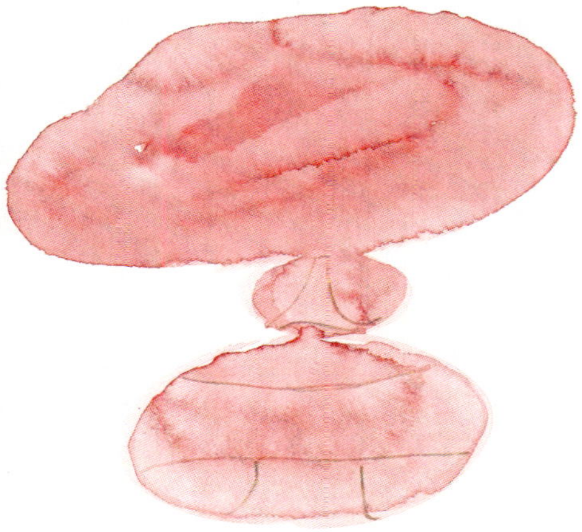

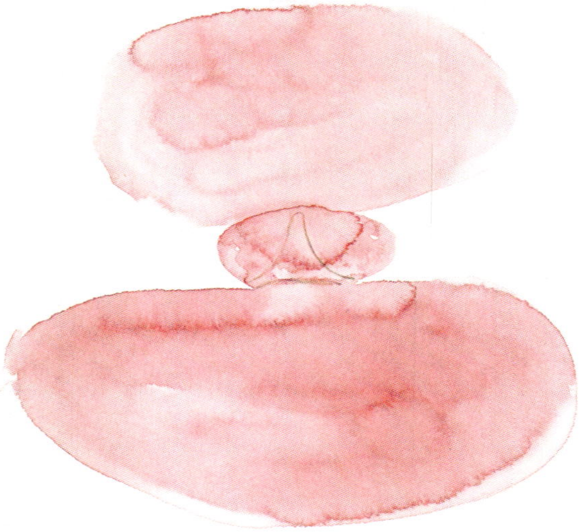

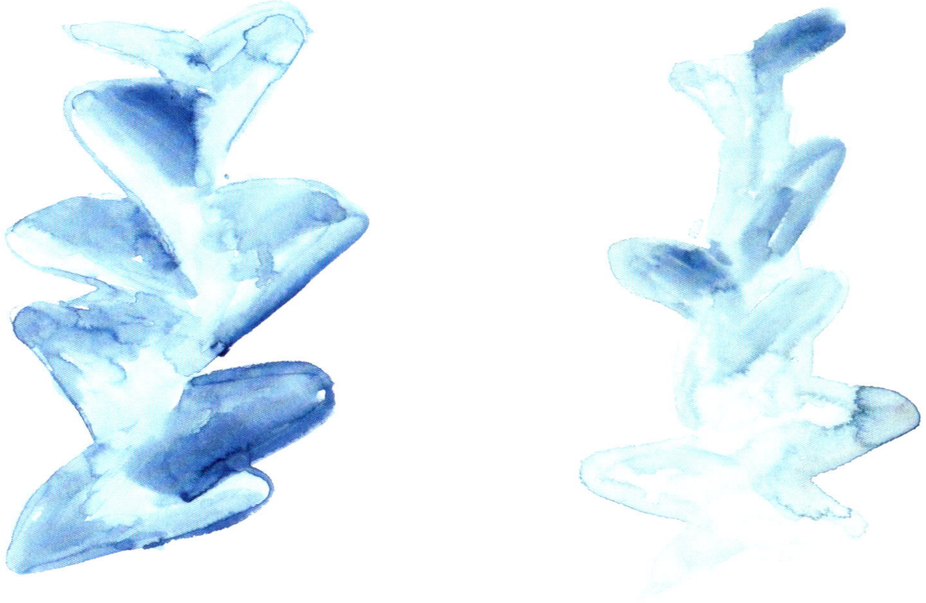

Jelly artist, 2006
Watercolor on paper
30.7 × 23 cm

Jelly artist, 2006
Watercolor on paper
23 × 30.5 cm

Jelly artist, 2006
Watercolor on paper
30.5 × 23 cm

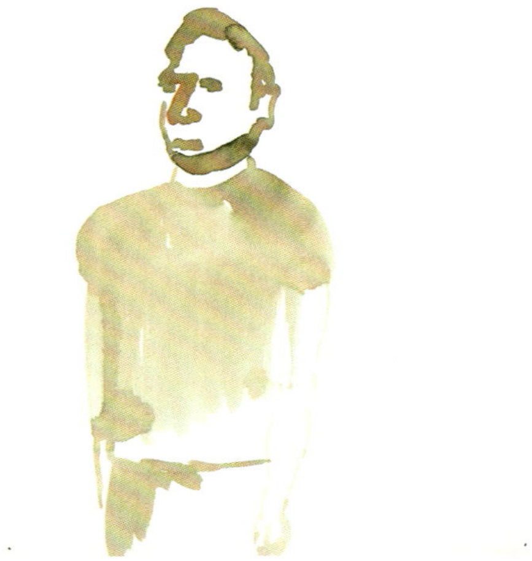

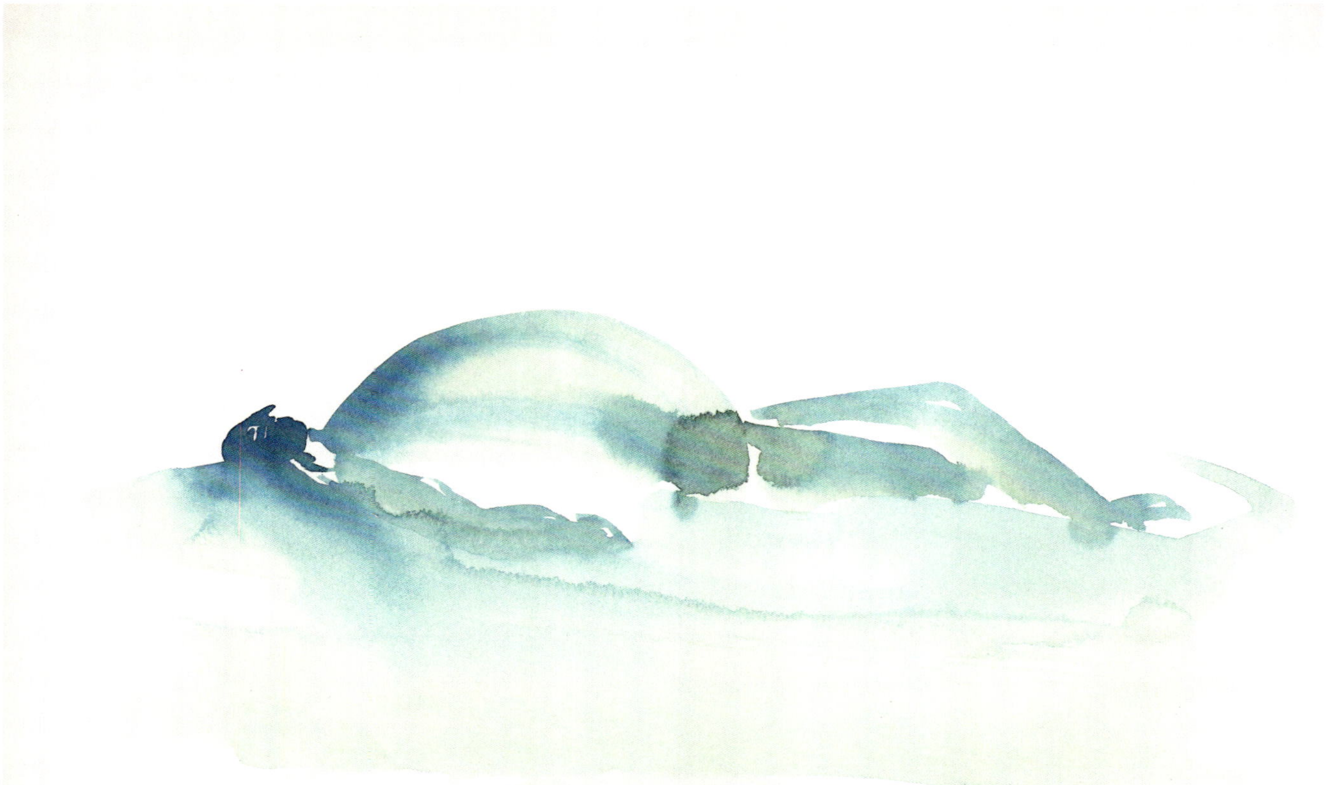

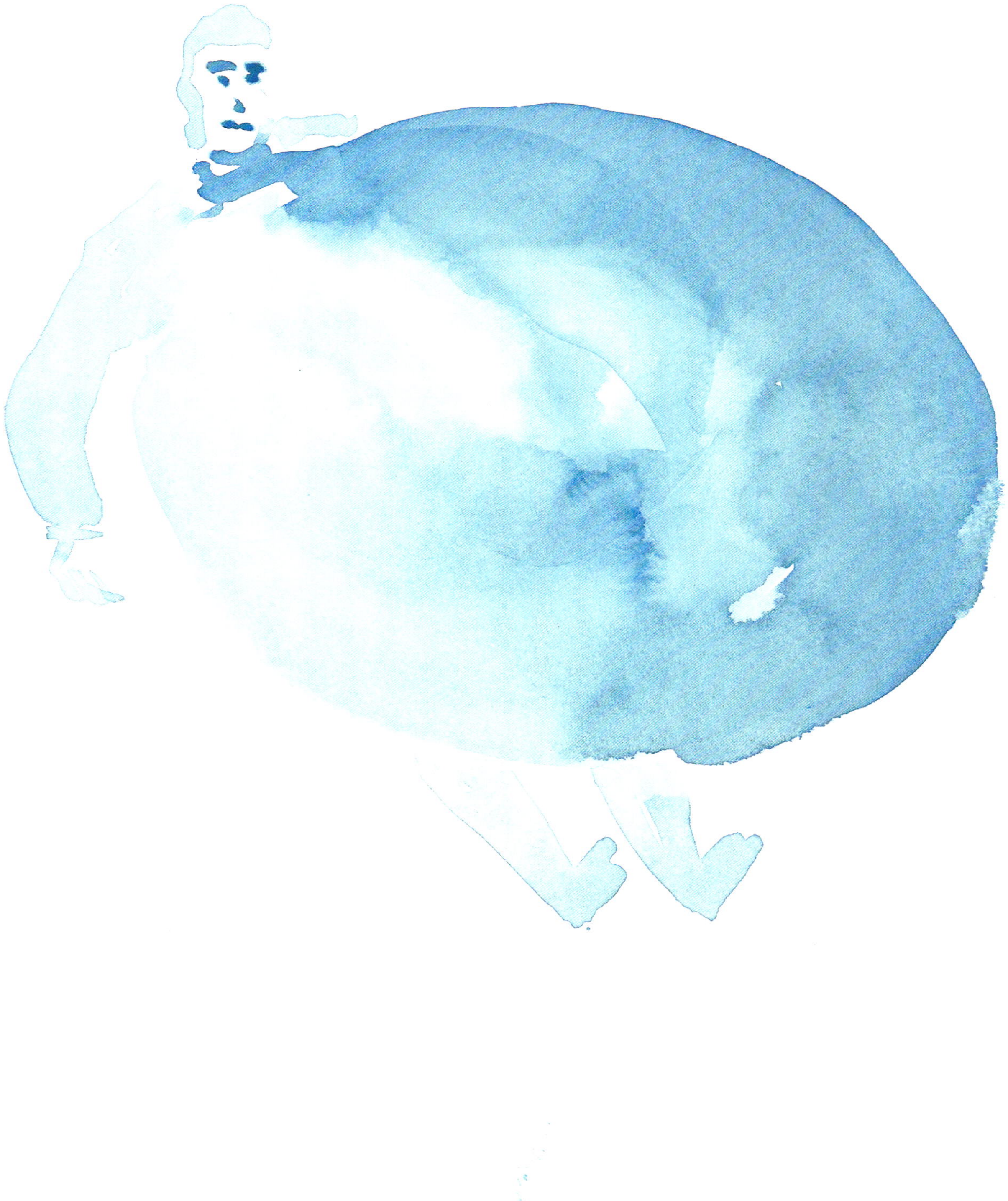

Performative sculpture, 2011
Photo: Elfie Semotan

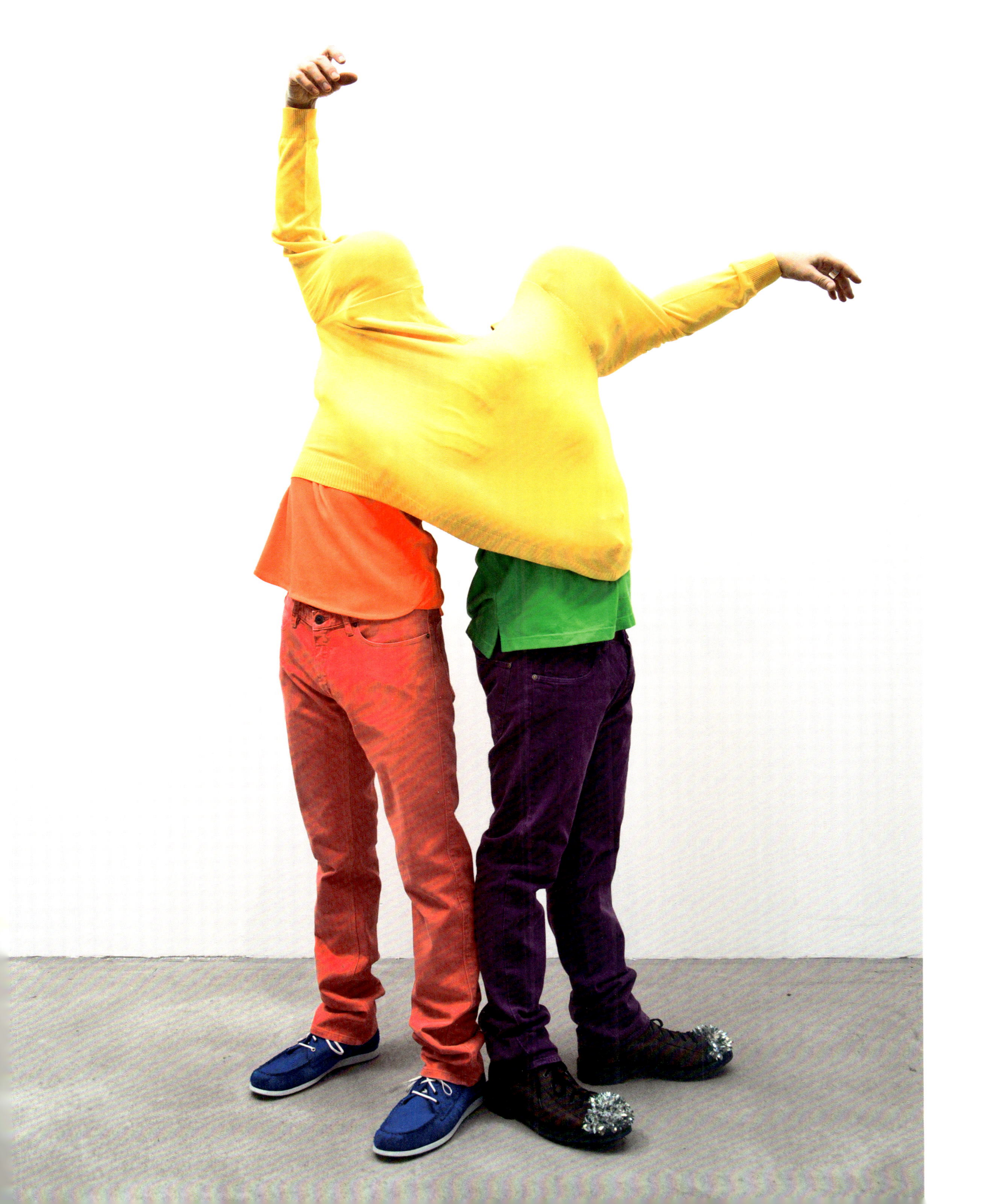

Performative sculpture, 2011
Photo: Elfie Semotan

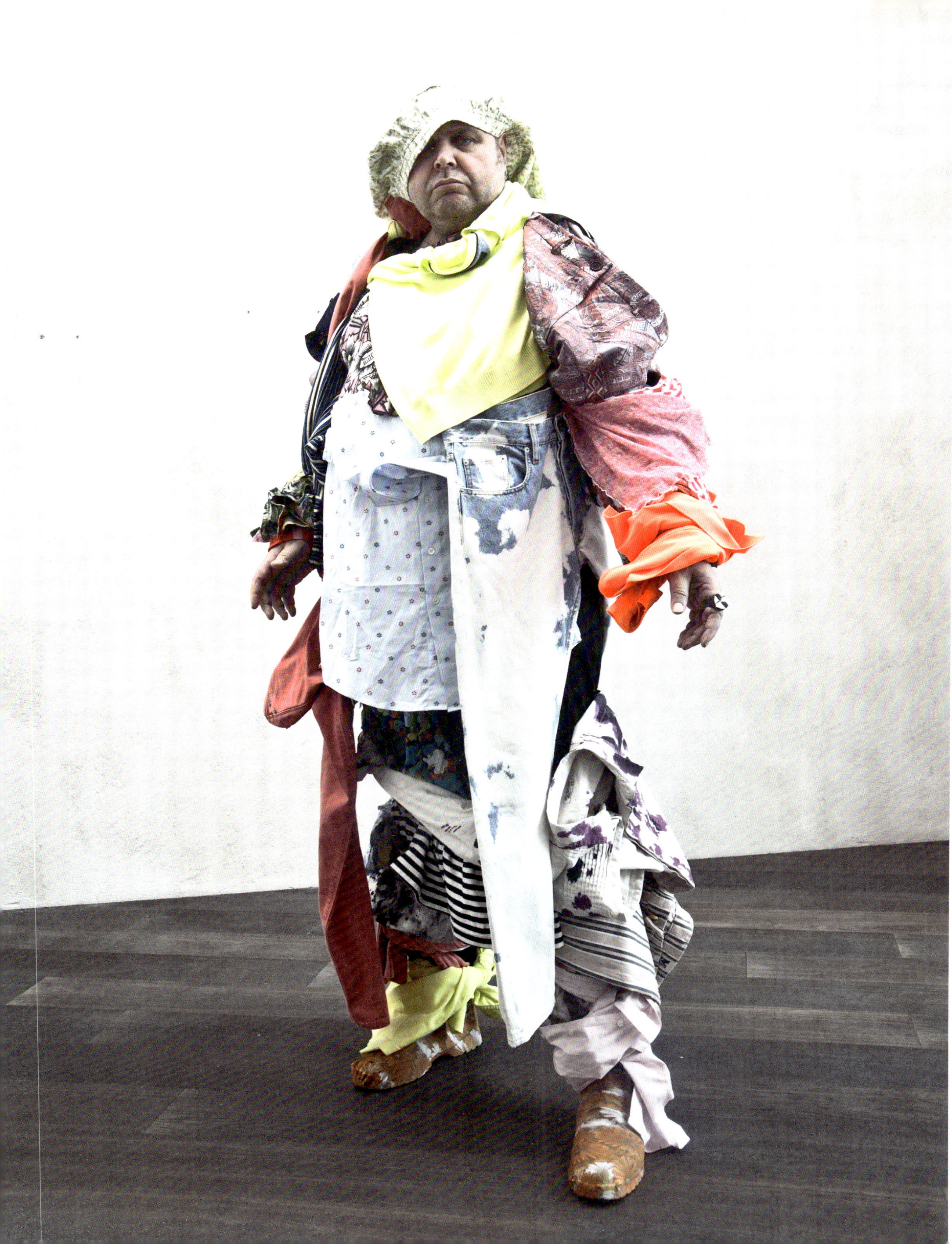

Ask Erwin Wurm

BT & LS Benno Tempel, Laura Stamps
SW Sara Weyns

BT & LS In every interview, you say that your work is an exploration of the potential of sculpture. As a result, over the last few decades your work has been one of the most interesting investigations of what sculpture means in today's world. Recently, you have also started to make furniture. How do these pieces fit with your exploration of the meaning of sculpture?

EW I'm obviously not the only one or the first one to explore furniture. A lot of people have done it before me. Many artists have worked with furniture. The first one was probably Brancusi, then all sorts of people right up to Franz West. What most drew my interest is the connection between an object and a person who has to do something. So there is a direct link with my *One Minute Sculptures*. There's something else that is specified right from the start, a user guide, which means that you're invited to sit down, or invited to sit at the bar stools, to open a cupboard or a cabinet door, and to take out a bottle, to pour a drink into a glass—as there is also a glass—and then to drink. On the one hand the process has a lot to do with instructions and with performative sculpture. The second thing that interested me was to use pieces of furniture as the starting point. I then make them into works of art by removing their function in a way. But in another way I give them a new function, that of furniture again. So it is almost a 360-degree rotation. The piece of furniture is removed from the furniture function, but then comes back again as an art object. It's like the sweater pieces, the really early ones, which worked with instructions for use specifying the order in which the sweaters had to be hung out. They were sweaters first and then they were hung up, and in a way they were transformed; and they functioned as art objects. And at the end of the hanging out period, the concept was restored to the object. It then became a normal sweater again. It's the same thing with furniture in that the functionality is first removed, totally reversed, virtually defunctionalized, deconstructed in a way, and is then restored again with another function. It is both things at the same time, it is a sculpture and a functional object, or an object on which someone can sit, and carry out a specific activity such as sitting, leaning back, crossing their feet, opening the cabinet, taking out a bottle,

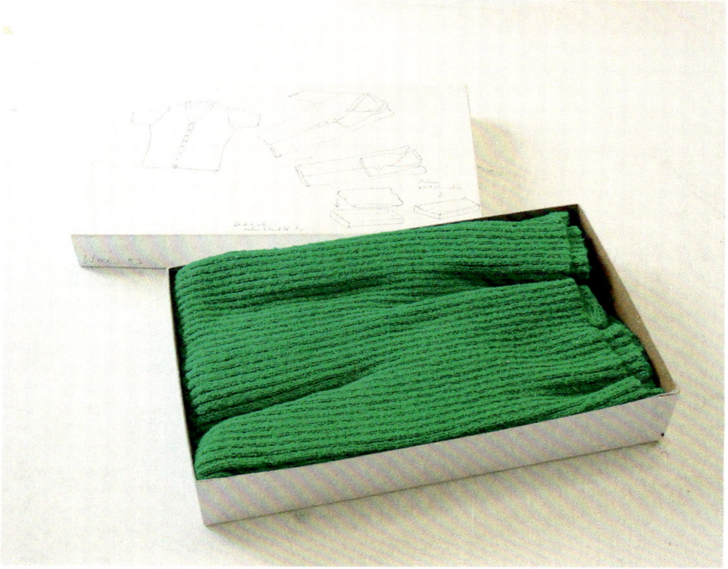

Instruction Drawing
Untitled, 1988
Pullover, cardboard, instruction drawing
7 × 28 × 17 cm

taking out a glass, and drinking; as long as the person is drunk—the piece is only finished when the person is drunk!

SW In your artistic practice, you seem to have the methodological approach of a scientist: you have determined the field of research, and are meticulously exploring it. How does that work? How does one work (or series) lead to the next one? And how would you—at this point—define your expertise?

EW That's because when there is a new group of works, the pieces develop during the process, and problems arise during the process that have to be remedied—solutions have to be found to the problems and implemented. In a way it's a kind of learning by doing. There is no determined path from the idea to the realized result, but during the creation of a work you examine the different possibilities that can be developed. The interesting thing about this—which is true for any work—is that when you explore the work and virtually follow it, it leads you to a certain extent. Gerhard Richter once said that his pictures were more intelligent than he was, and I think he meant much the same thing. You can plan a work in advance, or plan a picture, or a sculpture exactly in advance. But when you allow yourself the possibility, during the realization process or when developing the work, to accept and explore the possibilities that arise, this improves the work, even if there is a shift in focus.

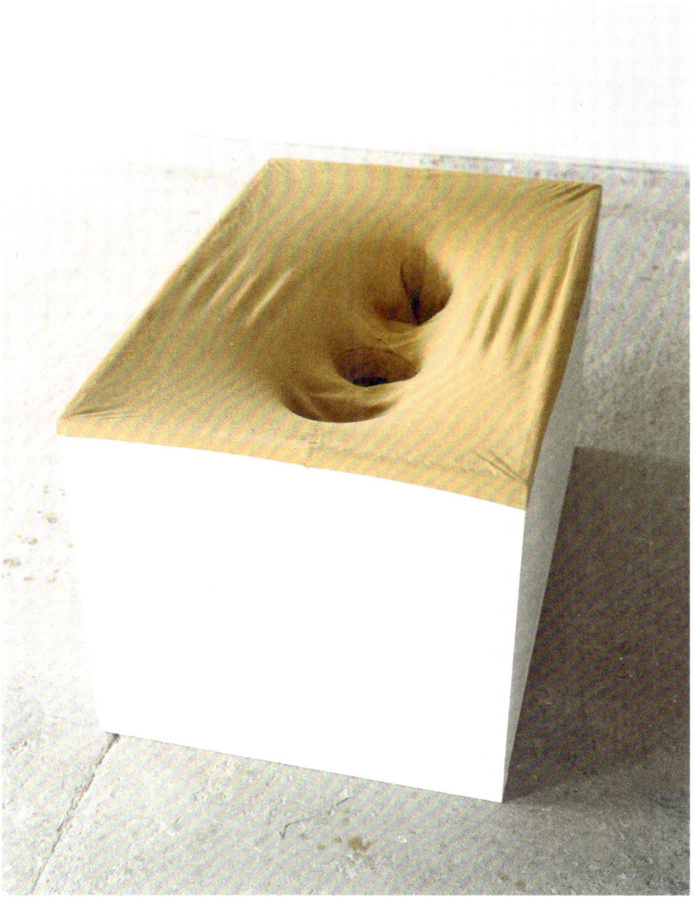

Untitled, 1992
T-shirt, pedestal
62 × 67 × 105 cm

BT & LS Can your furniture be compared to the sculptures in which you drape sweaters around boxes? Before they become art exhibits they are "only" clothes, and after the exhibition they could go straight back into the closet. Your pieces of furniture are made of leftover timber and bits of old furniture; if you dismantled the pieces after the exhibition could you produce something very different from these materials, or are the materials then just trash?

EW One could deconstruct them, but these furniture-sculptures have to be partially rebuilt, and that would demand too much effort. The works with the furniture are performative sculptures with the title *Möbeln — Furniture*. In any case, there is no intention to destroy them now. However, I have inserted the performative as an essential part of the work, and in doing so have created a direct connection with the *One Minute Sculptures*. The actual execution intended is something I still have to let go of, but it is intended. In any case it is also possible that the act is of a mental variety — in that it is not necessary that the piece is not realized by following the instructions, it can exist in the mind. But then the actual, real performative realization is still missing.

SW When I first saw the furniture pieces, I was very surprised. Your work often seems to deal with dysfunctionality, with not working, with inertia. To make functional art seemed like a strange step. But then it became clear that the original furniture pieces you use as the foundation to make the new ones have lost their original way of working. They become unusable in that sense. Yet I've seen you actually use your furniture pieces. Could you tell us something about the friction between functional and dysfunctional, and the status of these two pieces?

EW What I said above already partly answers this — the functionality and dysfunctionality — the reversal of functionality or the virtual 360-degree rotation, which makes the piece of furniture dysfunctional, and which then gets a function again as furniture, is like a circle which restores it. And I found this absurd rotation very amusing.

BT & LS You might also say that the sweaters are a second skin that the viewer could put on. In that sense, the pieces of furniture also embrace the viewer as soon as he or she sits on them. Can you say something about that?

EW These sweaters are a second skin and the house is like a third skin, in a way. It also has a protective function and envelops people, who feel safe inside it. As with the article of clothing both are reminiscent of traditional Greek and Roman sculptures cast in bronze, and other metal alloys. But the actual mass is missing, the volumes are defined by a very thin layer of bronze, so by a thin skin, such as a sweater or an article of clothing, which takes on and reproduces the human form, although the sweater does not have a plastic structure of its own. The desire to work with furniture actually comes from something I've been observing for years now, which are design magazines, for example, lifestyle magazines such as *Better Living*, and *Architectural Design*, which show individuals and people who are exclusively defined by their apartments, interiors, and furniture. That means that the actual individual is absent, is no longer required, but what this individual is, who this person is, what he or she represents, is represented by where he or she lives, by the furniture, by the collector's items, the pictures, the books, etc. That way the house, the interior and the furniture become an *Ersatz* — a cheap replacement for this person — it's as if this person doesn't matter anymore. The second reason is that I started with furniture that I grew up with in some ways; forties and fifties era furniture with round corners, furniture my grandparents lived with, and my parents too to some extent. So it is twice as emotionally charged and twice as interesting for me.

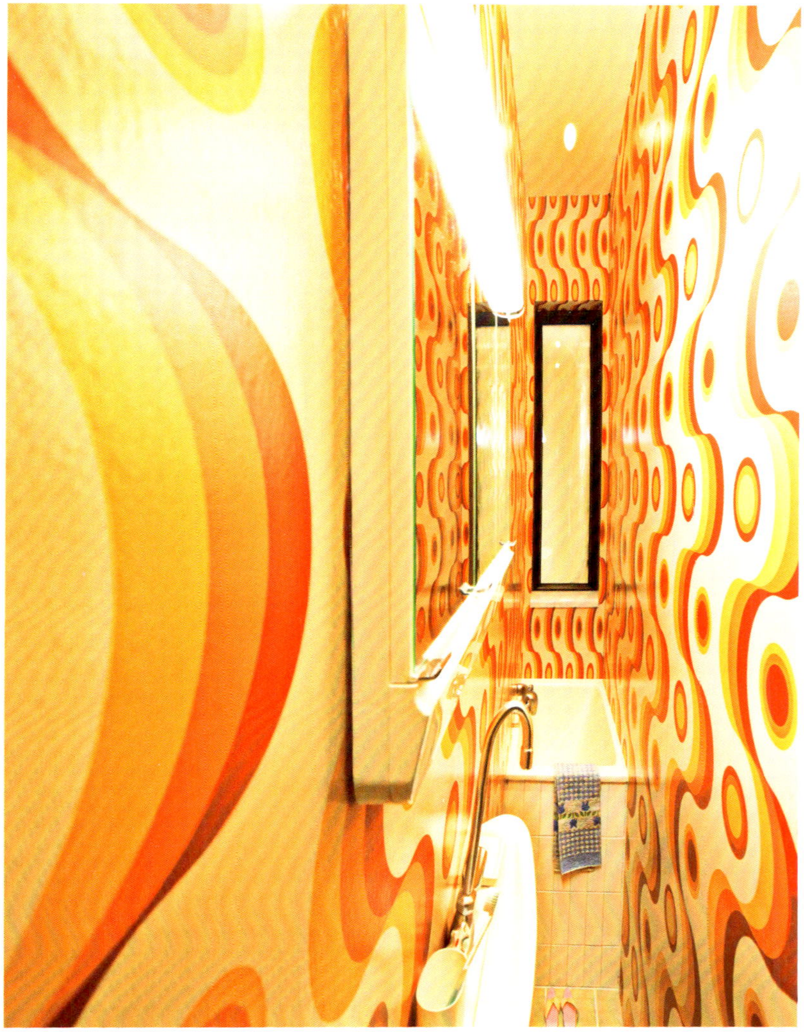

Narrow House, 2010
Mixed media
8 × 1.3 × 21 m
Photo: Mischa Nawrata

SW Are they in any way related to the instruction drawings and text works? The furniture pieces also seem to direct the position of the participant.

EW Yes, of course. There is a clear connection with the instruction drawings in graphic and text form. The furniture pieces also have information on how to use them, whether it's a bar stool or an *Untouchable*, or something else. So there's always a certain possibility of performative work.

BT & LS Or has the creation of furniture more to do with an exploration of the dividing lines between applied and autonomous art?

EW The dividing line between applied and autonomous art didn't interest me, doesn't interest me, and is also not a theme; what interests me is the object. I believe in any case that I move in the world of autonomous art even if there are sometimes objects that can also be used, but always in the sense of a performative concept, a performative sculpture.

SW By making furniture pieces, you inevitably enter into a long standing tradition in art history, leading through areas as diverse as the Renaissance, Marcel Duchamp, Russian Constructivism, Pop Art, Minimalism, and Post-Minimalism, adding to a very long list of names of celebrated artists who have made furniture and design pieces. Yet it always seems to be the world of applied arts that points out that tradition, and the art world seem to take it far less seriously, or has done so for a very long time. Why do you think that is? Are we experiencing a shift?

EW I never ask myself the question if what I make is applied art, fine art, or something else. It is all the same to me.

BT & LS Is there a direct connection between your series *The Idiot*, in which you linked Austrian architects to pieces of furniture, and the furniture-objects you are making now?

EW *The Idiot* was about Austrian artists who did not leave the country, who did not emigrate, and who have probably not achieved international success for the same reason as other Austrians, such as Schindler and Neutra. These pieces of furniture are partly icons in Austria—but not abroad—and one asks if it would have been different when their architects and designers would have emigrated. But my own new furniture pieces are about something different. They're not furniture icons. It's not designer furniture, but they are all actually rather anonymous pieces. For me it was about a piece of furniture that is very easy to place as far as time and social context go.

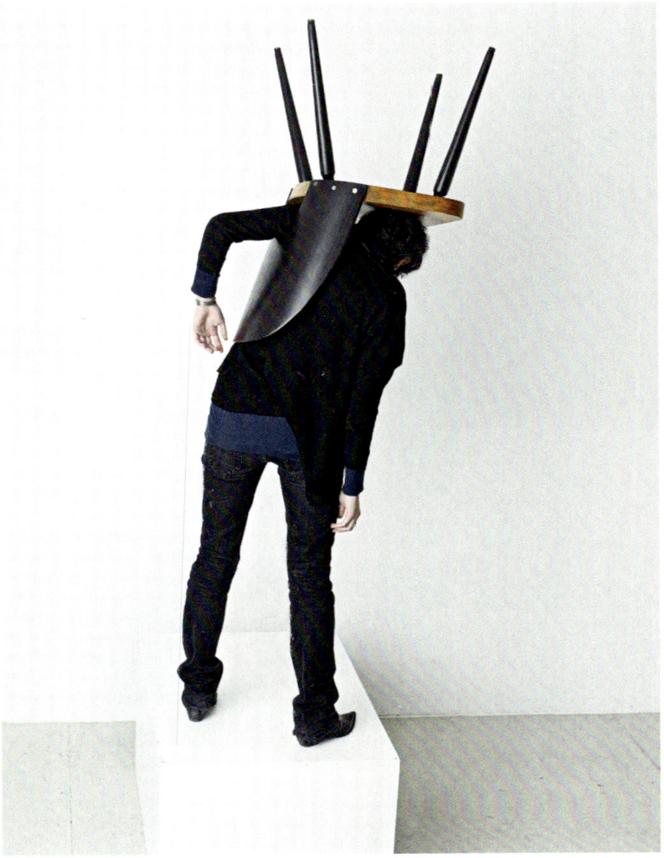

Idiot I, 2010
C-print
92 × 74.5 cm

BT & LS For the exhibition in Middelheim Museum, you are collaborating with Walter Van Beirendonck. Can you say something more about that? What does this collaboration entail, and are you consciously exploring the dividing lines between fashion and sculpture? Or is it about something entirely different?

EW What interests me most in this collaboration is that Walter Van Beirendonck is a fashion designer who has a lot of affinity with the graphic arts and also sometimes creates objects for exhibitions, and the fact that he—as he told me years ago—was inspired by some of my work and virtually let my work flow into his work in a way. That's the first reason. The second reason is that I'm interested in fashion, as it has to do with the phenomenon of hype and icons, which play a considerable part in our time. Apart from that I am also interested in clothing as an old sculptural theme on which I've worked for many years now, the double skin, the enveloping or filling of a volume with a skin or shell. Walter has brought the fashion aspect of it more to the front. I had given him drawings as specifications that left a false trace—his reaction to it, and what results from it and how, appeals to me.

SW You told me: "I love fashion and I want to destroy it." It seems like I find many examples of this conceptual ideal throughout your oeuvre: the duality between attraction and rejection. Can you elaborate on this?

EW I do really love great fashion and at the same time I'm interested in opening, shredding, undoing, and destroying it; so as to destroy, to deconstruct the functionality to make something else out of it. So you need to make a basic differentiation: on the one hand, there are the articles of clothing that I use. They are usually what I refer to as anonymous fashion, in parallel or as a counterpart to anonymous architecture, by which I mean architecture without an architect. It is anonymous fashion that interests me, as it is often the expression of the general public. Then there are naturally the high-fashion creations. Both interest me: the expressions of a high creative drive and creations by the general public.

BT & LS What struck me in the run-up to the exhibition, when you showed me the sketches for the clothing sculptures you have now produced in collaboration with Walter, was that the initial sketches, drawings of existing photographs from fashion magazines, resembled classic modern sculptures.

They reminded me of the work of sculptors such as Hans Arp. The fascinating thing is that the wearable objects that Walter has made are far less evocative of that sort of sculpture. What fascinates me is that the two-dimensional drawing evokes those associations with classic modern sculpture, while the final three-dimensional object does so far less. Can you say something about that?

EW For reasons of simplicity and speed I have taken pictures from fashion magazines and worked on those. That way, my specifications, and my drawings, shifted these magazine pictures from fashion photography towards modernist sculpture. In a way a wearable classic sculpture was created and the idea was that Walter would respond and react to that, which he did.

SW What are the advantages of working with other artists such as Elfie Semotan or Walter Van Beirendonck? What possibilities open up?

EW Elfie Semotan is a fashion photographer. Walter Van Beirendonck is a fashion designer. I wanted to connect them both, for reasons that I have explained above.

BT & LS In the last few years, you've stopped taking photographs and gone back to actual sculpture. At first sight, it's a surprising step for an artist who aims to explore the boundaries of sculpture. Can you say how that development has come about?

EW I took this step, as I was being sought after—sought after by gallery owners and collectors and so on—to endlessly further develop something that had worked well. And I noticed that the work does not benefit from endlessly repeating a few good ideas, on the contrary. I wanted to preserve the strength of these works and therefore have consciously drawn a line. Based on these considerations I have stopped photographing. If I still take the occasional *One Minute Sculpture* photo, then it'll be for a magazine or something else, but it'll not be included in my artistic work. I use photographers—such as for instance Elfie Semotan—to help me achieve this. I can explain the interest in magazines—and not just the interest in magazines, but also in the print media in general, and in TV and the new media because I believe that the place for art in public space was limited to squares, streets, and architecture up until a few years ago. I'm much more interested in the public space of the media, however. So art in public spaces in magazines, newspapers, on TV, etc. That I find essentially interesting.

BT & LS Your evolution can be described as expanding the language of sculpture. You question and research the parameters of sculpture. How does your more recent "traditional" work fit within that trend? In that sense, your work has moved from dematerialization to materialization.

EW From the start, I tried to develop a broad range of means of artistic expression and have continued to develop the various individual areas independently of one another. These are areas such as three-dimensional, traditional sculpture, and that is what led me to performance. This led me first to video, then photography, and at the same time to drawings, instructions for use, texts, and text work. And in all these areas, which have arisen from another one, I have tried to further develop in parallel to one another. The public focus was, however, directed more towards one element at one time, and on another at another time. But, and that is still true today, I have always made all parts in parallel up until now, i.e. there have never been solely performative sculptures or *One Minutes* at a given time. There has always also been traditional, and three-dimensional sculpture. Now that is no different, apart from the fact that I don't do photographs of the *One Minute Sculptures* anymore.

SW However, the new performative sculptures seem to contradict that trend. Also, there are the knitwear pieces you had the curators of some of your previous shows wear. And there are the big knitwear pieces; in situ installations that are made for a specific venue, and that are lost when the show ends. What interests you in this tension you can feel throughout your whole oeuvre, between the ephemeral works on one end of the spectrum and the bronzes on the other end, that are there for eternity?

EW I like this tension in an oeuvre, when a lot is possible, from the most short-lived work like dust sculptures right up to installations in which architectural parts are draped in knitwear via the performative sculptures of the *One Minute Works*, which dissipate collectively and disappear again, i.e. whose end is also defined, in comparison to the more durable pieces.

BT & LS Your *One Minute Sculptures* are the best-known part of your oeuvre. Their main features are that they can be executed by anyone and that they are temporary. But can't your later permanent sculptures like the *Anger and Envy Bumps*, and your *Fat Houses* and *Fat Cars* also be said to be about temporariness? A temporary situation (like being fat, or having an erect penis) that you have frozen in time? Or is that a too facile or one-sided conclusion?

EW I have attempted in my work both to treat or explore the concept of what is sculptural and have also attempted to connect daily life, my life, which surrounds me, in which I move, with the concept of "sculpturality," or to connect it in such a way as to create something new. I've also tried to draw unusual conclusions to get something new from both. I have given this example many times before: sculpture is working with volumes, you can also say that gaining or losing weight is working with volumes. So you can also conclude that gaining and losing weight is sculpture. That's how I arrived at the themes of fat and thin. But also when you approach it from the concept of what is sculptural, it's also natural to work with mass and volumes. It was exciting to bring both things together. Is it possible—that was actually the question—is it for instance possible to draw sculptural qualities from the increasing obesity that has a growing impact on our society? Or is it possible—it then went further—to transform some bodily conditions into sculptural qualities or further still, is it possible to transform mental or psychological limitations or states into sculptural qualities? To transform physical sensations or psychological states into sculptural qualities, sculptural forms? That's how the *Anger and Envy Bumps* came about. So short-term, short-lived, passing psychological states.

BT & LS If so, isn't it a wonderful metaphor for the absence of certainties in our contemporary world? The church, the state and marriage no longer offer the certainty (or the illusion of certainty) that people used to rely on. You appear to me to be more successful at capturing the present state of society than any other artist currently active. Is that something you deliberately try to do?

EW It wasn't the state of society that interested me but the phenomenon that I obtain by combining the concept of sculpturality with social phenomena and what results from that, that's what interested me. So if I asked a friend of mine to put on all the clothes in his entire closet at the same time, on top of each other, that's primarily a sculptural act. But it's also an instant reminder of how the homeless behave when

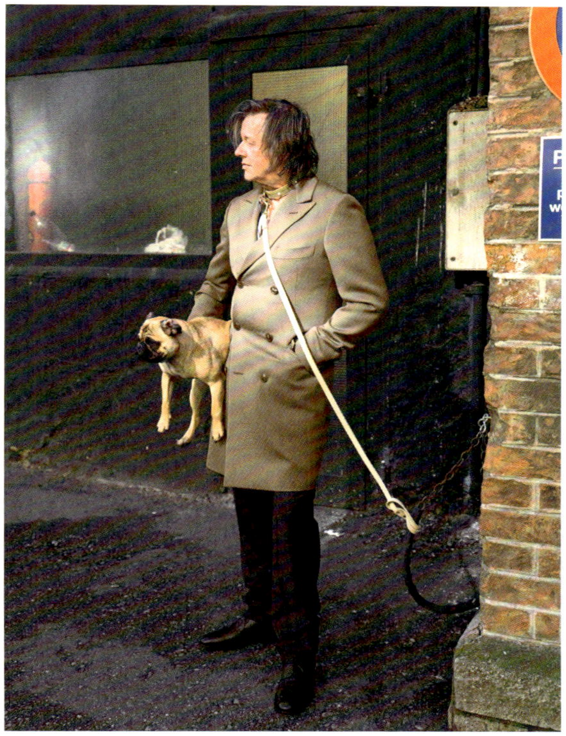

Hermès, The Psychoanalyst, 2008
C-print
150 × 112 cm

they carry their entire possessions around with them. Or with the work *Shopping* when I sent a couple into a shop and they could wear or take as much as they could put on: suddenly that has something to do with shopping, with wanting to have, to own, so with our consumer society and longing for things. So then they're really social, psychological, philosophical phenomena that emerge, but this was always based on quite a mundane investigation of sculptural phenomena, or considerations and basic structures.

BT & LS To what extent does time play a role in your thinking about sculpture?

EW Many of my works are based on the principle of time. There are the *One Minute Sculptures*, and then there are, of course, the works like *Stand West* when someone stands still for fourteen hours, hypnotized, as they wouldn't be able to do it otherwise. Stretching time functions as a delay: slowing down an act until it comes to a halt, and claims the status of a sculpture. That was an interesting turning point and pretty much the starting point for the question of how long something can be an action, and when something becomes sculpture? When does the sculptural in an action take control, and becomes so strong that it has to be read as a sculpture?

BT & LS You have never shied away from engaging with popular culture. For example, you worked with Claudia Schiffer on a photo-series for *Vogue*, your *One Minute Sculptures* formed the basis for a Red Hot Chili Peppers video clip, and you have worked on campaigns for Hermès. Do you go looking for these commissions in order to create a platform for your work outside the world of galleries and museums? And do you do so to connect with contemporary culture? Or is it the other way round, and do people in the commercial art world approach you because you clearly have a readier understanding of today's culture than they do?

EW I've never looked for orders or commissions outside the art world. I've always worked in a totally free manner. The Red Hot Chili Peppers, or actually Mark Romanek, the famous video director, contacted me and asked if it would be OK with me if they used my work. It was the same thing with Hermès and *Vogue*. At the same time, I thought to myself that it was good that this opportunity had opened up for me. As I said above, I'm very interested in the public space of the media, as it is a place where art can be placed in a different way. And Hermès I found exciting as a fashion icon. It was also them who approached me and asked if I would find it interesting to use Hermès fashion as the material for some of my works. It was never a campaign, nor intended as such. I just tried to make an artistic work with a fashion label, an icon of the fashion world as a medium.

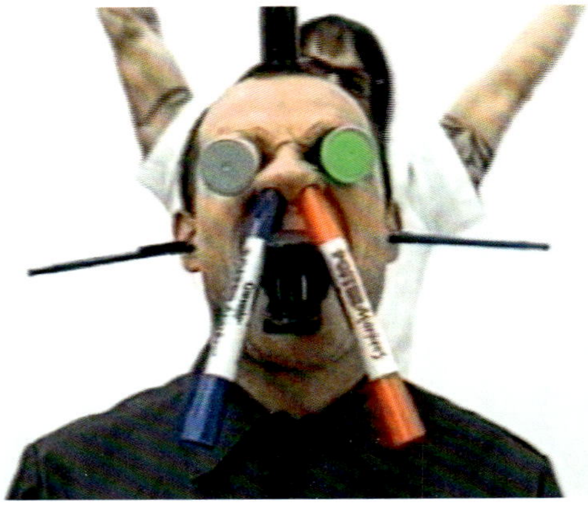

Red Hot Chili Peppers—Can't Stop, 2003
Video 4'35''
Courtesy: Red Hot Chili Peppers
Marc Romanek, Erwin Wurm
Photo: Mark Romanek

BT & LS And how do you ensure that you continue to be distinguishable from that commercial world? Or aren't you at all conscious of doing that?

EW There are a number of invitations from musicians, groups, and fashion labels, but I refused them all. I stick to these one-time collaborations. I will be making special works from time to time for magazines, dailies, or the Internet because I find it makes sense to create works for the public realm of the media.

BT & LS Do you think that the dividing lines between design, fashion, and autonomous art have become completely blurred?

EW I believe this boundary will always be there, but there are a lot of artists that are active in multiple fields at the same time, and transgress the boundaries with their work.

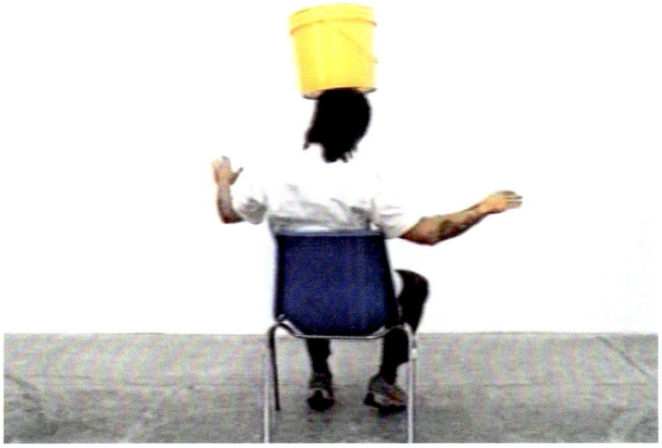

Red Hot Chili Peppers — Can't Stop, 2003
Video, 4'35'
Courtesy: Red Hot Chili Peppers
Marc Romanek, Erwin Wurm
Photo: Mark Romanek

BT & LS For example, I see a connection between your work and that of photographers like Martin Parr. Do you perceive a relationship between photography and what you do?

EW I know Martin Parr's interesting work. And of course there are many people who work in a similar field, and that make good art.

SW Your use of printed media not only of lifestyle or design magazines but also and, maybe more importantly, newspapers or other informative print as a "public space" is a powerful tool: people still tend to attach value to the printed word/image, whereas the Internet for instance might be considered very momentanous and less credible. How do you use that tool?

EW I've used daily newspapers, among which is *Die Zeit*, in Hamburg. I haven't yet personally used the Internet for artistic work. If I'd been twenty years younger, I would probably have used it a lot [in art work]. For my work *44 Vorschläge — Eine soziale Skulptur*, I was really attacked because the readers thought that all these xenophobe, misogynistic, and fascist statements I had collected were actually my own personal opinions. In fact I had collected and aggravated existing statements by contemporaries. But the overwhelming reactions have backed up my suspicion that I had chosen the right forum. In a gallery or museum space that would probably not have gone so deep — because then it is obvious that it is art.

SW You are known for your remarkable books. They have become somewhat legendary, even becoming collector's items. In detaching a book from a show, or a chronological survey it becomes more than a document. What kind of space is a book or can a book be? How is it different from the museum or gallery space?

EW Well yes, books have of course a longer validity than an exhibition. I'm quite pragmatic, and I think that anything which serves your work or which serves to bring your work to people, to make it known, to make it a topic of discussion, the work benefits from, and that is why publications are very important to me.

SW Talking about the use of space: What does a giant knitwear installation do with a room?

EW Knitwear in a way makes a space become part of an organism. Knitwear, or the enveloping of things immediately gives rise to an association with cover, protection, especially with a soft material as knitwear, which creates volume that accentuates and doubles the shapes of the body.

SW A big part of the big knitwear installation is the use of color. The more involved I am with your work, the more color becomes an obsession for me. It is everywhere in your work, and it is always an eye opener. Is color an obsession for you? Is that what you brought to sculpture of your adolescent dream to become a painter?

EW I don't really know. Maybe it was. It was obviously not conscious. The interest in color … at the start, the color in my work only emerged as the color of the material, and then I started to make more conscious use of color. No, that's wrong, it was much later. Right at the start, color was by all means a theme because I wanted to become a painter, and I painted my first sculptures. In the wooden sculptures,

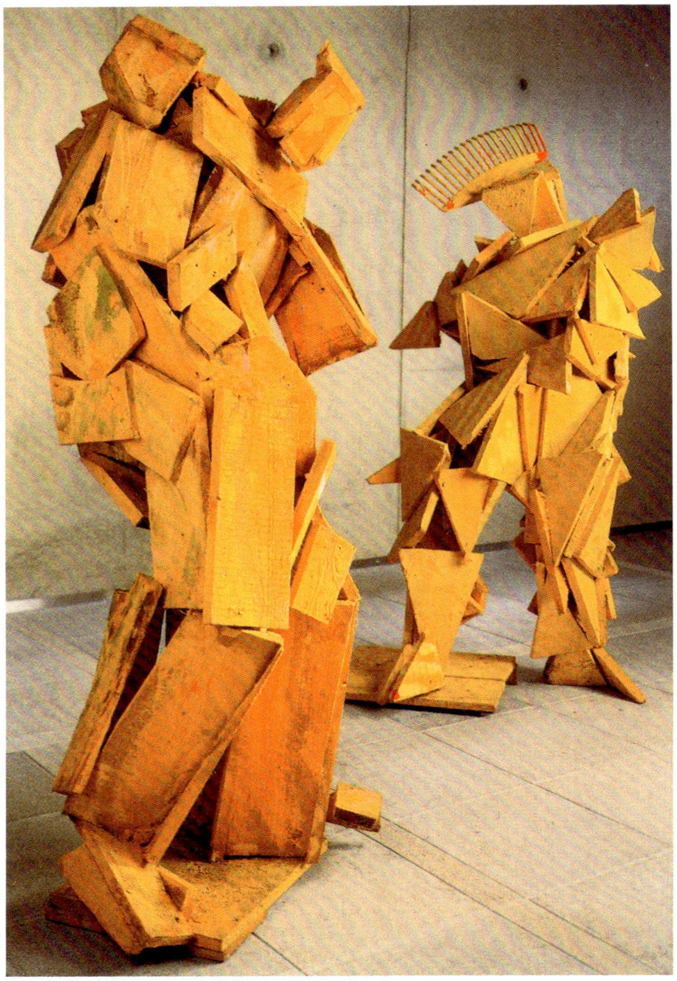

Gärtnerpaar, 1983
Wood, acrylic paint
170 × 80 × 70 cm (each of 2 figures)
Photo: Museum Beelden aan Zee, Scheveningen, The Hague

color was virtually a part of the skin. I could also use color as a sculptural quality and change the room with it, to open it up, or to close it. Color of course attracts because it can be used to evoke meanings and moods, separate the materiality from its origin, and it can leave traces that are partly false. You can let material disappear or present it as something different. I like that a lot. I've always had problems with the color of bronze material. That had far too many associations for me due to the many generations of artists who have worked with bronze. Only the possibility to paint bronze and to present it as something different permitted me to work with this material.

BT & LS Your *One Minute Sculptures* seem to me also very much in the spirit of today because of their do-it-yourself character. At this moment, with social media, they seem a very suitable form for something like the Internet. I wouldn't have been surprised if your *One Minute Sculptures* had become a craze on Facebook. What's your attitude to the artistic opportunities offered by the new media? Do you see a role for art in that area?

EW There are even fora about the *One Minute Sculptures*, where people can create *One Minute Sculptures* on the Internet. So that exists, to my great surprise. As mentioned above, there are unbelievable opportunities for art on the Internet. I'm just the wrong person. Other, younger people will use them. But there are huge opportunities, and we'll see lots of exciting things.

BT & LS What particularly makes me think of the Internet is the pointlessness of the *One Minute Sculptures*. Their very ridiculousness is their great strength. In that way, your work has actually predicted the consequences of the Internet for the visibility of the individual and how it can be manifested on the World Wide Web. But has the Internet changed your work too?

EW No, the Internet hasn't actually changed my work in any way. As I said, I've never made a conscious attempt to explore it artistically.

BT & LS You obviously want to make art more a part of everyday life, to give it a role in people's lives without it being taken too seriously. What do you think would be the ideal role for art in Western society?

EW I'm always surprised and amazed at how small the role of visual arts is in our Western society. It's especially blatant in Austria. Every other politician speaks about our nation of culture, but they're very poor when it actually comes down to putting things in place or getting things accepted. In my opinion, the average politician in Austria is not very well educated in terms of general culture, and is also not at all interested in art, or culture, which is disastrous of course. On one hand, they pay lip service to art, but if you inspect it closely, it often looks completely different. I remember being at a discussion about a year ago with the former Foreign Minister Spindelegger (now Vice Chancellor), by whom the future of the European Union and its opportunities was being discussed at a business forum, at the Vienna University for Economics and Business. He gave a forty-minute speech in which the word "culture" was mentioned one single time and the word "art" not once. And it was about the future of Europe. I asked him why that was, and the response was laughter. Everyone in the room laughed, not because the question or issue is interesting and justified, but because they thought it was an absurd question. What is art or culture supposed to mean in our world? And the well-dressed ladies and gentlemen sitting there, probably in tailor-made clothes, who drive expensive, well-designed cars, who probably live in villas with great furniture, and great art and great design pieces, who go to the opera and the theater, and probably to a fine arts museum, who visit other cities and probably admire the architecture there, so people who are highly involved in culture, but who are too ignorant to be aware of this and to be able to or want to articulate this.

SW Is it really possible to make art a part of everyday life? Is it too cynical to say that the best we can do, is make everyday life a part of art?

EW Art is quite simply part of everyday life for me. Art is also my everyday life. That means when you let something become everyday, it loses its special quality and it's not a luxury or something extraordinary any more. But that doesn't mean that the artwork itself no longer has anything special or extraordinary about it, only the way we deal with it. That means that it becomes something I spend time on everyday, and that is perfectly possible.

BT & LS To what extent are you inspired by slapstick film classics? The work of Buster Keaton—the man who never cracked a smile—seems to be reflected in your attitude.

EW Slapstick films, Stan Laurel, Oliver Hardy, Buster Keaton, Charlie Chaplin and many others, up to the German Karl Valentin, whom I find very funny with his very dry, very unusual humor. I'm not very interested in slapstick itself at all. What I find interesting is the cynical humor, the absurd. It is also something that is interesting for my work. The sufficient, the untenable, the amusing, the embarrassing, all that interests me. So the marginal, not the big names, like surrealism or Viennese Actionism, but the petty, the unimportant. Things that everyone can see for themselves, and that are always a part of us.

BT & LS The Gemeentemuseum has purchased a recent series of sculptures, *Small Psychos*. Eleven figures that are visible only thanks to the sweaters that conceal them. By adopting different attitudes, they constitute—as it were—"abstract" forms. The series is about the relationship between outward appearance and inner life. The externals are what dominate life today (a fact also reflected in *Fat Cars* and *Fat Houses*). This is often cited as one of the reasons for individualism. We think we can protect ourselves and distinguish ourselves from other people by thinking only about our own needs and desires, making money and investing it in our own few square meters, by buying expensive houses, cars, and clothes. But your work shows that, in fact, we all do exactly the same things; we are all the same sweaters, all in slightly different postures, but nevertheless trapped in our preoccupation with the external world. However individual we think we are, we are really more collective than ever; free will is a rare commodity. Prisoners of capitalism. Do you see your work as critical on society in that sense? If so, what message do you want it to convey?

EW That's precisely something that interests me a lot. Individuality or so-called individuality as a projection of the outside. Free will too as a projection of the outside. Brain scientists have been discussing recently, or up until a certain time ago, whether free will actually exists, the free will which we think we know or whether we are not actually dependent on, or shaped by genetic predisposition, preprogramming, determined by society and processes which start to take effect with our upbringing. So we are basically determined by the environment, our upbringing, and our genes. If we as Europeans look at the Americans, and we as Europeans look at the Japanese, we notice two basic differences. The American appears to act in a sovereign, individual way as an individual person. Even his laughter and sneeze are different and his table manners. It is much the same with the Japanese. With the Japanese, you have the feeling you are meeting a collective person. So a totally different assumption on the basis of specific behavior. But if you go to America and see the Americans together—and this is when the scales seem to have fallen from my eyes—the so-called highly individual, deep pitch of voice for American males has a social connection there. Or the American sneeze, and the American laugh. They are social models, like eating or the fact that businessmen who are always strictly dressed are allowed to wear jackets or trousers of a different color on Fridays. Even American individuality is actually represented as a collective form of behavior, which is interesting. It is much the same in Japan. But in Japan, the so-called collective individual also has individuality, and does not appear to act solely collectively.

BT & LS However humorous and light-hearted your work may appear, its themes are fairly serious. Isn't that true, in fact, of your whole oeuvre?

EW My work is about the drama of the pettiness of the existence, whether one approaches it with philosophy or a diet. We always draw the short straw.

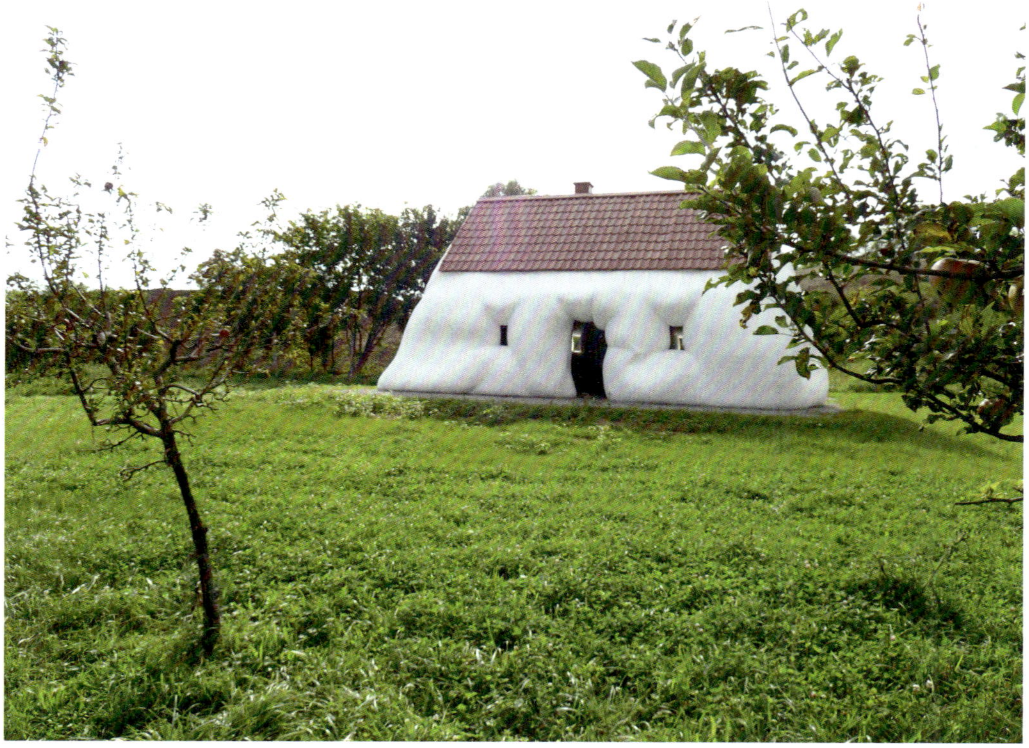

Fat House, 2003
Iron, wood, polystyrene, aluminium
4.5 × 10 × 7 m
Electric installation, video
8'40'' loop

SW Would you say that even when you are constantly pulling the viewer out of their comfort zone, it might be considered consoling that painfulness and inadequacy are omnipresent?

EW No, I don't find that at all consoling. What would be consoling would be to laugh about these things or much more to have the possibility to laugh about these things. If you have humor, if you can laugh at your own weaknesses, and joke about your insufficiency, I think that makes you strong. Laughing like that makes you strong.

BT & LS You once said in an interview that your work is based on comic strips and science fiction. Can you explain that?

EW The link between the work and comics lowers the threshold for the viewer even more. Yes, for instance for *Fat Car* I took a normal car and made it fat. This sculptural deformation has in a way created a simplification, has given the car an anthropomorphic shape. You could see a face in it. The simplified shape and the anthropomorphic aspect suddenly referred to comics—it reminded us of these cars that Walt Disney drew in the fifties.

SW Text is a big part of your work. There are drawings and photographs that include instructions; there are the text works such as the *Instructions On How To Be Politically Incorrect;* there are all those well-chosen titles; there are the works that refer directly to literature such as *Hamlet* and *Fountain for Arthur Rimbaud;* there are all these works on philosophers, especially on Wittgenstein, who did revolutionary work on language. Could you tell us what kind of a tool text is for you?

EW Text is an instrument for conveying content. That's why there are the videos too like *Tell* or talking cars and the talking house. That's very important for me.

SW Your work has been compared to the plays of Werner Schwab, who is said to be able to "present an abstract concept as a solid object." It has also been linked to authors as Thomas Bernhard and Samuel Beckett. Do you actually feel connected to their writing? Is it a coincidence that they all did texts for theatrical performance?

EW I'm very close to Werner Schwab. He was a childhood friend of mine and we were in close contact for a number of years. I also read a lot of Thomas Bernhard and Samuel Beckett. But I'm not an author. Language, for Werner, was a means of expression that he mastered like a virtuoso, but it's not like that for me. And with Thomas Bernhard, for instance, the endless parataxis is unique and brilliant. Or Beckett as well. I move in a quite different world and only make a few excursions into text. It's not true that I've written texts for the theater. I have taken texts for the *Die Zeit* newspaper. We have talked about that already. And I write the texts for my videos. That is not so much.

BT & LS Why, in your interviews, do you resist the importance attached to the body in relation to your oeuvre? Is it because you are not interested in the body as such (as material for art), but only in the possible condition in which a body can be? Whether it's your own body, that of the public or a created body?

EW Because it's the condition, the possible condition, the capacities too, and also the associated sociological, political, physical, and psychological possibilities which interest me. And especially the public body, so the body of the public, and the scientific body. I find both very interesting. The body of the public, the public body or also for instance the body in Christianity — I was brought up as a Catholic, but am no longer a believer—it also refers to the body as bread and bread as the body. I really don't know how you can translate *Leib/Laib* [body/bread], but it's an incredible reduction of a human person. For me, the body is always a unit, part of a unit that makes up the human person. And it's only one part. That's why I miss the rest, but don't want to do without the rest so to speak. It's incredible how you can reduce a person to a body. It's fascinating.

BT & LS To what extent is your work about identity? And how does this relate to authenticity?

EW Identity, the concept of identity, and the preoccupation with it comes up again and again in my work, as it's the reflection of ourselves. How do I see myself? Is what I see the same as how others see me? It is about projections, conceptions, precepts, and all those things. And then of course it is also about authenticity, to the same extent.

BT & LS Does it worry you that many people appreciate your work for its externals? Or do you see that as the ultimate confirmation of its real meaning?

EW The question running through my work for a few decades was always: Can I by means of the connection of sculpturality to an everyday theme of our time, achieve a new perspective or a new way of interpreting this theme? Because they were general themes or themes from our time, which went much further than the art world, I reached many more people with them. The readability of the artwork is enhanced by the partial kinship to comics (as mentioned above) that lowers the threshold.

BT & LS But then comes the next question: Don't you think that you've perhaps hit the nerve of the times better than some other artists?

EW When you're dealing with time, you're suddenly likely to position your work in your time, and so you come across something like the sprit of the age, or that you create something in part, you make something that also produces the spirit of the age. That's true for the most varied themes and interest groups. It's exactly the same with sociology, philosophy, with themes from religion, fashion, architecture, the concept of icons, which is a twentieth-century phenomenon.

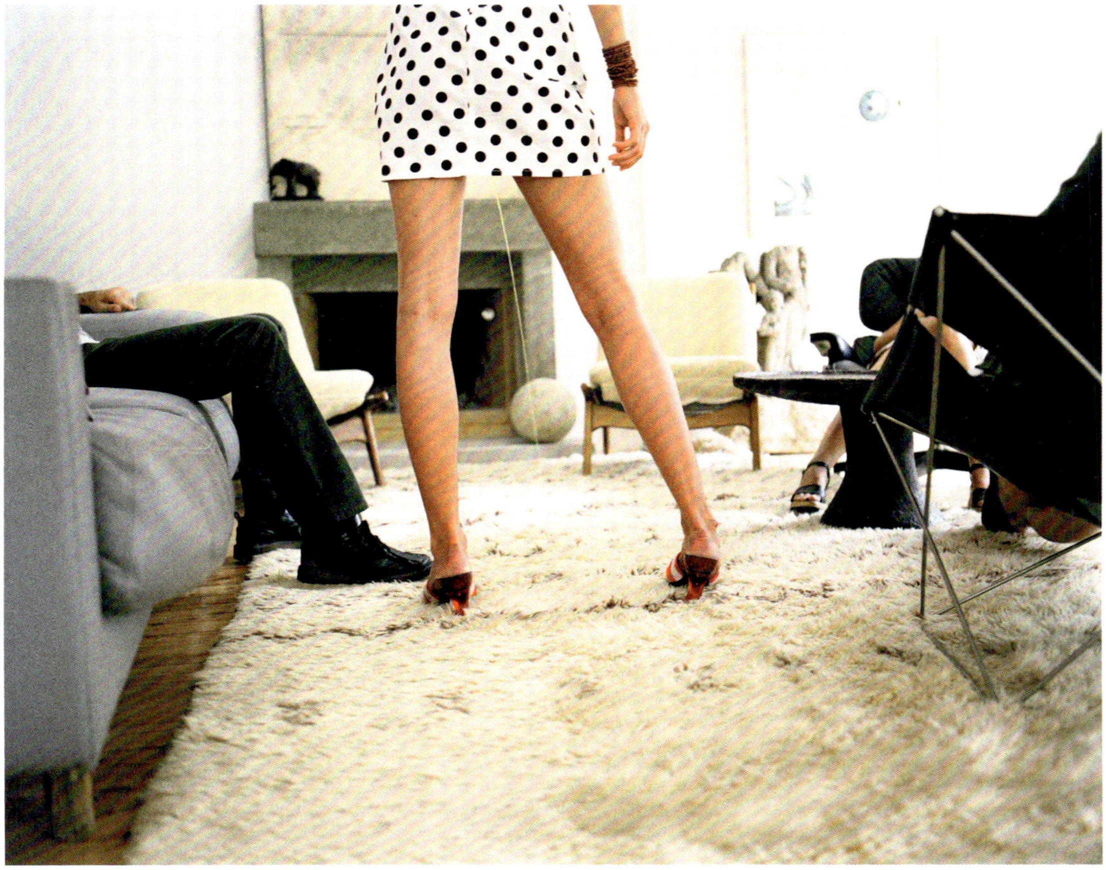

Instructions on how to be politically incorrect, Pee on Someone's Rug, 2003
C-print
126 × 159 cm

Vragen aan Erwin Wurm

BT & LS Benno Tempel, Laura Stamps
SW Sara Weyns

BT & LS Uw werk is een onderzoek naar het potentieel van beeldhouwtechnieken. In de laatste decennia gold het als een van de interessantste onderzoeken naar de betekenis van de beeldhouwkunst in de wereld van vandaag. Onlangs bent u ook begonnen met het maken van meubelen. Hoe passen deze stukken in dat onderzoek?

EW Uiteraard ben ik niet de enige en ook niet de eerste die zich bezighoudt met meubelen. Hierin zijn mij al heel wat anderen voorgegaan. De eerste die zich hiermee bezighield, was waarschijnlijk Brancusi en daarna eigenlijk iedereen die je je maar indenken kan, tot zelfs Franz West. Er zijn er dus heel wat. Wat mij aan dit thema interesseert, is enerzijds het verband tussen een object en een persoon die een handeling moet uitvoeren. Dit hangt eigenlijk rechtstreeks samen met mijn *One Minute Sculptures.* Die bevatten namelijk ook een soort van richtlijn, een gebruiksaanwijzing. Dit wil zeggen: men wordt uitgenodigd om te gaan zitten of, in het geval van de drinkstoelen, om een deur of een kastdeur te openen, er een fles uit te halen, een glas in te schenken – want er is ook een glas voorzien – en te drinken. Deze handeling heeft heel veel te maken met gebruiksaanwijzingen en beeldhouwkunst. Het tweede wat ik daar zo interessant aan vind, is meubelen als uitgangspunt nemen en er kunstwerken van maken door er de functie gedeeltelijk aan te onttrekken. Maar tegelijk geef ik ze opnieuw een functie, namelijk de functie van een meubel. Het is een soort van cirkelbeweging: het meubelstuk en de meubelfunctie worden gescheiden en komen dan terug samen als kunstobject. Dit is analoog aan de werken met de truien – die heel vroege – waar een gebruiksaanwijzing bij zat en waarbij men de truien moest ophangen volgens bepaalde instructies. Eerst waren het gewoon truien die men had opgehangen. Daarna werden ze getransformeerd: het concept van het object werd gescheiden om daarna als kunstwerk te functioneren. Eenmaal de truien verwijderd werden, waren het concept en het object opnieuw verenigd. Ze werden weer gewoon truien. Ook bij de meubelen wordt de functionaliteit eerst weggenomen, maar dan omgekeerd; de meubelen worden als het ware ontdaan van hun functie en gedeconstrueerd, om daarna weer een andere functie te krijgen. Ze zijn tegelijk sculptuur en functioneel object. Iemand kan er

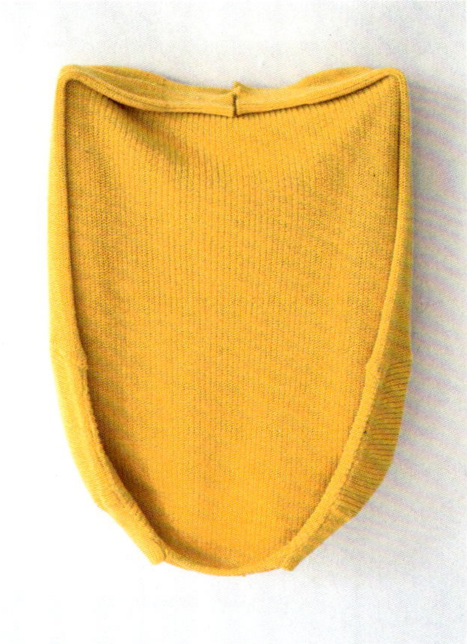

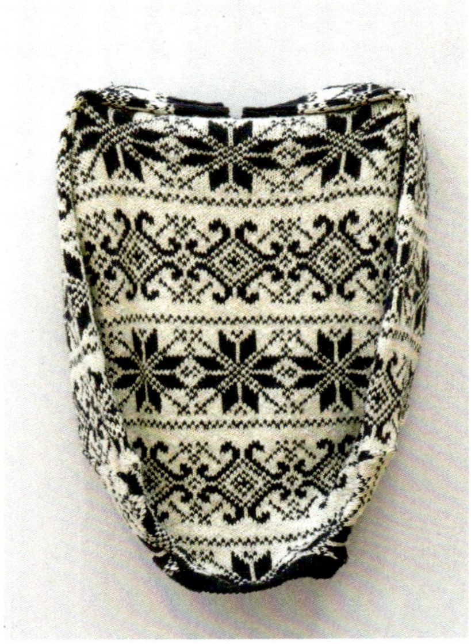

Untitled, 1994
Pullover, nails
53 × 38 × 8 cm

Untitled, 1990
Pullover, nails
50 × 30 × 12 cm

op zitten en een bepaalde handeling uitvoeren: zitten, leunen, de benen kruisen, de kast openmaken, een fles nemen, een glas nemen, inschenken, drinken, alles terugzetten, rechtstaan en weggaan.

SW U lijkt in uw artistieke bezigheden als een wetenschapper te werk te gaan. U heeft uw onderzoeksgebied afgebakend en onderzoekt het uiterst nauwkeurig. Hoe gaat dat in zijn werk? Hoe leidt een werk (of een reeks van werken) tot een ander werk? Hoe zou u vandaag uw ervaring hiermee omschrijven?

EW Bij een nieuwe reeks van werken ontwikkelen de werken zich tijdens de uitvoering. Tijdens de uitvoering duiken er problemen op en wordt daaraan gewerkt. Die problemen worden vervolgens opgelost. Het gaat in zekere zin om 'learning by doing': leren door te doen. Er is geen vaste weg van het idee naar het uitgevoerde resultaat, maar tijdens de uitvoering wordt onderzocht welke mogelijkheden ontwikkeld kunnen worden. Het interessante hieraan is dat als men het werk onderzoekt en als het ware volgt, men in zekere zin door het werk wordt geleid. Gerhard Richter zei ooit dat zijn werken intelligenter zijn dan hijzelf. Ik denk dat hij hier ongeveer hetzelfde mee bedoelde. Een werk kan je vooraf plannen: zoals met een schilderij of een sculptuur. Als je echter de mogelijkheid openlaat om tijdens de uitvoering of ontwikkeling van het werk andere mogelijkheden die zich voordoen aan te grijpen en te onderzoeken, wordt het werk beter, ook al verschuift het zwaartepunt hierdoor.

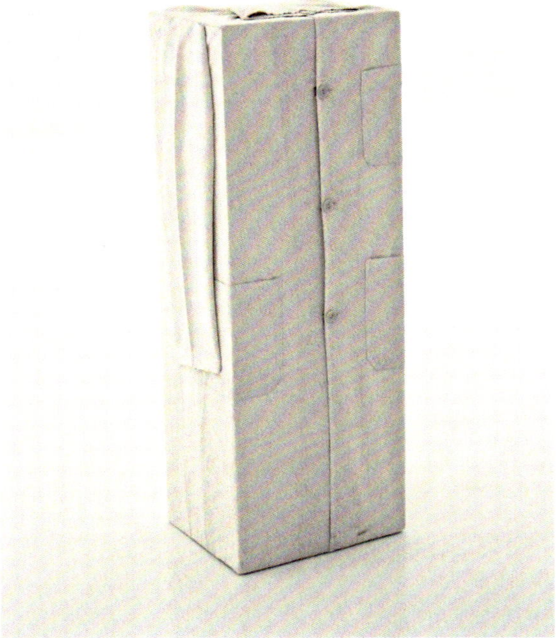

Untitled, 1988
Coat, wood
83 × 30 × 24.5 cm

BT & LS Kunnen uw meubelen vergeleken worden met de sculpturen waarbij u truien rond kisten drapeert? Voor ze artistieke tentoonstellingsstukken worden, zijn ze 'maar' kledingstukken. Ook na de tentoonstelling kunnen ze rechtstreeks terug in de kleerkast gehangen worden. Uw meubelen worden gemaakt uit afvalhout en uit delen van oude meubelen. Als u de meubelen na de tentoonstelling demonteert, zou u met het materiaal dan iets totaal anders kunnen maken of rest er dan enkel afval?

EW Men zou ze wel kunnen demonteren, maar deze meubelsculpturen moet men voor een deel opnieuw bouwen. En dat zou te kostelijk zijn. De werken met de meubelen zijn Performative Sculptures – performance gerelateerde sculpturen – met de titel *Meubelen.* In elk geval is het niet de bedoeling ze te vernietigen. Toch heb ik het performatieve als wezenlijk onderdeel van het werk ingebouwd en daarmee een directe verbinding gemaakt naar de *One Minute Sculptures*. De vooropgestelde uitvoering moet ik uit handen geven, maar bedoeld is ze wel. Alleszins is ze ook als mentale variant mogelijk. Maar dan ontbreekt nog de feitelijke, echte, performatieve uitvoering.

SW Toen ik uw meubelen voor het eerst zag, was ik heel verrast. In uw werk leek het vaak om disfunctionaliteit te gaan, om niet-functioneren, om traagheid. Functionele kunst maken, leek een vreemde stap. Maar dan werd duidelijk dat de originele meubelstukken die als basis dienen voor de creatie van de nieuwe werken, hun oorspronkelijke functie verloren hebben. In dat opzicht zijn ze onbruikbaar geworden. Toch heb ik gezien dat u uw meubelstukken effectief gebruikt. Kunt u iets zeggen over de spanning tussen functioneel en disfunctioneel en over de status van deze nieuwe werken?

EW Die vraag heb ik hiervoor al gedeeltelijk beantwoord. De spanning tussen functionaliteit en disfunctionaliteit bestaat uit het omkeren van de functionaliteit. Ofwel de bijna cirkelvormige omkering waarbij de functionaliteit aan het meubelstuk onttrokken wordt, waarna het opnieuw een functie als meubel krijgt. Het is als een cirkel waarbij het meubel opnieuw naar het uitgangspunt teruggebracht wordt. Deze absurde omkering vind ik erg leuk.

BT & LS Men zou ook kunnen stellen dat de truien een tweede huid zijn die de toeschouwer kan aantrekken. In die zin omarmen de meubelen ook de toeschouwer zodra die plaatsneemt. Kunt u hierover iets meer vertellen?

EW De truien zijn een tweede huid en het gebouw is in zekere zin de derde huid. Het heeft ook een beschermende functie, het omhult de mensen die zich er geborgen in voelen. Net zoals bij het kledingstuk verwijzen beide elementen naar de traditionele Griekse en Romeinse beeldhouwwerken, gegoten in brons en andere metaallegeringen. De eigenlijke massa ontbreekt, het volume wordt gedefinieerd door een heel dunne laag van brons, door een dunne huid. Net zoals een trui of een kledingstuk de vorm van het menselijke lichaam aanneemt en weergeeft, hoewel de trui zelf geen plastische structuur bezit. Het verlangen met meubelen te werken komt ook voort uit een jarenlange observatie van designertijdschriften en woonmagazines, zoals "Schöner wohnen", "AD" enz., waarin mensen getoond worden die uitsluitend gedefinieerd worden door hun huis, hun interieur en hun meubelen. De persoon zelf is afwezig, hij is niet meer essentieel. Maar wie deze persoon is of waar hij of zij voor staat, komt tot uiting via hoe die persoon woont, via de meubelen, de verzamelobjecten, de schilderijen, boeken enz. Zo worden de woning, het interieur en de meubelen een Ersatz voor die persoon – de persoon zelf is niet meer belangrijk: men ervaart het grootste deel van hem zo ook wel. Een andere reden om met meubelen te werken, was dat het oorspronkelijk meubelen waren waarmee ik in zekere zin ben opgegroeid, namelijk die jaren veertig-, respectievelijk jaren vijftigmeubelen met afgeronde hoeken. Dat zijn de meubelen van mijn grootouders en voor een deel ook nog van mijn ouders. Die meubelen zijn hierdoor dubbel beladen en voor mij dubbel zo interessant.

SW Is er een verband tussen de meubelen enerzijds en de uitvoeringsschetsen en teksten anderzijds? De meubelen lijken ook de positie van de deelnemer te sturen.

EW Ja, uiteraard. Er is een heel duidelijk verband tussen de getekende en geschreven gebruiksaanwijzingen. De meubelen zelf geven ook aanwijzingen met betrekking tot de uitvoering: of het een drinkmeubel is of een *Untouchable* of iets anders. Er wordt altijd verwezen naar een bepaalde performatieve mogelijkheid ervan.

BT & LS Of heeft het maken van meubelen meer te maken met een onderzoek naar de grenzen tussen toegepaste en autonome kunst?

EW Nee, dat interesseert me niet. Het is voor mij ook geen thema van het werk. Ik ben enkel geïnteresseerd in het object. Ik beweeg me in de wereld van de autonome kunst, ook wanneer het om gebruiksobjecten gaat, maar altijd in de zin van een performatieve voorstelling, een performatieve sculptuur.

SW Bij het maken van de meubelstukken treedt u onvermijdelijk in het spoor van een oude traditie in de kunstgeschiedenis. Eén die voorkomt in de meest uiteenlopende stromingen zoals de renaissance, Duchamp, het Russische constructivisme, de popart, het minimalisme en het postminimalisme. Hiermee plaatst u zichzelf in de lange

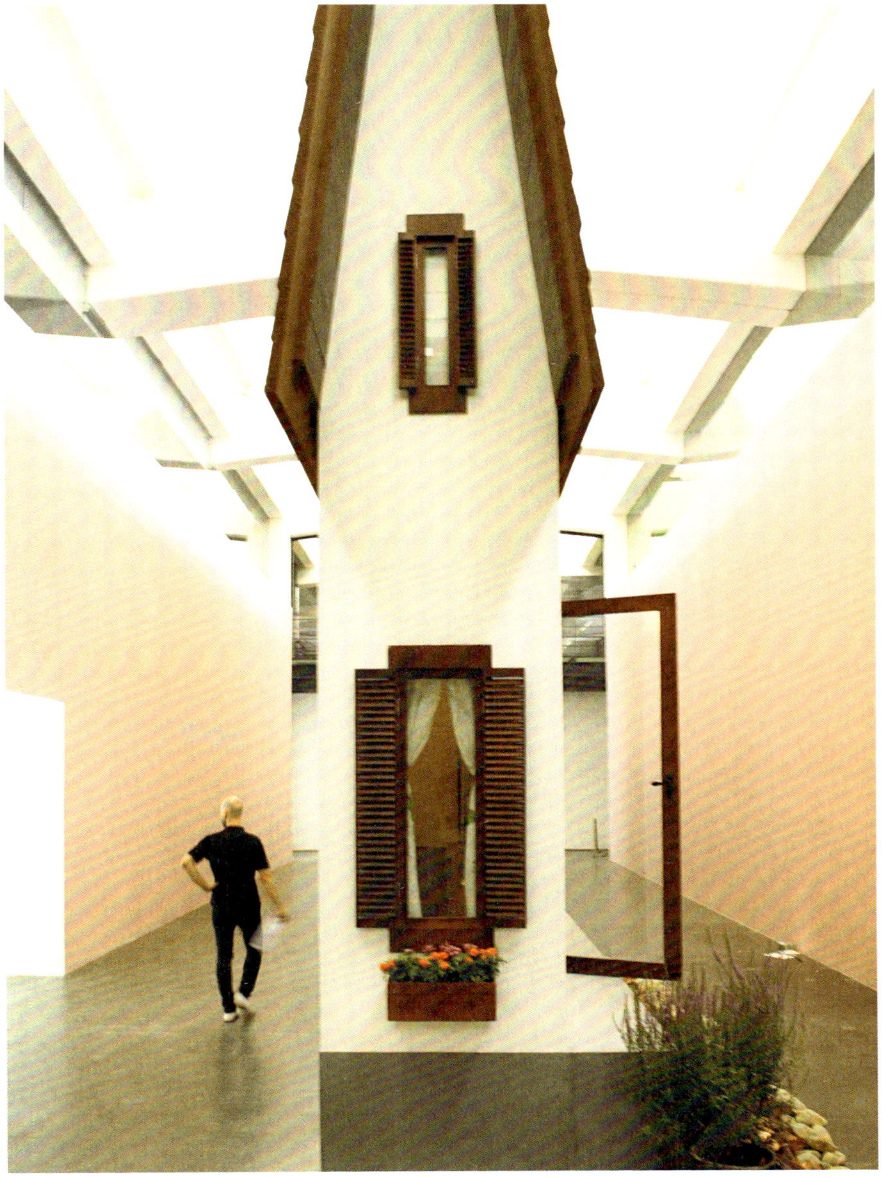

Narrow House, 2010
Mixed media
8 × 1.3 × 21 m
Installation view, 2011
Ullens Center for
Contemporary Art Beijing
Photo: Tang Xuan

rij van gevierde kunstenaars die meubel- en designobjecten gemaakt hebben. Toch lijkt het altijd weer de wereld van de toegepaste kunsten te zijn die deze traditie op de voorgrond plaatst, terwijl de artistieke wereld deze traditie veel minder ernstig lijkt te nemen, of lange tijd niet ernstig heeft genomen. Waarom is dat zo, denkt u? Is er een verandering gaande?

EW Ik stel me de vraag niet of dat wat ik maak toegepaste kunst, vrije kunst of iets anders is. Dat is me volkomen eender.

BT & LS Is er een direct verband tussen uw serie *The Idiot*, waarin Oostenrijkse architecten gelinkt worden aan meubelstukken, en de meubelen die u nu maakt?

EW Bij The Idiot ging het om Oostenrijkse architecten die niet geëmigreerd zijn en waarschijnlijk daarom geen internationaal succes gekend hebben. In tegenstelling tot het werk van andere Oostenrijkers, zoals Schindler en Neutra enz. zijn deze meubelen in Oostenrijk grotendeels iconen, maar niet in het buitenland. En dan stelt men zich de vraag of het anders was geweest als de architecten en designers die deze meubelen ontworpen hebben, wél geëmigreerd waren. Maar bij mijn nieuwe meubelsculpturen gaat het ergens anders om. Daar gaat het niet om meubeliconen. Het zijn geen designmeubelen, maar stuk voor stuk relatief anonieme meubelen. Mij ging het om een meubel dat wat tijd en maatschappelijke context betreft, makkelijk te plaatsen is.

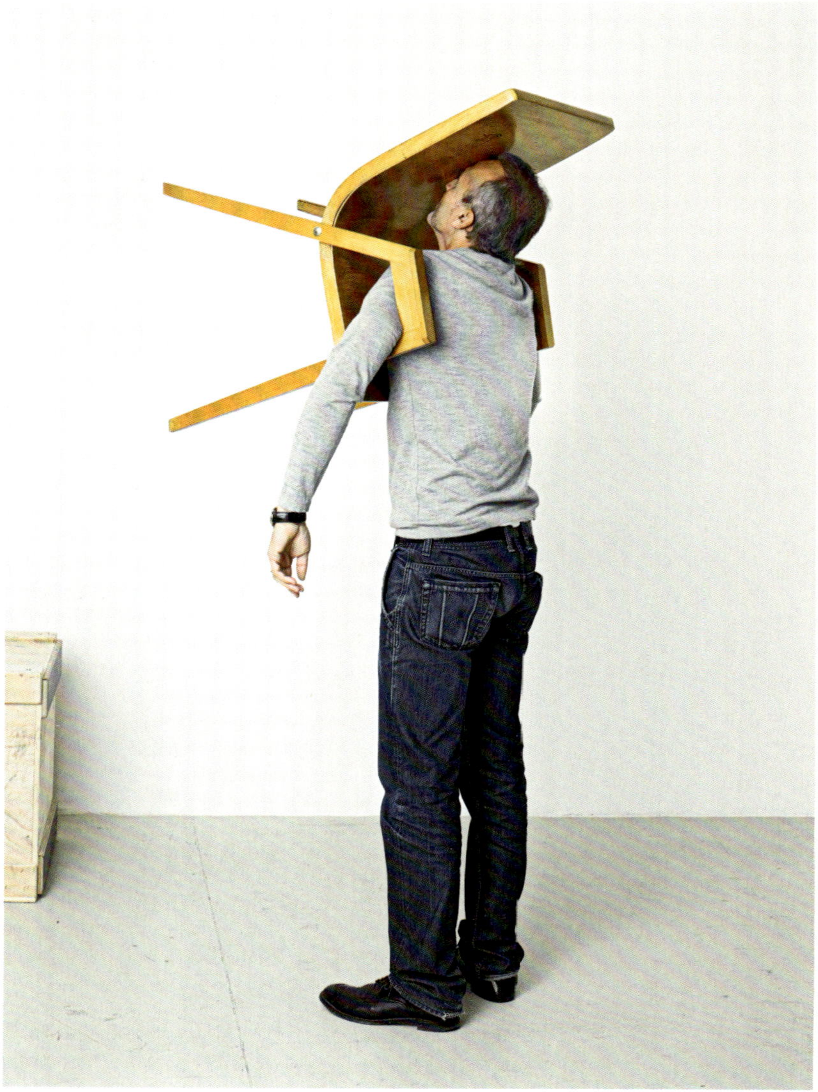

Idiot II, 2010
C-print
92 × 74.5 cm

BT & LS Voor de tentoonstellingen in het Middelheimmuseum werkt u samen met Walter Van Beirendonck. Wat houdt deze samenwerking in? Onderzoekt u bewust de grenzen mode en beeldhouwkunst? Of gaat het om iets totaal anders?

EW Wat ik in de eerste plaats interessant vind aan de samenwerking, is dat Walter Van Beirendonck een modeontwerper is met een grote affiniteit met de beeldende kunsten en dat hij ook soms zelf objecten maakt voor tentoonstellingen. Daarnaast liet hij – en dat heeft hij me zelf enkele jaren geleden gezegd – zich door enkele van mijn werken inspireren, waardoor mijn werk in zekere zin ook al infiltreerde in zijn werk. Een tweede reden ligt in het feit dat ik geïnteresseerd ben in mode, omdat mode samenhangt met de fenomenen hype en iconen, die in onze tijd een belangrijke rol spelen. Daarnaast ben ik ook geïnteresseerd in kleding als een oud thema van de beeldhouwkunst, waarmee ik al enkele jaren bezig ben: de dubbele huid, het omhullen van een volume door een huid, door een omhulsel. Door Walter komt het mode-aspect meer op de voorgrond. Ik had voor hem tekeningen gemaakt als specificaties, die een vals spoor leggen, zijn reactie en wat en hoe dat iets doet ontstaan, trekt me aan.

SW U zei: “Ik hou van mode en ik wil ze vernietigen.” Die dualiteit van aantrekking en afstoting komt op veel plaatsen in uw werk terug.

EW Ik ben inderdaad gefascineerd door mode, maar ik voel tegelijk de drang om ze te verstoren, te versnijden, te vernietigen; de functionaliteit ervan teniet te doen, te deconstrueren en er iets anders van te maken. Er moet een onderscheid gemaakt worden tussen het volgende: enerzijds zijn er de kledingstukken die ik gebruik. Dat is meestal wat ik ‘anonieme mode’ noem, parallel aan of als tegenhanger van de anonieme architectuur, met name de architectuur zonder architect. De anonieme mode interesseert me, omdat ze vaak een uitdrukking is van de brede massa. Anderzijds is er ook de mode van de bovenste plank. Mij interesseren ze allebei: de uitdrukkingen van een creatieve drang en de vormgeving voor de brede massa.

BT & LS Toen u me uw ontwerpen voor de kledingsculpturen toonde die u samen met Walter maakte, viel me op hoe erg de oorspronkelijke schetsen – tekeningen van bestaande foto’s uit modetijdschriften – leken op de klassieke modernistische sculpturen. Ze deden me denken aan het werk van beeldhouwers als Hans Arp. De draagbare objecten die Walter heeft gemaakt, doen echter veel minder denken aan dit soort sculpturen. Wat mij fascineert is dat de tweedimensionale tekening deze associatie met klassieke modernistische sculpturen oproept, terwijl het finale driedimensionale object dat veel minder doet.

EW Omwille van de eenvoud en de vaart heb ik foto’s uit modemagazines gehaald, en die bewerkt. Mijn specificaties, mijn tekeningen verschoven de modefoto’s op die manier in de richting van modernistische sculpturen. Er ontstond op een bepaalde manier een draagbaar klassiek beeldhouwwerk en het was de bedoeling dat Walter daarmee iets deed, dat hij daarop reageerde.

SW Wat zijn de voordelen van de samenwerking met andere kunstenaars, zoals Elfie Semotan of Walter Van Beirendonck? Welke mogelijkheden bieden deze samenwerking?

EW Elfie Semotan komt uit de modefotografie, Walter Van Beirendonck is modeontwerper. Ik wou beide mogelijkheden met elkaar verbinden, net om bovengenoemde redenen.

BT & LS De laatste jaren bent u gestopt met fotografie en bent u teruggekeerd naar de eigenlijke beeldhouwkunst. Op het eerste gezicht is dat een verrassende stap voor een kunstenaar die de grenzen van de beeldhouwkunst wil onderzoeken. Hoe is deze verschuiving tot stand gekomen?

EW Ik heb deze stap gezet omdat ik steeds gevraagd werd door galeriehouders en verzamelaars om iets wat goed gefunctioneerd had, te perfectioneren en eindeloos verder te bewerken. Ik heb gemerkt dat de eindeloze terugkeer van enkele goede ideeën het werk niet beter maakt, integendeel. Ik wilde de kracht van deze werken bewaken, wilde het werk vasthouden. Daarom heb ik er heel bewust een streep onder getrokken. Op basis van deze overwegingen moest ik stoppen met fotograferen. Als ik nog een of andere *One Minute Sculpture*-foto maak, dan is dat enkel voor tijdschriften of zo, maar niet meer als deel van mijn artistieke werk. Daarbij doe ik beroep op fotografen, zoals bijvoorbeeld Elfie Semotan, die me helpen om mijn idee in de praktijk om te zetten. Mijn interesse voor tijdschriften – en voor gedrukte media in het algemeen, maar ook voor televisie en de nieuwe media – verklaar ik door het feit dat de plaats voor artistiek werk, kunst in de publieke ruimte, tot voor enkele jaren in de eerste plaats beperkt was tot pleinen, straten en bouwwerken. Ik ben meer geïnteresseerd in de publieke ruimte van de media. Kunst in de publieke ruimte vindt voor mij plaats in magazines, tijdschriften, op de televisie enz. Dat vind ik het wezenlijk interessante.

BT & LS Uw ontwikkeling kan omschreven worden als de uitbreiding van de taal van de beeldhouwkunst. U stelt de parameters van de beeldhouwkunst in vraag en onderzoekt ze. Zo te zien heeft in uw werk een verschuiving van dematerialisering naar materialisering plaatsgevonden. Hoe past uw huidige 'traditionelere' werk in deze trend?

EW Van begin af aan heb ik geprobeerd om een breed spectrum van artistieke uitdrukkingsvormen te ontwikkelen. Ik heb deze onderling zeer verschillende domeinen onafhankelijk van elkaar verder ontwikkeld. Hierbij gaat het om domeinen zoals de driedimensionale klassieke sculptuur. Via dit domein ben ik dan tot de performance gekomen. Via de performance kwam ik dan eerst terecht bij video, dan bij fotografie en parallel daarmee bij het tekenen, bij gebruiksaanwijzingen, tekst, en werken met tekst. Al deze domeinen, waarbij het ene uit het andere ontstaan is, heb ik parallel verder proberen te ontwikkelen. De blik van het publiek werd echter soms meer op het ene, soms meer op het andere element gericht. Maar, en dat geldt ook vandaag nog, ik heb altijd alle delen parallel gemaakt. Dat wil zeggen: ik heb nooit uitsluitend performatieve sculpturen of *One Minutes* gemaakt. Daarnaast heb ik ook altijd klassieke driedimensionale sculpturen gemaakt. Nu is dat niet echt anders, behalve dan dat ik geen foto's van de *One Minute Sculptures* meer maak.

SW De nieuwe performatieve sculpturen lijken deze trend toch tegen te spreken. Bijvoorbeeld de gebreide stukken die u de curatoren van enkele van uw vroegere tentoonstellingen liet dragen. Of de grote, gebreide stukken, in-situ-installaties, die ontworpen werden voor een specifieke plaats en die verloren gaan zodra de tentoonstelling afgelopen is. Wat vindt u zo interessant aan de spanning – die overigens in heel uw oeuvre voelbaar is – tussen de vergankelijke stukken enerzijds en de voor de eeuwigheid gecreëerde bronzen figuren anderzijds?

EW Het bevalt me wanneer er in een oeuvre een voelbare spanning is, waarbinnen heel veel mogelijk is. Dan denk ik aan werken met een minimale levensduur, zoals de stofsculpturen, over installaties waarbij bouwonderdelen door breigoed ommanteld worden, tot performatieve sculpturen en *One Minutes* enz. Werken die als het ware oplossen en verdwijnen – waarin het einde gedefinieerd is – zorgen voor frictie met duurzame werken.

BT & LS Uw *One Minute Sculptures* vormen het bekendste deel van uw oeuvre. Hun belangrijkste kenmerken zijn dat ze door iedereen gemaakt kunnen worden en dat ze vergankelijk zijn. Maar kunnen we ook niet stellen dat ook uw latere 'blijvende' sculpturen zoals de *Anger Bumps*, *Envy Bumps*, *Fat Houses* en *Fat Cars* 'vergankelijk' zijn? Een vergankelijke situatie (zoals dik zijn, een erectie hebben enz.) die u bevroren heeft in de tijd? Of is dat een te eenvoudige of eenzijdige conclusie?

EW Ik heb in mijn werk, naast het onderzoek van het sculpturale, geprobeerd om het alledaagse leven – mijn leven dus, dat me omringt en waarbinnen ik me beweeg – in verband te brengen met de idee van dat sculpturale. Of zo te verbinden dat er iets nieuws uit ontstaat. Ik heb ook geprobeerd om ongebruikelijke conclusies uit beide aspecten te trekken. En op die manier iets nieuws van allebei te verkrijgen. Ik heb dit voorbeeld al vaak gegeven: als de beeldhouwkunst kan omschreven worden als werken met volumes, dan kunnen we ook zeggen dat toevoegen en wegnemen werken met volumes is. Dus kunnen we ook besluiten dat toevoegen en wegnemen beeldhouwkunst is. Op die manier ben ik enerzijds tot die dik/dun-thema's gekomen. Anderzijds gaat het – als we de idee van het beeldhouwen verlaten – om werken met massa en volume. Die beide aspecten samenbrengen was ontzettend spannend. Is het mogelijk – en dat was ook de vraagstelling – om bijvoorbeeld uit de toenemende zwaarlijvigheid die steeds vaker

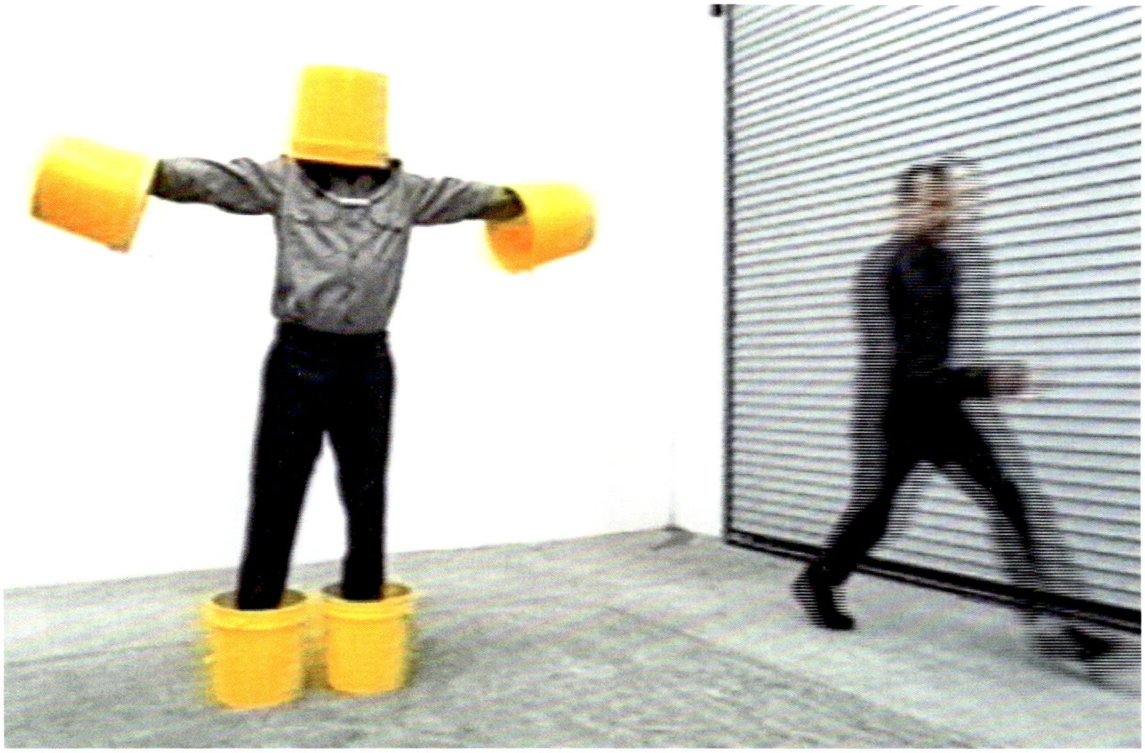

Red Hot Chili Peppers — Can't Stop, 2003
Video, 4'35"
Courtesy: Red Hot Chili Peppers
Marc Romanek, Erwin Wurm
Photo: Mark Romanek

in onze samenleving voorkomt, sculpturale kwaliteiten te halen? Of is het mogelijk – om nog een stap verder te gaan – om bepaalde lichamelijke toestanden om te vormen tot sculpturale kwaliteiten? Of – nog een stap verder – is het mogelijk om spirituele of geestelijke condities of toestanden om te vormen tot sculpturale kwaliteiten? Fysieke gewaarwordingen of psychische toestanden op hun sculpturale kwaliteiten te onderzoeken? De vraag was: is het mogelijk om toestanden als nijd en woede in een sculpturale vorm te gieten? Op die manier kwamen de verschillende werken met de titel *'Ärgerbeule'* (woedebuilen) en *'Neidbeule'* (afgunstbuilen) tot stand. Kortstondige, vluchtige psychische toestanden dus.

BT & LS Als dit zo is, is dit dan geen fantastische metafoor voor het gebrek aan zekerheden in onze huidige wereld? De kerk, de staat, het huwelijk bieden niet meer de zekerheid (of de illusie van zekerheid) die ze de mensen vroeger boden. Ik denk dat het u beter lukt dan om het even welke andere actuele kunstenaar, om de huidige toestand van de samenleving te vatten. Is dit iets wat u bewust doet?

EW Niet de toestand van de samenleving interesseert me, maar het fenomeen dat ik creëer door het samenbrengen van de idee van het sculpturale met sociale fenomenen. Als ik dus een vriend vraag om al zijn kleren over elkaar aan te trekken, dan is dat in eerste instantie een sculpturale handeling. Anderzijds doet het meteen denken aan de daklozen die hun volledige hebben en houden met zich meedragen. Of nog bij het werk *Shopping*, waar ik een koppel in een winkel stuur en ze zoveel mochten dragen en meenemen als ze konden aantrekken. Dan heeft het plotseling te maken met bezit en dus met onze consumentenmaatschappij, met de begeerte. En dan treden maatschappelijke, sociale, psychologische, filosofische fenomenen op de voorgrond. Maar de reden hiervoor was steeds het banale verbuigen van sculpturale fenomenen of overwegingen en basisstructuren.

BT & LS In hoeverre speelt tijd een rol in uw ideeën over beeldhouwkunst?

EW Veel van mijn werken zijn gebaseerd op het principe van tijd. Er zijn de *One Minute Sculptures*, daarnaast zijn er natuurlijk de werken als *Stand West*, waarbij iemand veertien uur stilstaat. Gehypnotiseerd, omdat hij het anders niet zou volhouden. Het rekken van tijd functioneert als een vertraging: de vertraging van een handeling tot ze helemaal tot stiltand komt en de status van een beeldhouwwerk krijgt. Dat was een interessant keerpunt en bijna ook het uitgangspunt van de vraag over hoe lang iets een handeling is en wanneer iets sculptuur wordt. Wanneer wordt het sculpturale in de handeling zo sterk dat men het als sculptuur kan beschouwen?

BT & LS U heeft er nooit voor teruggedeinsd om zich bezig te houden met de populaire cultuur. U heeft bijvoorbeeld met Claudia Schiffer samengewerkt aan een fotoreeks voor Vogue, uw *One Minute Sculptures* lagen aan de basis van een videoclip van de Red Hot Chili Peppers en u werkte mee aan campagnes voor Hermès. Zoekt u naar dergelijke opdrachten om naast de wereld van de galeries en de musea een platform te creëren voor uw werk en op die manier een link te leggen met de hedendaagse cultuur? Of is het net omgekeerd en komen de mensen uit de wereld van de commerciële kunst naar u omdat u duidelijk een bredere kennis heeft van de hedendaagse cultuur dan zij zelf?

EW Ik heb nooit naar opdrachten of opdrachtgevers buiten de kunstwereld gezocht. Ik heb echt nooit naar opdrachtgevers gezocht. De Red Hot Chili Peppers, of beter Mark Romanek, de beroemde videoregisseur, heeft mij benaderd en gevraagd of ik het goed vond dat ze mijn werk zouden gebruiken voor een videoclip van de Red

Hot Chili Peppers. Hetzelfde scenario bij Hermès en Vogue. Daarnaast heb ik wel gedacht: wat goed dat ik deze kansen krijg. Zoals ik hierboven beschreven heb, ben ik erg geïnteresseerd in de publieke ruimte van de media, omdat men kunst hierin anders kan positioneren. En Hermès als mode-icoon vond ik spannend. Ze hebben me benaderd en gevraagd of het me zou interesseren de mode van Hermès te gebruiken als materiaal voor enkele werken. Het was nooit een campagne of als zodanig bedoeld, ik heb nooit reclame gemaakt. Ik heb geprobeerd om met het modelabel als medium, als icoon in de modewereld, artistiek werk te maken.

BT & LS En hoe kunt u verzekeren dat u zich ook in de toekomst van de commerciële wereld kunt onderscheiden? Of bent u zich hiervan niet bewust?

EW Er zijn een aantal uitnodigingen van muzikanten, groepen en modelabels, maar die heb ik allemaal geweigerd. Ik hou het op deze eenmalige samenwerkingen. Ik ga wel van tijd tot tijd nog speciale werken maken voor magazines, dagbladen of het internet, omdat ik het zinvol vind om werken te maken voor de mediale publieke ruimte.

BT & LS Denkt u dat de grenzen tussen design, mode en autonome kunst ondertussen volledig vervaagd zijn?

EW Ik denk dat deze grens altijd zal bestaan, maar dat er veel kunstenaars zijn die op meerdere domeinen tegelijk actief zijn en grensoverschrijdend werken.

BT & LS Ik zie bijvoorbeeld een verband tussen uw werk en het werk van fotografen zoals Martin Parr. Ziet u een verband tussen de fotografie en wat u doet?

EW Ik ken het boeiende werk van Martin Parr. En uiteraard zijn er tal van mensen die op gelijkaardige domeinen werken, en die goede kunst maken.

SW Uw gebruik van de geprinte media – niet enkel van lifestyle of designmagazines, maar ook, en dat is misschien nog belangrijker – van dagbladen en andere informatieve geprinte media als 'publieke ruimte' is een krachtig instrument. Mensen zijn nog steeds geneigd om belang te hechten aan het gedrukte woord/beeld, in tegenstelling tot het internet, dat als heel vluchtig en minder geloofwaardig beschouwd zou kunnen worden. Hoe gebruikt u dit instrument?

EW Met dagbladen heb ik gewerkt, onder andere met *Die Zeit* Hamburg. Het internet heb ik persoonlijk nog niet veel ingezet voor artistiek werk. Mocht ik 20 jaar jonger zijn, dan zou ik waarschijnlijk ook hier heel sterk aanwezig zijn. Voor mijn werk *44 Vorschläge – Eine soziale Skulptur* ben ik echt aangevallen, omdat de lezers dachten dat al de xenofobe, vrouwonvriendelijke en fascistische uitlatingen die ik verzameld

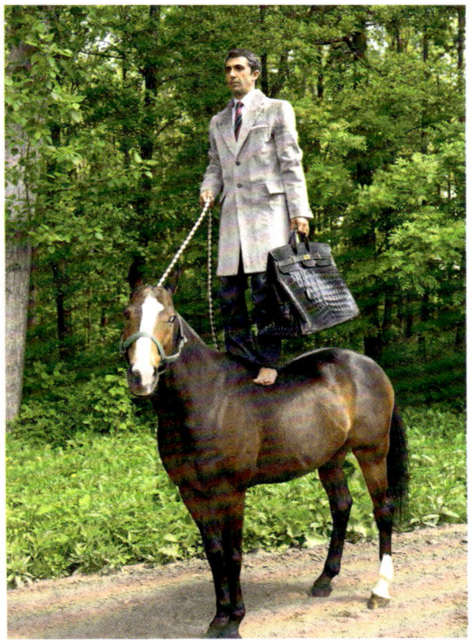

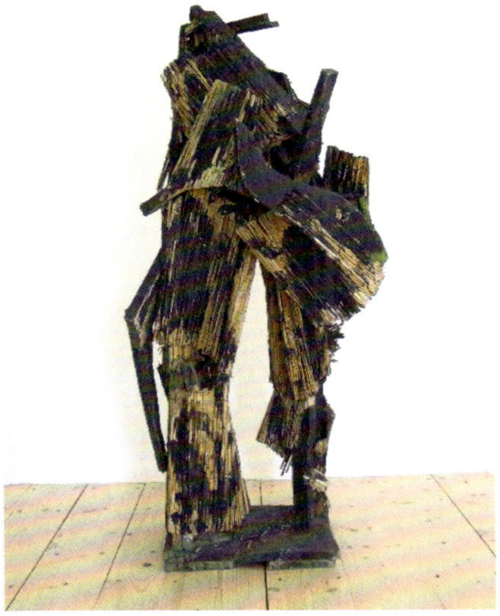

Hermès, The Anarchist, 2008
C-print
150 × 112 cm

Untitled, 1997
Wood, paint
130 × 60 × 70 cm

had echt mijn mening weergaven. In feite verzamelde en verergerde ik bestaande uitspraken van tijdgenoten. Maar de overdonderende reacties hebben mijn vermoeden gestaafd dat ik de juiste ruimte gekozen had. In een galerie of museumruimte was dat waarschijnlijk niet zo diep gegaan – omdat het dan overduidelijk kunst is.

SW Laat ons hier nog even op verder gaan: u staat bekend voor uw opmerkelijke boeken. Die zijn legendarisch en zijn intussen zelfs verzamelobjecten geworden. Door een boek los te koppelen van een tentoonstelling of een chronologisch onderzoek, wordt het meer dan zomaar een boek. Welke ruimte is een boek of kan het zijn? Hoe onderscheidt het zich van de ruimte van een museum of een galerie?

EW Wel ja, boeken hebben natuurlijk een veel langere houdbaarheid dan een tentoonstelling. Ten eerste omdat ze een langere geldigheid hebben dan een tentoonstelling. Ik ben relatief pragmatisch van aard en ik vind dat alles wat het werk ondersteunt of wat dient om het werk bij de mensen te brengen, bekend te maken of ter discussie te stellen, het werk ook ten goede komt. Daarom zijn publicaties ook heel belangrijk voor mij.

SW Nu we het over het gebruik van ruimte hebben: wat doet een enorme breigoedinstallatie met een ruimte?

EW Door het breigoed wordt de ruimte in zekere zin deel van een organisme. Breigoed of het omhullen van dingen brengt meteen de associatie mee van bekleden, bescherming zoeken, in het bijzonder met een zacht materiaal als breigoed, dat een volume creëert dat de lichaamsvormen sterk accentueert en verdubbelt.

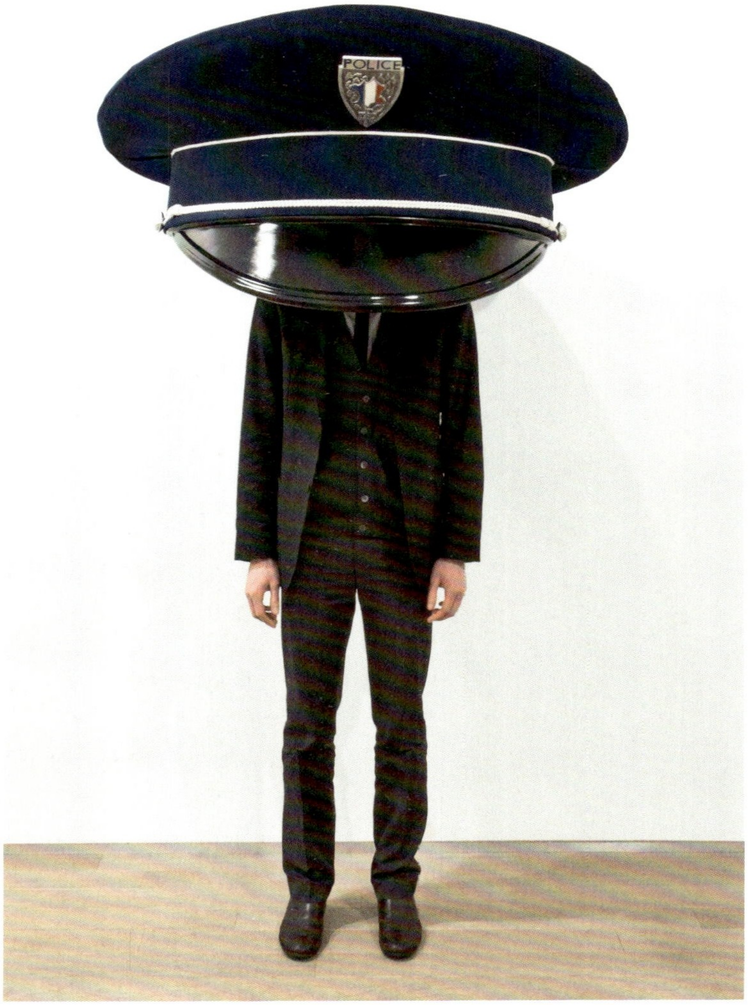

French Police Cap, 2010
Styrofoam, epoxy resin, textile fabric
150 × 115 × 110 cm
Installation view, 2011
Galerie Thaddaeus Ropac, Paris

SW Een groot deel van de breigoedinstallatie is gebaseerd op het gebruik van kleur. Hoe meer ik me in uw werk verdiep, hoe meer kleur voor mij een obsessie wordt. Kleur is overal aanwezig in uw werk, kleur opent steeds opnieuw de ogen. Is kleur voor u een obsessie? Is kleur datgene wat u uit uw jeugddroom om schilder te worden in de beeldhouwkunst overneemt?

EW Ik weet het niet. Misschien is dat zo. Maar dat is natuurlijk ook onbewust. De interesse voor kleur… Aanvankelijk was de kleur in mijn werk vaak enkel de kleur van het materiaal. Daarna ben ik kleur bewuster gaan gebruiken. Nee, dat is niet juist, dat was al veel vroeger het geval. Helemaal in het begin was kleur alleszins een thema, omdat ik eigenlijk schilder wilde worden. Mijn eerste sculpturen heb ik beschilderd. Bij de houtsculpturen functioneert kleur als een soort van huid. Ik kan kleur ook sculpturaal inzetten en daarmee de ruimte veranderen, opentrekken en sluiten. Kleur is natuurlijk aantrekkelijk, omdat men met kleur betekenis en stemmingen kan oproepen, de materialiteit van haar oorsprong kan losmaken en sporen kan leggen die ook ten dele vals zijn. Men kan materiaal laten verdwijnen of het voor iets anders laten doorgaan. Dat vind ik erg fijn. Ik heb bijvoorbeeld altijd problemen gehad met de kleur van brons. Dat was voor mij zo beladen met de vele generaties kunstenaars die met brons gewerkt hebben. Toen ik de mogelijkheid kreeg om brons te lakken of te beschilderen, boden zich voor mij andere kansen aan. Slechts toen ik brons kon beschilderen en als iets anders voorstellen, kon ik met dit materiaal werken.

BT & LS Uw *One Minute Sculptures* lijken op basis van hun do-it-yourself-karakter in grote mate te beantwoorden aan de huidige tijdgeest. Momenteel lijken ze – samen met de sociale media – een heel geschikte vorm te zijn voor het internet bijvoorbeeld. Ik zou er niet van geschrokken zijn mochten uw *One Minute Sculptures* een hype geworden zijn op Facebook. Hoe staat u tegenover de artistieke mogelijkheden die de nieuwe media bieden? Ziet u op dit vlak een rol weggelegd voor kunst?

EW Er zijn zelfs fora over *One Minute Sculptures* waarop mensen *One Minute Sculptures* creëren op het internet. Dus die bestaan, tot mijn grote verrassing. Zoals al gezegd, biedt het internet uiteraard ongelooflijk veel mogelijkheden voor de kunst. Maar hiervoor ben ik niet de juiste man. Die – eindeloze – mogelijkheden zullen andere, jongere kunstenaars onderzoeken. Er staan ons nog spannende dingen te wachten.

BT & LS In het bijzonder de zinloosheid van de *One Minute Sculptures* doet me aan het internet denken. Hun belachelijkheid is tegelijkertijd hun sterkte. In dat opzicht heeft uw werk inderdaad voorspeld welke gevolgen het internet heeft voor de zichtbaarheid van het afzonderlijke en hoe dat via het world wide web bekendheid kan krijgen. Heeft het internet ook uw werk veranderd?

EW Nee, het internet heeft mijn werk eigenlijk niet veranderd. Omdat ik mij, zoals reeds gezegd, op artistiek vlak daar nooit bewust mee beziggehouden heb.

BT & LS Blijkbaar wilt u kunst tot een groter deel maken van het dagelijkse leven, een rol laten spelen in het leven van de mensen zonder dat kunst al te ernstig genomen wordt. Wat is volgens u de ideale rol die de kunst in de westerse samenleving kan spelen?

EW Ik ben telkens weer verrast en sta er altijd van versteld hoe beperkt de rol van de beeldende kunst in onze westerse samenleving is. In het bijzonder in Oostenrijk is dit heel frappant. Bijna elke politicus neemt het woord ‘cultuurnatie’ in de mond, maar als het erop aankomt om theorieën in de praktijk om te zetten en door te voeren, komt er niet veel van in huis. Volgens mij is de doorsnee Oostenrijkse politicus wat betreft algemene cultuur erg onderontwikkeld, en artistiek volkomen ongeïnteresseerd. Wat natuurlijk fataal is. Het gaat enerzijds over lippendienst bewijzen aan de kunst, maar bekijkt men dat van dichterbij, dan ziet het er vaak helemaal anders uit. Ik herinner me een discussie van ongeveer een jaar geleden met de toenmalige minister van Buitenlandse Zaken (nu vicekanselier), Spindelegger, die over de toekomst en de mogelijkheden van de Europese Unie sprak aan de Weense Universiteit voor Toegepaste Economische Wetenschappen. Hij heeft een voordracht van veertig minuten gegeven. Eén keer heeft hij het woord cultuur gebruikt, het woord 'kunst' nam hij niet in de mond. En het ging om de toekomst van Europa. Ik heb hem gevraagd hoe dat kwam en hij lachte. Iedereen in de zaal lachte. Niet omdat de vraag en de kwestie interessant en gerechtvaardigd waren, maar omdat ze dachten: "Wat voor een absurde vraag is dat?" Welke rol moet kunst of cultuur in onze wereld spelen? En daar zitten dan dames en heren, waarschijnlijk in op maat gemaakte kleding, die met dure en goed ontworpen auto's rijden, die waarschijnlijk in villa's wonen met chique meubelen en kunst en design, die naar de opera en naar het theater gaan, waarschijnlijk ook naar het kunsthistorisch museum, die andere steden bezoeken en daar wellicht de architectuur bewonderen. Mensen dus die deelnemen aan cultuur, maar te onwetend zijn om zich daar ook van bewust te zijn en dit ook te kunnen of te willen uitspreken.

SW Is het echt mogelijk om kunst tot deel van het dagelijkse leven te maken? Is het te cynisch om te zeggen dat we in het beste geval het dagelijkse leven tot deel van de kunst kunnen maken?

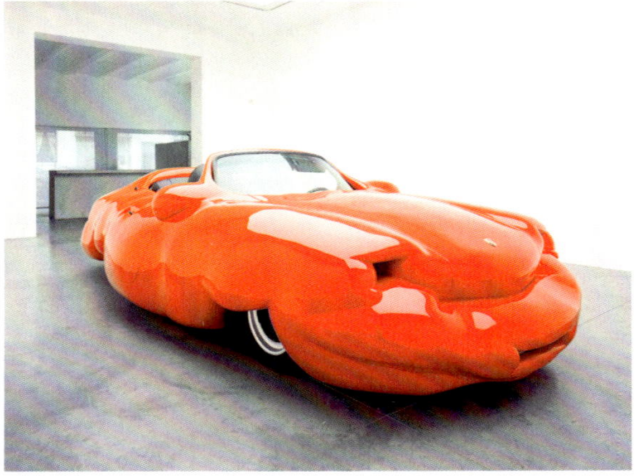

Fat Convertible, 2005
Mixed media
130 × 239 × 469 cm
Photo: Xavier Hufkens Gallery, Brussels

EW Voor mij maakt kunst gewoon deel uit van het dagelijkse leven. Kunst is ook mijn alledaagse leven. Dat wil zeggen dat als men iets opneemt in het alledaagse, het zijn bijzondere karakter verliest en niet langer luxe uitstraalt en buitengewoon is. Dat wil echter niet zeggen dat het kunstwerk zelf niets bijzonders of buitengewoons meer heeft. Ik heb het enkel over de omgang met het kunstwerk. Het kunstwerk wordt iets waarmee ik me dagelijks bezighoud, en dat is zeker mogelijk.

BT & LS In hoeverre wordt u geïnspireerd door de klassiekers onder de slapstickfilms? Het werk van Buster Keaton – de man die nooit lachte – lijkt in uw standpunt weerspiegeld te worden.

EW Slapstickfilms, Stan Laurel, Oliver Hardy, Buster Keaton, Charlie Chaplin en vele anderen, tot en met de Duitser Karl Valentin, die ik heel grappig vind met zijn droge, heel schuine humor. Slapstick op zich interesseert me bitter weinig. Wat mij interesseert is de cynische humor, het belachelijke. Dat is iets dat ik ook voor mijn werk opzoek. Het toereikende, het zwakke, het belachelijke, het pijnlijke: het zijn de dingen die me interesseren. Het bijkomstige zelfs, niet de grote successen zoals het Surrealisme of het Weens Actionisme, maar het bekrompene, het onbelangrijke. Dat waar iedereen zich in herkent. Dat is altijd een deel van ieder van ons.

BT & LS Het Gemeentemuseum heeft een recente reeks sculpturen gekocht: de *Small Psychos*. Elf figuren die enkel zichtbaar zijn door de trui die hen verbergt. Doordat ze verschillende houdingen aannemen geven ze – bij wijze van spreken – 'abstracte' vormen weer. Bij deze reeks gaat het om het verband tussen uiterlijke verschijning en innerlijk leven. Het uiterlijke bepaalt vandaag het leven (een feit dat zich ook weerspiegelt in de *Fat Cars* en *Fat Houses*). Dit wordt vaker aangevoerd als een van de redenen van individualisme. Wij denken dat we onszelf kunnen beschermen en ons van andere mensen kunnen afschermen door enkel aan onze eigen noden en wensen te denken, geld te verdienen en het in onze eigen paar vierkante meter te investeren door dure huizen, auto's en kleren te kopen. Uw werk illustreert echter dat we in feite allemaal hetzelfde doen. We zijn allemaal dezelfde truien, in licht verschillende houdingen, maar toch gevangen in onze aandacht voor uiterlijkheden. Hoe individueel we ook denken te zijn, we zijn in feite collectiever dan ooit tevoren. De vrije wil is zeldzaam geworden. We zijn gevangenen van het kapitalisme. Beschouwt u uw werk in dit opzicht als maatschappijkritisch? Indien ja, welke is dan de boodschap die u wilt overbrengen?

EW Dat is inderdaad de kwestie: individualiteit of zogenaamde individualiteit als projectie van het uiterlijke. En ook de vrije wil als projectie van het uiterlijke. Hersenwetenschappers hebben onlangs, of enige tijd geleden, gediscussieerd over de vraag of de vrije wil echt bestaat, de vrije wil zoals we die denken te kennen. Of zijn we veeleer afhankelijk van of worden we gevormd door genetische voorbestemming, voorprogrammering, maatschappelijke determinatie, processen die door de opvoeding in gang gezet worden? Het ging er dus over of we in de grond bepaald worden door omgeving, opvoeding en onze genen. Als men als Europeaan de Amerikanen en de Japanners bekijkt, vallen twee fundamentele dingen op. De Amerikaan geeft een soevereine, individuele indruk, lijkt een onafhankelijke persoon. Zelfs zijn lach en zijn nies zijn anders, net zoals zijn

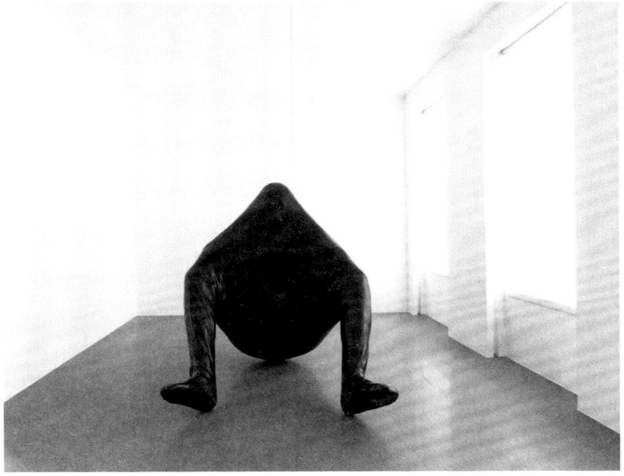

Philosophers, Big Gulp, 2009
Bronze, dark patina
180 × 159 × 200 cm
Photo: Xavier Hufkens Gallery, Brussels

tafelmanieren. Bij de Japanner is dat niet zo. Bij een Japanner heeft men het gevoel een collectief persoon te ontmoeten. Een totaal andere veronderstelling dus op basis van een speciaal gedrag. Gaat men echter naar Amerika en ziet men de Amerikaan niet individueel – en mijn ogen gingen open – dan is dit zogenaamd zeer individuele en diepe stemregister bij de mannelijke Amerikanen een maatschappelijk fenomeen. Hetzelfde geldt voor de Amerikaanse nies en de Amerikaanse lach. Dat zijn maatschappelijke modellen, net zoals het eten of het feit dat op vrijdag de zakenmannen – die anders altijd een das dragen – een anderskleurig colbertjasje of een anderskleurige broek mogen dragen. Ook de Amerikaanse individualiteit is in werkelijkheid een collectieve houding. Dat is heel interessant. In Japan is de situatie vergelijkbaar. Maar in Japan stelt men vast dat het zogenaamde collectieve individu toch ook een individualiteit heeft en niet enkel collectief lijkt te handelen.

BT & LS Hoe humoristisch en lichthartig uw werk ook mag lijken, uw onderwerpen zijn altijd heel ernstig. Geldt dat inderdaad niet voor uw volledige oeuvre?

EW Mijn werk gaat over het drama van de belachelijkheid van het zijn, of men dat zijn nu benadert met filosofie of met een dieet. We trekken aan het kortste eind.

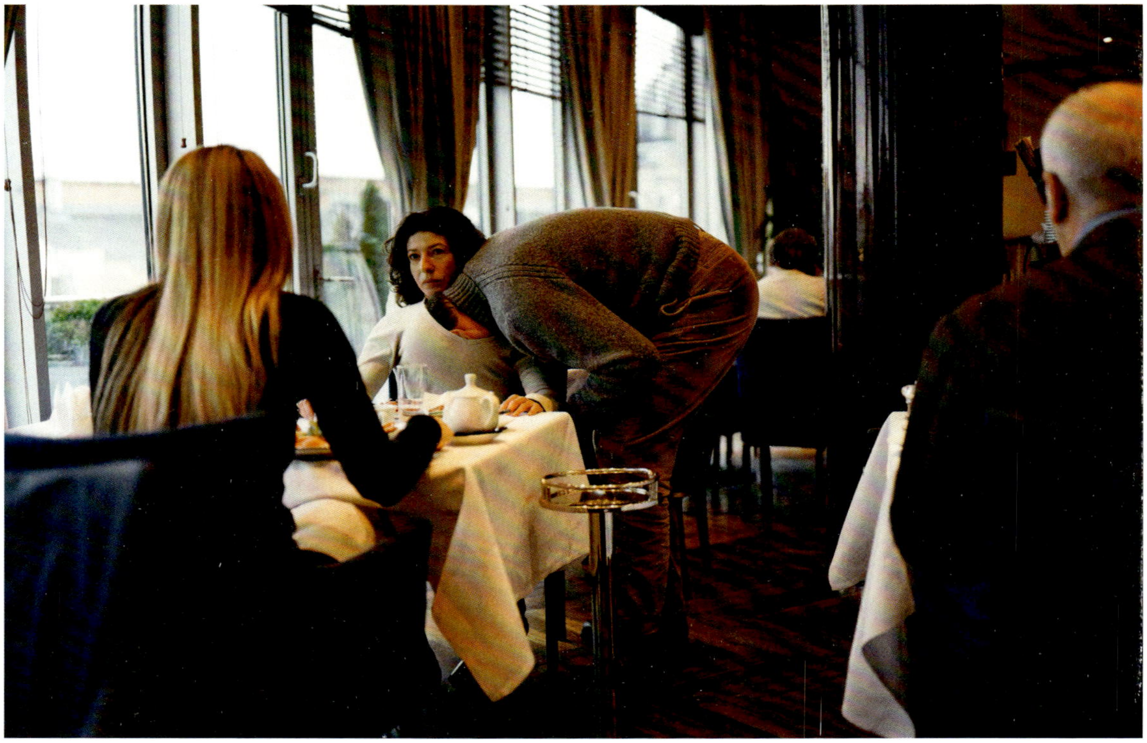

Instructions on how to be politically incorrect, Inspection, 2002
C-print
126 × 184 cm

SW Zouden we kunnen zeggen dat het – ook al trekt u de toeschouwer voortdurend uit zijn comfortzone – als troostend beschouwd kan worden? Dat pijn en ontoereikendheid alomtegenwoordig zijn?

EW Nee, nee, ik vind dat niet troostend. Het zou troostend zijn om met deze dingen te lachen – of meer nog de mogelijkheid te hebben met die dingen te lachen. Als je humor hebt, en lacht om je eigen zwakheden, en grappen maakt over je eigen ontoereikendheid, maakt dat je sterk, denk ik. Dat lachen maakt je sterk.

BT & LS In een interview zei u ooit dat uw werk gebaseerd is op stripverhalen en science-fiction. Kan u dat uitleggen?

EW Door het verband van het werk met comics, daalt de drempel voor de toeschouwer nog verder. Bijvoorbeeld voor de *Fat Car* heb ik een normale auto genomen, en die dik gemaakt. En door deze sculpturale vervorming heeft er een zekere vereenvoudiging plaatsgevonden, kreeg de auto een antropomorfe gedaante. Men kon er een gezicht in zien. Door die vereenvoudigde vorm en het antropomorfe karakter ervan, was er plotseling een verwijzing naar comics: het deed ons denken aan die auto's die door Walt Disney werden getekend in de jaren '50.

SW Tekst maakt een groot deel uit van uw werk. Er zijn de tekeningen en foto's met aanwijzingen, teksten zoals *'Instructions On How To Be Politically Incorrect'* en al die markante titels van werken die rechtstreeks verwijzen naar de literatuur (Hamlet, Fountain for Arthur Rimbaud enz.), en de werken over filosofen, in het bijzonder over Wittgenstein, die zelf revolutionaire werken schreef over taal. Welk soort instrument is tekst voor u?

EW Tekst is een instrument om inhoud over te brengen. Daarom zijn er ook die video's als Tell of de sprekende auto's, het sprekende huis enz. Dat is voor mij heel belangrijk.

SW Uw werk werd vergeleken met de stukken van Werner Schwab, van wie wordt gezegd dat hij 'een abstract concept als een massief object kan voorstellen'. U werd ook in verband gebracht met auteurs als Thomas Bernhard en Samuel Beckett. Voelt u zich verbonden met hun schrijfkunst? Is het toeval, dat zij juist theaterteksten geschreven hebben?

EW Er is natuurlijk de sterke band met Werner Schwab. Hij was een jeugdvriend van mij met wie ik meerdere jaren intensief contact heb gehad. Uiteraard heb ik veel van Thomas Bernhard gelezen en ook van Samuel Beckett. Maar ik ben geen auteur. Voor mij is taal niet zoals bij Werner een uitdrukkingsmiddel, dat hij virtuoos beheerst. Ook Thomas Bernhard, met zijn eindeloos lange nevenschikkingen, is uniek en fantastisch. Dat zijn taaluitvinders en taalkunstenaars. Ik beweeg me in een heel andere wereld en maak slechts hier en daar een excursie naar tekst. Het is niet juist dat ik teksten voor theater geschreven heb. Ik heb teksten uit het tijdschrift *Die Zeit* gehaald. Daar hebben we het al over gehad. En ik schrijf de teksten voor mijn video's. Dat is niet zo veel.

BT & LS Waarom verzet u zich in interviews tegen het belang dat men – met het oog op uw werk – toeschrijft aan het menselijke lichaam? Is het omdat u geen interesse heeft voor het lichaam op zich (als materiaal voor kunst), maar enkel voor de mogelijke toestand waarin een lichaam zich kan bevinden? Of het nu gaat om uw eigen lichaam, het publieke lichaam of een artistiek gecreëerd lichaam?

EW Omdat ik geïnteresseerd ben in de toestand, de mogelijke toestand en ook de bevoegdheid en de hiermee samenhangende sociologische, politieke, filosofische en psychologische mogelijkheden ervan. En in het bijzonder in het publieke lichaam, dus het lichaam van de openbaarheid, en het wetenschappelijke lichaam. Het publieke lichaam, het lichaam van de openbaarheid of ook in de christelijke betekenis – ik ben katholiek opgevoed, maar ben niet meer gelovig – met Leib/Laib (lichaam/brood) verwijst het naar het lichaam als brood en brood als lichaam. Ik weet helemaal niet hoe je Leib/Laib moet overbrengen, maar het is natuurlijk een ongelooflijke reductie van het menselijke individu. Voor mij is het lichaam altijd een eenheid, dus deel van een eenheid die het menselijke individu uitmaakt. En dat is slechts één deel. Ik mis het andere maar ik mag het bij wijze van spreken niet missen. Het is verbazingwekkend hoe men de mens tot een lichaam kan herleiden. Dat is fascinerend.

BT & LS In hoeverre gaat uw werk over identiteit? En wat is het verband met authenticiteit?

EW Identiteit, de idee van identiteit en de omgang daarmee, keert in mijn werk altijd terug, omdat het de reflectie van onszelf is. Hoe zie ik mij? Zie ik mezelf op dezelfde manier als anderen me zien? Dan gaat het om projecties, om voorstellingen, richtlijnen en zo. En dan gaat het uiteraard evenzeer om authenticiteit.

BT & LS Verontrust het u dat veel mensen uw werk slechts waarderen wegens de uiterlijkheden? Of ziet u dit als de ultieme bevestiging van de echte betekenis?

EW De vraag, doorheen verschillende jaren van werken, is altijd de volgende geweest: kan ik door middel van de verbinding van het sculpturale met een alledaags thema van onze tijd, een nieuw perspectief of een nieuwe interpretatiemogelijkheid geven aan dat thema? Omdat dat thema's uit onze tijd waren die veel verder gingen dan de kunstwereld, heb ik daar veel meer mensen meer bereikt. De leesbaarheid van het werk wordt vergemakkelijkt door de gedeeltelijke verwantschap aan comics (hierboven vermeld) waardoor de drempel verlaagt.

BT & LS Maar denkt u niet dat u misschien beter de kern van de tijdgeest raakt dan veel andere kunstenaars?

EW Wel ja. Als men zich met de tijd bezighoudt, dan ligt het plots voor de hand dat men zijn eigen werk in de tijd positioneert en hierdoor ook zoiets als de tijdgeest raakt of ten dele iets creëert dat ook tijdgeest produceert. Dat heeft te maken met de meest uiteenlopende thema's en doelgroepen. Het is net als bij sociologie, filosofie en ook bij thema's uit de godsdienst, de mode, de architectuur, de idee van het icoon, wat een fenomeen uit de 20e eeuw is.

Erwin Wurm was born in 1954 in Bruck an der Mur in Austria. He lives and works in Vienna and Limberg.

A comprehensive biography and bibliography of books, articles and reviews in the media, Internet, and TV can be found at: www.erwinwurm.at

This book is published in conjunction with the exhibitions

Erwin Wurm: Wear Me Out
Middelheim Museum, Antwerp
May 29 to September 25, 2011

Acknowledgments
Philip Heylen, Alderman for Culture and Tourism, Antwerp; Bruno Verbergt, Director Culture, Sports and Youth, Antwerp; Steven Thielemans, General Director Museums and Heritage, Antwerp

Director
Menno Meewis

Curator
Sara Weyns

Exhibitions
Sara Weyns, Pieter Boons (heimat.be)

Education
Greet Stappaerts, Greet Cooreman

Collection management
Lucie Bausart

Documentation center
Jeannine Schools, Johan Vermariën

Administration and secretary Middelheim promoters
Filip Janssens, Eddy Van Gasse, Linda Willems, and Maggy Troffaes

Production and technical services
Étoile Mécanique (www.etoilemecanique.com)

Supervisor production and technical services Middelheim Museum
Ludo Scherer

Production and technical services
Mohamed Ach-chak, Nico Amey, Francine Bettens, Willy Dams, Dirk Dellen, Willy De Vreeze, Rik Gosselin, Patrick Heyrman, Filip Maes, Germaine Maieu, Linda Mulkens, Marc Nouwynck, Frank Rubbens, Danny Sluyts, Rita Steukers, Thibaud Van Agtmael, Jef Van Beurden, Carl Van Craen, Victor Vandyck, Paul Venesoen, Theo Verschooten

Maintenance
Saniye Baleci, Bouchra Haddouyate

Safety
Mohammad Madadi, Werner Verhaert, René Wuyts

Press and communication
Laurence De Bolle, Nadine Plehiers, Nadia De Vree, Miranda De Boel

Middelheim promotors
Ackermans & van Haaren, Allen & Overy Belgium, BASF Antwerpen NV, BNP Partibas Fortis, CMB, DEME, Duvel Moortgat, Ernst & Young, Gimv, Inno.com CVA, KBC Global Services NV, Leasinvest Real Estate, Umicore, Van Breda Risk & Benefits

Middelheim Museum
Middelheimlaan 61
2020 Antwerp, Belgium
Tel. +32 3 288 33 60
Fax +32 3 288 33 99
middelheimmuseum@stad.antwerpen.be

Erwin Wurm: The Beauty Business
GEM, museum voor actuele kunst, The Hague
June 25 to September 18, 2011

Director
Benno Tempel

Curator
Laura Stamps, Mandy Prins

GEM, museum voor actuele kunst
Stadhouderslaan 43
2517 HV The Hague
The Netherlands
Tel. +31 70 33 811 33
Fax +31 70 33 811 55
www.gem-online.com

Erwin Wurm is represented by the following galleries:

Xavier Hufkens
Rue Saint-Georges 6-8
1050 Brussels, Belgium
Tel. +32 02 639 67 30
Fax +32 02 639 67 38
www.xavierhufkens.com

Galerie Thaddaeus Salzburg
Mirabellplatz 2
5020 Salzburg, Austria
Tel. +43 662 881 393
Fax +43 662 881 3939
www.ropac.net

Galerie Thaddaeus Paris
Rue Debelleyme 7
75003 Paris, France
Tel. +33 1 4272 9900
Fax +33 1 4272 6166
www.ropac.net

Lehmann Maupin
540 West 26 Street
New York, NY 10001
USA
Tel. +1 212 255 2923
Fax +1 212 255 2924

201 Chrystie Street
New York, NY 10001
USA
Tel. +1 212 254 0054
Fax +1 212 254 0055
www.lehmannmaupin.com

Catalogue

Coordination
Leni Michl, Sander Vermeulen, Sara Weyns,
Pieter Boons (heimat.be)

English copyediting
Leina Gonzalez

Dutch copyediting
Marjorie Blomme, Patrick De Rynck

English translations
datatra.be, Kevin Martley

Dutch translations
datatra.be

Graphic design
BaseDesign, Brussels

Typeface
Janson

Production
Christine Emter, Hatje Cantz

Reproductions
Repromayer GmbH, Reutlingen

Printing
Offsetdruckerei Karl Grammlich GmbH, Pliezhausen

Paper
LuxoArt Samt, 150 g/m²

Binding
Lachenmaier GmbH, Reutlingen

Exhibition Photography Middelheim Museum
Ottomura Photography Collective (www.ottomura.be)

Printed in Germany

Cover illustration
Performative Sculpture, 2011
Photo: Elfie Semotan

Published by
Hatje Cantz Verlag
Zeppelinstrasse 32
73760 Ostfildern
Germany
Tel. +49 711 4405-200
Fax +49 711 4405-220
www.hatjecantz.com

You can find information on this exhibition
and many others at www.kq-daily.de.

Hatje Cantz books are available internationally at selected
bookstores. For more information about our distribution
partners, please visit our website at www.hatjecantz.com.

ISBN 978-3-7757-3218-5

With special thanks to

Erwin Wurm, the artist;
Leni Michl
Johanna Lakner
and Claudia Salzer at Studio Wurm;
the Austrian Cultural Forum, Brussels;
Ben Van den Berghe
and all the performers at the Middelheim Museum;
Walter Van Beirendonck
Dirk Van Saene
Elke Hoste
Joost Jansen
Tools & Dies
Ilke
Ruth
Sandra
Masha
Alice
Rose
Trinka
Jain
Marc
Gunter
Bernadette
Rosalinde
Thérèse
Lisa
Cecile
Livina
Kirsten
Hilde
Peter
Yolande en Moses

STAD ANTWERPEN
Cultuur, sport & jeugd

Met steun van de
Vlaamse overheid

österreichisches kulturforum bru

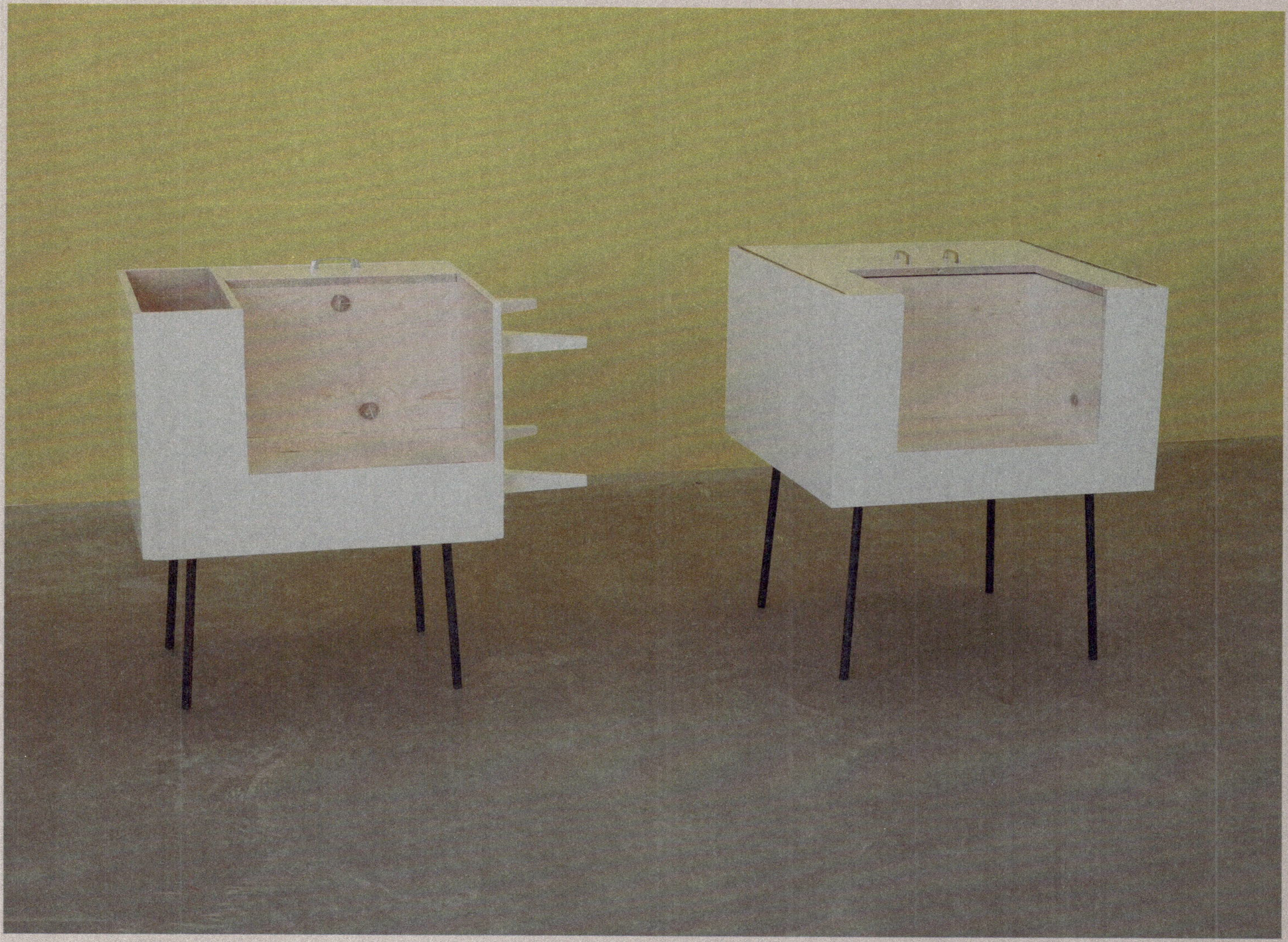

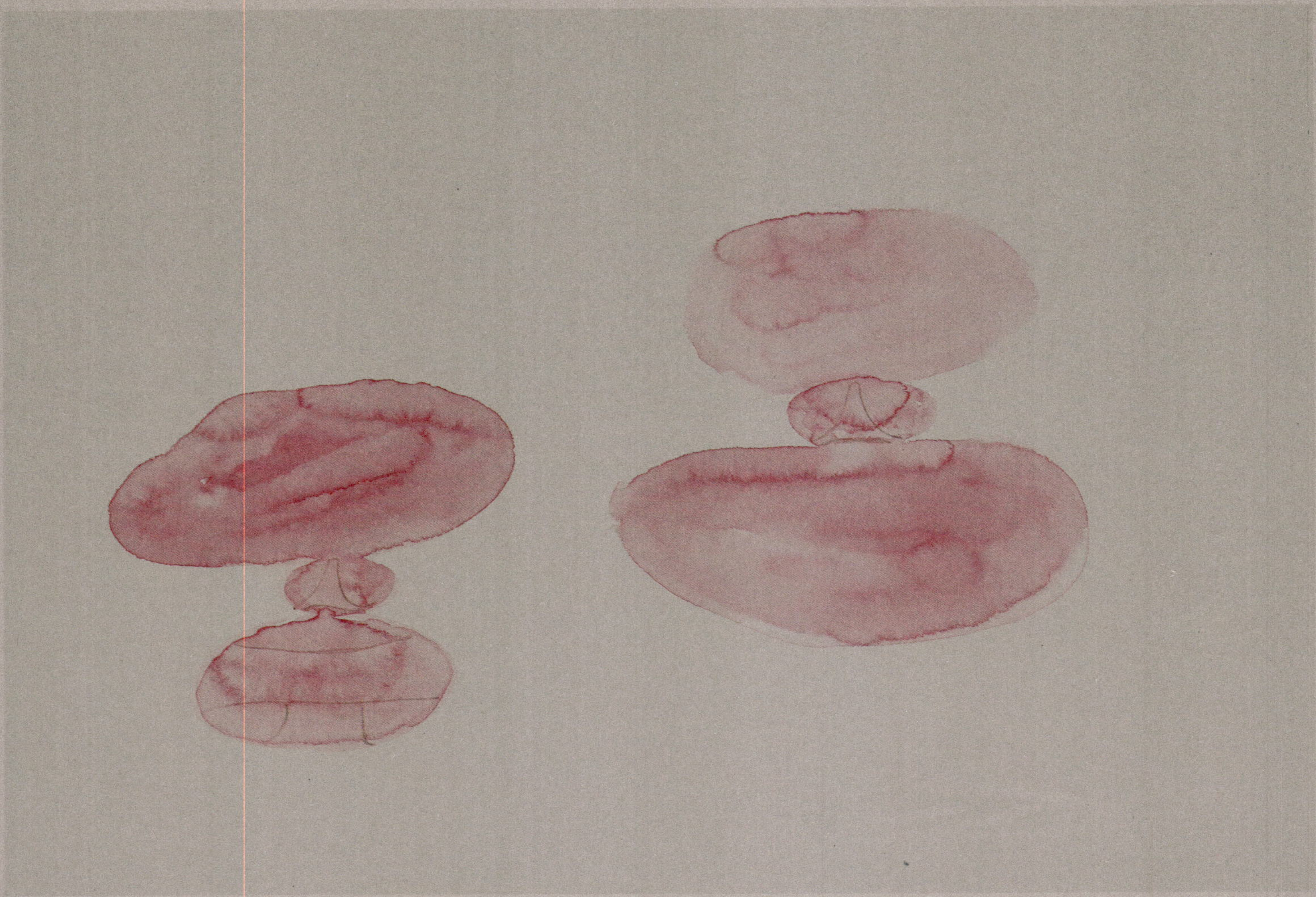